CW00703976

# DERBY DAYS

### FIFTY YEARS OF THE EPSOM CLASSIC

STEWART PETERS

# DERBY DAYS

## FIFTY YEARS OF THE EPSOM CLASSIC

TEMPUS

FRONTISPIECE – Secreto (20) outlasted the hot favourite El Gran Senor in a
pulsating finish to the 1984 Derby.

FRONT COVER – North Light comes home first in the 2004 Derby.
BACK COVER – Reference Point holds off Most Welcome (noseband) and Bellotto to win the 1987 Derby.

First published 2004

Tempus Publishing Ltd
The Mill, Brimscombe Port
Stroud, Gloucestershire GL5 2QG
www.tempus-publishing.com

© Stewart Peters, 2004

The right of Stewart Peters to be identified as the Author
of this work has been asserted by him in accordance with the
Copyrights, Designs and Patents Act 1988.

All rights reserved. No part of this book may be reprinted
or reproduced or utilised in any form or by any electronic,
mechanical or other means, now known or hereafter invented,
including photocopying and recording, or in any information
storage or retrieval system, without the permission in writing
from the Publishers.

British Library Cataloguing in Publication Data.
A catalogue record for this book is available from the British Library.

ISBN 0 7524 3202 8

Typesetting, design and origination by Tempus Publishing.
Printed in Great Britain

# INTRODUCTION

An aerial view of Epsom racecourse taken in 1929.

The Derby, run at Epsom Downs racecourse in Surrey, is proudly and justifiably known as the 'Blue Riband of the Turf'. Traditionally run on a Wednesday, the race now takes place on the first Saturday in June, and holds command as the jewel in the crown of flat racing. It has long been, and always will be, the race that owners, trainers and jockeys most want to win, such is the rich history and worldwide recognition attached to the event.

Ever since the very first running of the race back in 1780 – worth £1,065 15s to the victor – the Derby has escalated in fame and fortune, so much so that connections of the winning horse can now expect to scoop in excess of £1 million in prize money.

For the contestants, there is simply no place to hide in the white-hot cauldron of the Derby battle, thanks to the unique, extremely challenging and unforgiving characteristics of the racecourse. Run over a stamina-sapping distance of a mile-and-a-half, often at breakneck speed, there are multiple twists, turns and undulations to conquer in order to achieve victory at Epsom. Run left-handed, the horses encounter a right-hand bend directly after the start, together with a steep rise of 140 feet before levelling off for the next three furlongs when the runners have reached the top of the hill. From that point onwards, those runners that are really able to adapt to the course come to the fore, as the field begin the descent to the famous Tattenham Corner. Free-wheeling downhill all the time, horses must get into position here, as the finishing straight of three-and-a-half furlongs arrives at the conclusion of the corner, and here the ground gradually levels out again before rising slightly once more on the final charge to the line.

Accompanying the unique test on Derby day is the atmosphere created by the vast crowd, an atmosphere that gives off contrasting energies of tension, mystery, colour and fever-pitch excitement. With the main, towering grandstand on one side, it is the opposite 'Downs' that really bring the event to life, offering the most unusual but enchanting scene of any race day in the year. It is a tradition on Derby day for the Downs to be packed with 'everyday people', many of whom mark the occasion by travelling to Epsom by open-top buses, which line-up side by side on the Downs overlooking the home straight. In this same area, a huge funfair with all sorts of attractions can be found, making the Derby a carnival-like spectacle like no other in the racing calendar.

Literally steeped in tradition, the town of Epsom was famous for its natural mineral water before the Derby. The water was discovered on the Downs by Henry Wicker – a local farmer – while he was taking his cattle to drink at a watering hole. The water gathered a reputation as a healing, rejuvenating property, attracting polluted citygoers wishing to escape to the country.

Having encountered the undulations Epsom presents as well as Tattenham Corner,
Derby runners then face the home straight – a brutal three-furlong fight to the line.

Open-top buses are a common sight on Derby day.

Racing first took place on the Downs long ago in 1661, but it was not until 1779 that Edward Smith Stanley, the twelfth Earl of Derby, devised a race for himself and his friends to run their three-year-old fillies over a mile-and-a-half. The race was named the Oaks after the inventor's estate, and proved to be a huge success – so much so that the following year, another race was invented for both three-year-old colts and fillies. For the name of the new race, the Earl of Derby and his friend Sir Charles Bunbury – a well-recognized racing figure of the time – flipped a coin, and instead of the greatest Flat race of all being christened the Bunbury, the victorious Earl ensured the race was named after him, and the Derby was born.

Ironically, it was Sir Charles Bunbury's horse, Diomed, that won the first ever Derby in 1780, though the race was then run over a mile, with Tattenham Corner introduced – together with a new distance of a mile-and-a-half – in 1784.

Ever since Diomed's victory in the inaugural event, the Derby has risen to fantastic and much-cherished heights. Some of the horses that grace the roll of honour leave one inspired. In modern times, the awesome Nijinsky – who was the last horse to win the English Triple Crown of the 2,000 Guineas, Derby and St Leger; the brilliant, tough and charismatic Mill Reef and the scintillating but tragic Shergar – to name a few – have written their names into Epsom history,

Top hats are traditionally worn in the members' enclosure at the Derby.

while the French wonder horse, Sea Bird II, won the Derby in wonderful, graceful style before putting up the performance of a lifetime in France's Prix de l'Arc de Triomphe to generally be considered the best Derby winner of the modern era.

Whereas the horses will always be the key components to any Derby, many human schemers and warriors have forged strong, heart-warming bonds with the great race. Trainers like the hugely respected Sir Noel Murless, the legendary Irishman Vincent O'Brien, and more recently, his young, unrelated namesake, Aiden O'Brien, have carved lasting associations with the Derby. Then there are the jockeys, brave and daring in this often-ferocious event. Sir Gordon Richards – twenty-six times Champion Jockey, but not a Derby winner until his very last, ultra-emotional attempt at the race; the highly charged Scot Willie Carson and the soft-spoken but undoubted Epsom genius Pat Eddery – all of whom will forever be remembered in Derby recollections. Of course, one must not forget the greatest Derby jockey of them all, a man with such a knack for guiding his mounts round the unique test that it froze the blood – the record-breaking, nine-time winner, the incomparable Lester Piggott.

The Derby, once a year, brings together all that is best with Flat racing, and every year a fresh chapter is written; a new touching, romantic, classic episode for the history books, joining the catalogue of memorable battles that have previously taken place on the famous Epsom Downs. They are magical battles on magical days. They are *Derby Days*.

French jockey Olivier Peslier shows what it means to win the Derby.

The Queen's horse, Aureole, exercises in preparation for the Derby.

# PINZA

The 1953 Derby took place in Coronation year and, fittingly, there were extremely high hopes of a Royal winner. Trained by Captain Boyd-Rochfort, the Queen's horse Aureole – bred at Sandringham – was a talented chestnut colt by the brilliant 1933 Derby winner Hyperion. Aureole was one of the few horses in the race that possessed proven form over the full Derby distance. Versatility too was a trait of jockey Harry Carr's mount, with Aureole having won on firm going at York as a two-year-old, and in the recent Lingfield Derby Trial, had been successful on heavy going. Adding to his Epsom prospects was the fact that the Lingfield Derby Trial had also been won by April The Fifth in 1932, Mid-day Sun in 1937 and, most recently, Tulyar in 1952, before all three went on to glory in the Derby itself.

While the chances of a Royal success were certainly reasonable, two other horses were more strongly fancied in the betting market. The first of these was the Great Northern Stakes (held at York in May) winner, Premonition. Despite being a notoriously lazy worker at home and considered an inferior Epsom prospect to his stablemate Aureole by Captain Boyd-Rochfort, Premonition was a powerfully-built individual with stamina to suggest he would more than see out the taxing distance of the Derby.

Starting as 5/1 joint-favourite with Premonition was another powerfully-built animal in Pinza, a bay colt with a white face. Trained at Newmarket by Norman Bertie and owned by Shanghai businessman Sir Victor Sassoon, Pinza had caught the eye in emphatic style at Newmarket on his latest start by winning with the ease of a very good horse. Additionally, the colt had been pleasing his trainer tremendously in the build-up to the Derby. But perhaps the most interesting aspect of Pinza's bid for glory came from the presence in the saddle of one of the best (if not the best) jockeys in Flat racing history. The jockey in question was Sir Gordon Richards, who had received his knighthood in The Queen's Coronation and Birthday Honours List the week before the Derby. Twenty-six times in thirty-three years the forty-nine-year-old Richards had been Champion Jockey, and he had won an abundance of Classics during a glittering career. Yet the Derby had proved, time and again, to be his nemesis, despite having ridden many favourites in the race. In Pinza though, Richards believed he finally had the colt that could fulfil his lifelong ambition.

Having won the 2,000 Guineas at Newmarket, the Captain Charles Elsey-trained Nearula had shot to the top of the ante-post list for the Derby. But with twelve days to go before the race, the colt was struck with lameness, leaving his participation in grave danger. However, a few days prior to the event, Captain Elsey reported the horse to be working well again on his Malton gallops. Despite this news, the horse had slipped behind Pinza, Premonition and Aureole in the market, and the sight of Nearula arriving at Epsom the day before the race with his legs bandaged did little to encourage those who still believed the colt could win the Derby.

Pinza returns to the winner's circle having won the 1953 Derby.

As the runners descended into Tattenham Corner, Shikampur was still prominent, but here, despite being well placed, Nearula found nothing – perhaps feeling the effects of a troubled preparation. It was also at this point that Pinza began to make his mark on the race. The horse had been lying seventh at the top of the hill before beginning his challenge down the inside. Rounding Tattenham Corner and coming in to the home straight, Pinza started to accelerate and quickly put eight lengths between himself and his nearest pursuer, Aureole.

Pinza was now in full flight, and although The Queen's horse was staying-on bravely, Aureole was no match for Pinza – a bigger and stronger colt. To an emphatic roar, Pinza crossed the line a comfortable four-length winner from Aureole.

Two French-trained horses came next in Pink Horse and Shikampur, the latter holding off the persistent threat of Chatsworth. Nearula had flattered to deceive and eventually came home in ninth place, while the major disappointment of the race was undoubtedly Premonition, who only beat two home. Premonition's jockey, Eph Smith, later reported the horse had come down the hill poorly, losing his balance in the process. The talented colt would have his moment of glory later in the season, however, winning the fifth and final English Classic of the year, the St Leger.

At last, Sir Gordon Richards had broken the hoodoo that had plagued him in the Derby, and in truth, his victory on Pinza had never looked in doubt from the moment he had asked his mount for an effort, with the colt galloping home powerfully. It was a wonderful, crowning moment for Richards and all who shared a passion for racing, and the reception he was given on being led back in was as thunderous as it was deserved. Even The Queen was overjoyed by Richards' success, despite it coming at the expense of her horse. Here was a man finally realising his dream, a dream that was a culmination of an unrivalled career, which by its close, would see Richards amass 4,870 winners, while his English Classic record boasted three wins in the 2,000 Guineas, three in the 1,000 Guineas, two in the Oaks and five St Leger's. Despite hinting at retirement prior to the Derby, Richards carried on riding until eventually calling time in July 1954 after an accident at Sandown. Fittingly, his ride on Pinza was his last ever in the Derby.

Pinza's win gave owner Sir Victor Sassoon his first Derby after twenty-five years of trying. Sassoon had seventy horses in training at the time, the majority with Pinza's handler Bertie and some with Noel Murless.

Pinza – whose breeder, the great Fred Darling, sadly died a week after the Derby – had been involved in a bad accident after a highly successful juvenile campaign. The horse had slipped in roadwork and cut his back end. This injury required two surgeries to have flint removed from the wound. But thankfully,

Among the other interesting contenders for the 1953 Derby – a race that had originally attracted an entry of 446 – were the Chester Vase winner Empire Honey, partnered by Bill Rickaby; Chester's Dee Stakes winner Victory Roll and Shikampur, trained in France by Richard Carver (who had trained the 1948 winner My Love). Shikampur – one of three French challengers – was owned by the Aga Khan of the time, a man who had owned five previous Derby winners, including the previous year's victor, Tulyar.

On ground described as 'fairly good', the huge field of twenty-seven were sent off on the quest for Blue Riband glory, and it was one of the French raiders, Shikampur, that set the early pace together with Star Of The Forest.

As the race progressed, there appeared to be an absence of the shouting and jostling that so often accompanies the Derby in the heat of the battle. Indeed, after the race, the jockeys reported that this particular running of the greatest Classic had been pure and clean with no hard-luck stories – surprising, considering the substantial size of the field.

Sir Gordon Richards is congratulated by The Queen.

**1953 DERBY RESULT**

| FATE / HORSE | WEIGHT | JOCKEY | ODDS |
|---|---|---|---|
| **1st – Pinza** | 9-0 | Gordon Richards | 5/1* |
| **2nd – Aureole** | 9-0 | W.H. Carr | 9/1 |
| **3rd – Pink Horse** | 9-0 | W.R. Johnstone | 33/1 |
| 4th – Shikampur | 9-0 | C. Smirke | 100/6 |
| 5th – Chatsworth | 9-0 | S. Clayton | 100/6 |
| 6th – Pharel | 9-0 | J. Doyasbere | 22/1 |
| 7th – Timberland | 9-0 | G. Littlewood | 100/1 |
| 8th – Prince Canerina | 9-0 | E.C. Elliott | 50/1 |
| 9th – Nearula | 9-0 | E. Britt | 10/1 |
| 10th – Good Brandy | 9-0 | D. Smith | 100/8 |
| 11th – Mountain King | 9-0 | T. Gosling | 33/1 |
| 12th – Windy | 9-0 | F. Barlow | 100/1 |
| 13th – Fellermelad | 9-0 | A. Breasley | 22/1 |
| 14th – Empire Honey | 9-0 | W. Rickaby | 40/1 |
| 15th – Prince Charlemagne | 9-0 | L. Piggott | 66/1 |
| 16th – Novarullah | 9-0 | C. Spares | 100/8 |
| 17th – Durham Castle | 9-0 | A. Roberts | 100/1 |
| 18th – Jaffa II | 9-0 | J. Egan | 100/1 |
| 19th – Gala Performance | 9-0 | E. Mercer | 100/1 |
| 20th – Fe Shaing | 9-0 | S. Wragg | 100/1 |
| 21st – Scipio | 9-0 | J. Lindley | 100/1 |
| 22nd – Victory Roll | 9-0 | M. Beary | 50/1 |
| 23rd – Peter-So-Gay | 9-0 | P. Evans | 100/1 |
| 24th – Star Of The Forest | 9-0 | K. Gethin | 22/1 |
| 25th – Premonition | 9-0 | E. Smith | 5/1* |
| 26th – City Scandal | 9-0 | A.P. Taylor | 100/1 |
| Last – Barrowby Court | 9-0 | T. Carter | 100/1 |

All horses are three-year-old colts or fillies
*Denotes favourite
++ Weight is in stone & pounds

6 June 1953
Going – Fairly Good
Winner – £19,118 10s
Time – 2 mins 35 ⅗ secs
Joint Favourites – Pinza & Premonition
27 Ran

| | |
|---|---|
| Pinza | Bay colt by Chanteur II – Pasqua |
| Aureole | Chestnut colt by Hyperion – Angelola |
| Pink Horse | Bay colt by Admiral Drake – Khora |

Winner bred by Mr F. Darling
Winner trained by N. Bertie at Newmarket

Pinza recovered to be able to demonstrate to the racing world his enormous ability as a three-year-old. The colt proved his Epsom superiority by taking the King George VI and Queen Elizabeth Stakes at Ascot later in the season, again in convincing style.

Soon after his win at Ascot, Pinza broke down and was retired to stud. His place in the Derby record books was assured. A great horse, and one that had helped a great jockey realise a lifelong ambition.

# NEVER SAY DIE

The 1954 Derby certainly had a very open look about it. Whereas the year before had seen the likes of Pinza and Aureole dominate both the betting market and the race, the Derby on this occasion was primed for a surprise result, such was the uncertainty that surrounded a number of the leading contenders.

As it was in Pinza's year, 1954 would feature joint favourites. The first of these was the Harry Peacock-trained Rowston Manor, a big, well-built horse that seemed suited to the Derby trip. Rowston Manor had leapt into consideration for Epsom after winning the Lingfield Derby Trial in May. In that trial, Rowston Manor took the scalp of the one-time Derby favourite Ambler II, a defeat that ultimately led to that American colt's withdrawal from Epsom.

The other joint favourite was the speedy Ferriol, trained in France by Willy Clout. Although the colt had finished a solid runner-up in the 2,000 Guineas at Newmarket, there were doubts regarding his staying power; although the firm ground present in 1954 certainly allowed him a greater chance of lasting home. In Ferriol's favour was the fact that he was a low-actioned horse with fine balance, the sort that typically responded well to the undulations of the Downs. Additionally, the colt – partnered by Rae Johnstone – had not been over-raced during the season by Clout.

Another with suspect stamina was the winner of the 2,000 Guineas, Darius. The bay colt had won at Newmarket in grand style, displaying the ability that had seen him conquer Rowston Manor in the Champagne Stakes as a two-year-old. However, there were plenty that questioned Darius' ability to last home at Epsom. Although he was by a speedy Derby winner in the 1945 hero Dante, Darius' dam, Yasna, had not produced any winners that stayed twelve furlongs.

The Queen and Queen Mother watch the 1954 Derby.

While his chance was not as strong as Aureole's had been the year before, Landau was a decent Royal representative for The Queen. The colt had gathered his fair share of critics during the season, having disappointed in general, but Landau had undeniably been one of the leading juveniles of his generation. Landau was trained for The Queen by Noel Murless and was ridden in the Derby by twenty-six-year-old Billy Snaith, who had been a late replacement for Sir Gordon Richards, who was sidelined with injury.

No horse though was giving off as many good vibes in the days leading up to the race as the chestnut outsider Never Say Die. Trained by the seventy-four-year-old Joe Lawson, the horse had been quoted as high as 200/1 by some bookmakers towards the end of May. The American-bred challenger had won only one of six races as a two-year-old and had disappointed in his three races in the current campaign, although all came over distinctly shorter distances than the Derby. However, on the gallops in the week before the Derby, Never Say Die consistently looked the pick of the Newmarket contenders, sparkling

Never Say Die was the first of Lester Piggott's record-breaking nine Derby winners

in his work and depicting the prototype of a progressive, stronger horse. The colt was partnered in the Derby by an eighteen-year-old named Lester Piggott, who had been runner-up in the 1952 Derby aboard Gay Time.

Among the other interesting contenders from the field of twenty-two were the Captain Boyd-Rochfort-trained and American-owned Blue Prince II, a horse that was partnered by Harry Carr as a consequence of Ambler II being withdrawn; the Chester Vase winner Blue Rod and Valerullah – an own-brother to the 1,000 Guineas and Oaks winner of 1949, Musidora. Of the three, Blue Prince II had Epsom form on his side, having won the Woodcote Stakes on the course as a two-year-old.

As the field broke away, it was an outsider in Moonlight Express that was the first to show from Rowston Manor and Alpenhorn. In the early stages, Landau, Never Say Die, Darius and the Eph Smith-ridden L'Avengro were in close proximity to the leaders, but the hotly fancied Ferriol was behind and, from there, never seemed likely to threaten for honours. Then, after half a mile, L'Avengro took control from Rowston Manor and the two disputed the lead to the top of the hill.

As the field swarmed round Tattenham Corner, all the main players – with the notable exception of Ferriol – were still in contention, and while L'Avengro soon stumbled his way out of the leading places, it was the big horse, Rowston Manor, that threw down his challenge from Landau, Darius and Blue Sail, with Never Say Die's white face beginning to show menacingly on the wide outside.

The gallop had been strong and those with stamina limitations were beginning to crack. As Rowston Manor faltered, Darius briefly took over in the straight, but game as the 2,000 Guineas winner was, he was soon swallowed alive by Piggott on the charging Never Say Die, and the chestnut quickly shot four lengths clear.

The challenge from the fancied pair of Rowston Manor and Landau had been quashed – although both were staying-on at one pace – while Darius too was now struggling, and it was left to another outsider in Arabian Knight to attack the leader.

Arabian Knight, for a horse that favoured softer conditions, was eating up ground towards the finish, yet there was simply no stopping Never Say Die, and at the end, he crossed the line a comfortable two-length winner. Arabian Knight held second by a neck from Darius with the fancied horses finishing back in the field. Rowston Manor came seventh, Landau eighth and the disappointing Ferriol eleventh.

Never Say Die became the first American-bred horse to win the Derby since Iroquois in 1881 and the first American-owned to win since Mr H. Duryea's Durbar II in 1914. The man who bred and owned Never Say Die was Mr R.S. Clark and although this was Mr Clark's first Derby triumph, he had tasted glory at Epsom before, courtesy of his 1939 Oaks heroine Galatea II.

As trainer Joe Lawson celebrated his first Derby winner, most of the accolades went to Piggott for his fantastic ride on Never Say Die. The youngster had experienced his first ride in the Derby in the 1951 race on the Ken Cundell-trained Zucchero, then at the extremely tender age of fifteen. Zucchero had been left at the start in that race after digging his heels in and had lost valuable ground. Even then though, the mastery that Piggott would display in future years at Epsom was apparent as the jockey weaved his hopeless cause through the field to eventually finish thirteenth of thirty-three. Lester Piggott had ridden his first-ever winner at the age of thirteen and in the mid-1950s, after Never Say Die's win, he was awarded the much-envied job of stable jockey to the powerful Noel Murless yard. It was a situation that would only aid the incredible love affair that Piggott would establish with the Derby in the future.

Although the 1954 Derby field was considered average at best, Never Say Die had won well. He was beaten on his next start in the King Edward VII Stakes at Royal Ascot – a race where Piggott was suspended for riding an overly aggressive race – but the colt bounced back to win a St Leger later in the season. Never Say Die went on to sire two horses that became Classic winners: the 1962 Derby hero Larkspur and the 1,000 Guineas and Oaks heroine of 1960, Never Too Late II.

## 1954 DERBY RESULT

| FATE / HORSE | WEIGHT | JOCKEY | ODDS |
|---|---|---|---|
| **1st – Never Say Die** | 9-0 | L. Piggott | 33/1 |
| **2nd – Arabian Night** | 9-0 | T. Gosling | 33/1 |
| **3rd – Darius** | 9-0 | E. Mercer | 7/1 |
| 4th – Elopement | 9-0 | C. Smirke | 9/1 |
| 5th – Narrator | 9-0 | F. Barlow | 66/1 |
| 6th – Blue Prince II | 9-0 | W.H. Carr | 33/1 |
| 7th – Rowston Manor | 9-0 | D. Smith | 5/1* |
| 8th – Landau | 9-0 | W. Snaith | 100/7 |
| 9th – L'Avengro | 9-0 | E. Smith | 25/1 |
| 10th – Blue Sail | 9-0 | J. Longden | 100/6 |
| 11th – Ferriol | 9-0 | W.R. Johnstone | 5/1* |
| 12th – Moonlight Express | 9-0 | J. Mercer | 50/1 |
| 13th – Blue Rod | 9-0 | F. Durr | 33/1 |
| 14th – Kingsloe | 9-0 | W. Anderson | 100/1 |
| 15th – Court Splendour | 9-0 | W. Nevett | 28/1 |
| 16th – Alpenhorn | 9-0 | M. Beary | 40/1 |
| 17th – Hylas | 9-0 | F. Payne | 100/1 |
| 18th – Dark Corsair | 9-0 | J. Marshall | 100/1 |
| 19th – Valerullah | 9-0 | K. Gethin | 100/9 |
| 20th – Ruwenzori | 9-0 | E. Britt | 66/1 |
| Last – Rokimos | 9-0 | J. Egan | 100/1 |
| Pulled Up – Cloonroughan | 9-0 | W. Rickaby | 50/1 |

2 June 1954
Going – Firm
Winner – £16,959 10s
Time – 2 mins 35 ⅘ secs
Joint Favourites – Ferriol & Rowston Manor
22 Ran

| | |
|---|---|
| Never Say Die | Chestnut colt by Nasrullah – Singing Grass |
| Arabian Night | Bay colt by Persian Gulf – Faerie Lore |
| Darius | Bay colt by Dante – Yasna |

Winner bred by Mr R.S. Clark in the USA
Winner trained by J. Lawson at Newmarket

The field at the mile post in the 1955 race.

# PHIL DRAKE

Without a doubt, the most dominant and imposing horse in the field for the 1955 Derby was the George Colling-trained Acropolis. Colling had trained Nimbus to win the 1949 Derby while Acropolis, a giant chestnut, was by Donatello II, the same stallion that would be responsible for the legendary Crepello two years later. Acropolis was a machine and had fittingly pulverised his opposition – albeit moderate in standard – in two races as a juvenile. After taking the Classic Trial at Thirsk earlier in the current season, Acropolis headed for the Newmarket Stakes where he was to register one of the most incredible – and in some ways, ludicrous – of Derby trial wins ever seen. The time the colt posted was phenomenal, but the bizarre fact was that he ran the race by himself after his only opponent, Rowland Ward, had run off the course. Critics pointed to the fact that Acropolis had beaten nothing of note – and in this instance he literally had not – but he was undeniably a mighty horse with staying power that would prove most difficult to beat at Epsom. One worrying aspect surrounding Acropolis' bid for glory was that two weeks prior to the Derby, he jarred himself in work, damaging a shoulder, and despite reports to the contrary, there were those that questioned the colt's fitness come the big day.

There were plenty ready to challenge Acropolis on Derby day, with the French holding a particularly strong hand. Hafiz II was one of five colts – Acropolis, True Cavalier, Daemon and Tippecanoe were the others – that lined-up for the race unbeaten. Hafiz II was somewhat temperamental and highly strung, but was ridden by the talented Roger Poincelet and owned by the Aga Khan, a man looking for his sixth Derby success.

To many though, the really interesting challenge from France came from the tall, dark-bay colt with a big white blaze, Phil Drake. The horse was trained by Francois Mathet and was originally targeted at Epsom as a second-string to his stablemate, the Prix Juigne winner Datour. But in the days leading up to the race, the whispers of encouragement for Phil Drake began to get increasingly strong and it came as no surprise when Datour was eventually withdrawn. Phil Drake had been runner-up to Datour in the Prix Juigne earlier in the season having never run as a two-year-old; indeed, the colt had been nowhere in the betting lists in the middle of the May. It was not until the horse delivered an exquisite performance in the Prix La Rochette at Longchamp (over a distance of a mile and three furlongs) shortly before the Derby that his star began to shine with serious intent. Phil Drake was partnered at Epsom by one of France's finest jockeys, Fred Palmer.

Doubts surrounded a number of the other leading contenders, including Our Babu and True Cavalier. The former was the 2,000 Guineas winner whose stamina was suspect at best, while True Cavalier had emerged as a somewhat puzzling winner of the Lingfield Derby Trial, when the winning time appeared too slow to be true. Additionally, a blow was struck to Irish hopes on the eve of the race when their main challenger, Hugh Lupus, injured his near-fore foot when stumbling at the road that crosses the course while preparing for his Tuesday morning gallop. The injury resulted in his withdrawal; a crying shame

Jockey Fred Palmer and the 1955 Derby winner Phil Drake.

for a talented horse that had won his previous race well and had only been beaten a short head by Our Babu in the Middle Park Stakes as a two-year-old.

Hugh Lupus aside, twenty-three did line-up beneath glorious sunshine, with the going perfect. It was to be Noble Chieftain that led the field in the early stages, tracked by True Cavalier, Starlit II, Our Babu and My Smokey.

The pace had not been spectacular early on, and as the field descended in to Tattenham Corner, there appeared no sign of it picking up. The race looked set to favour those with a strong finishing burst, and would conversely be detrimental to the true, out-and-out stayers. As it was, coming down the hill, the likes of Our Babu and Acropolis were well positioned and were travelling sweetly, while on the other hand, the Chester Vase winner Daemon was totally unable to cope with the unique descent and dropped back from a useful position. Looking towards the rear of the field as they came round Tattenham Corner, the white face of Phil Drake could be spotted, the French raider apparently in a hopeless position, and it was the huge outsider Cardington King that swept into the straight in command.

The slow pace had been a thorn in the side to the likes of the staying horses Acropolis and True Cavalier, and as that pair struggled to quicken, it was another outsider in the form of the Irish horse Panaslipper, ridden by Jas Eddery, that wrestled the lead from Cardington King.

Panaslipper soon shot well clear and a shock win looked on the cards. However, passing an amazing sixteen other horses in the straight and showing true Classic speed and stamina in doing so, Phil Drake was being fired like a missile at the leader under a beautiful ride from Palmer. Finishing like a train, the inexperienced French horse overtook his game Irish opponent in the last hundred yards to win by a length-and-a-half, with the favourite Acropolis three lengths away in third.

It was a scintillating performance by Phil Drake, who was having only the third run of his life, and although he understandably ran very green in the early stages, he positively exploded once in the home straight.

Although the mediocre pace had resulted in one of the slowest winning times ever, the jubilation could not be taken away from Phil Drake's connections, including the horse's owner and breeder, Madame Volterra, and his trainer Mathet, for whom this Derby win was almost like a signature moment after he had received a 'Legion d'Honneur' earlier in May for his contributions to racing.

## 1955 DERBY RESULT

| FATE / HORSE | WEIGHT | JOCKEY | ODDS |
| --- | --- | --- | --- |
| 1st – Phil Drake | 9-0 | F. Palmer | 100/8 |
| 2nd – Panaslipper | 9-0 | Jas Eddery | 100/1 |
| 3rd – Acropolis | 9-0 | D. Smith | 11/4* |
| 4th – Cardington King | 9-0 | W. Nevett | 100/1 |
| 5th – True Cavalier | 9-0 | R. Fawdon | 100/8 |
| 6th – Bryn | 9-0 | W. Rickaby | 50/1 |
| 7th – National Anthem | 9-0 | A. Breasley | 50/1 |
| 8th – Kookaburra | 9-0 | E.J. Cracknell | 50/1 |
| 9th – Our Babu | 9-0 | E. Mercer | 8/1 |
| 10th – Praetorian | 9-0 | K. Gethin | 33/1 |
| 11th – Hafiz II | 9-0 | R. Poincelet | 100/8 |
| 12th – Noble Chieftain | 9-0 | F. Barlow | 66/1 |
| 13th – Windsor Sun | 9-0 | L. Piggott | 33/1 |
| 14th – National Holiday | 9-0 | J. Wilson | 100/1 |
| 15th – Marwari | 9-0 | P. Canty | 100/1 |
| 16th – Tippecanoe | 9-0 | E. Britt | 25/1 |
| 17th – Starlit II | 9-0 | J. Mercer | 100/1 |
| 18th – State Trumpeter | 9-0 | E. Smith | 25/1 |
| 19th – Point Gamma | 9-0 | J. Deforge | 33/1 |
| 20th – Daemon | 9-0 | C. Smirke | 15/2 |
| 21st – Solarium | 9-0 | W. Snaith | 28/1 |
| 22nd – My Smokey | 9-0 | T. Gosling | 25/1 |
| Last – Bicester | 9-0 | W.H. Carr | 100/1 |

25 May 1955
Going – Good
Winner – £18,702
Time – 2 mins 39 ⅘ secs
Favourite – Acropolis
23 Ran

| Phil Drake | Bay colt by Admiral Drake – Philippa |
| Panaslipper | Chestnut colt by Solar Slipper – Panastrid |
| Acropolis | Chestnut colt by Donatello II – Aurora |

Winner bred by Owner (Madame Volterra)
Winner trained by F. Mathet in France

Alec Head, trainer of Lavandin (pictured in 2000).

# LAVANDIN

When Phil Drake had won the 1955 Derby, it had signalled the commencement of countless quality French raiders at the English Classics. It seemed that for every Derby in the upcoming years, there would be at least one or two French horses that would dominate the betting market. In contrast, the late 1950s and early '60s – with some notable exceptions – could be considered a somewhat poor period for English-trained horses. Indeed, even excluding Phil Drake's performance of the year before, six of the ten forthcoming Epsom Derbys would be won by horses trained outside the host country, with the winners coming from either France or Ireland.

In early May, the betting market for the 1956 Derby had a decidedly Gallic edge to it. Directly at the top of the lists were Philius II – also favourite for the 2,000 Guineas at Newmarket – Valcares III, Lavandin and Tanerko. All four were trained in France, while rounding out the top five was the Irish-trained Milesian. However, after a distinctly puzzling and uninformative series of trials, only Lavandin would actually line-up for the Blue Riband come Derby day.

Having been ante-post favourite for both the 2,000 Guineas and the Derby, Philius II was beaten at Newmarket by a 50/1 outsider named Gilles de Retz. Despite his foreign sounding name, Gilles de Retz was trained in Berkshire by Charles Jerdein, but after his proud moment in the Guineas, the horse then disappointed badly when flopping in the Lingfield Derby Trial, leaving Lavandin to head the market for Epsom. Despite his defeat at Lingfield, Gilles de Retz still headed for the Derby, together with his stablemate Affiliation Order, an unraced two-year-old, but a winner on his latest start over thirteen furlongs at three.

Where as many of his compatriots had fallen by the wayside, Lavandin arrived at Epsom as favourite, albeit a fairly unsteady one. The bay colt had only managed third place on his latest start in the Prix Hocquart in France and there were some worries that the ground may be too firm for him at Epsom. But there was extreme confidence in the ability of Lavandin's young trainer, Alec Head, who was considered a genius of his time, and one who would go on to saddle countless Derby contenders in future years. Additionally aiding Lavandin's chance was the fact he was partnered by Australian Rae Johnstone, already a two-time Derby winner aboard My Love in 1948 and Galcador in 1950. As well as Lavandin, Head also trained Buisson Ardent, a speed merchant that had finished third in the 2,000 Guineas and had then won the French equivalent. Against Buisson Ardent was that his sire, Relic, was a pure sprinter, similar to the sire of Gilles de Retz – Royal Charger – and therefore there were severe questions regarding stamina.

In a very open Derby field of twenty-seven, several other horses stood out, including Induna, Full Measure, Roistar and Pirate King. Induna was the convincing winner of the Lingfield Derby field and was ridden at Epsom by Charlie Smirke. Smirke was a three-time winner of the Derby, partnering victors Windsor Lad in 1934, the record-breaking Mahmoud in 1936 and Tulyar in 1952. Full Measure was a big, imposing horse that was unbeaten in the only two races of his life, while the electric Roistar – sixth in the Guineas and bred to stay – was the big hope of Ireland. One horse that was thriving in his pre-race workouts was the H.L. Cottrill-trained Pirate King. The colt was a rugged, powerful animal with stamina on his side and had won his latest two starts, including the Newmarket Stakes over a mile-and-a-quarter.

Although the going was firm, wind and rain accompanied the race as the runners were sent on their way. As the gates went up, both Induna and the outsider Idle Rocks were rooted to the turf, giving up valuable ground. The Billy Snaith-ridden Monterey was the first to show from 100/1 shot Stoney Ley and the strapping Pirate King. The latter was cut like a diamond and looked

Monterey has a clear lead rounding Tattenham Corner. Lavandin (white cap and sleeves) lies about eighth.

Lavandin crosses the line first in 1956 ahead of Roistar and Hornbeam. Out of the picture is runner-up Montaval.

like a wall of muscle in the preliminaries, clearly primed for the occasion. The Guineas hero Gilles de Retz was among those towards the rear early on.

Although he was obviously in top physical condition, the unique Epsom course – so often the undoing of a large, big-striding horse – seemed to get the better of Pirate King as the field came down the hill, and although he was in second place at the time, he began to lose both his balance and his place among the leaders as the surprising Monterey increased his lead over King David II, Tenareze, Roistar, Pearl Orama, Lavandin and Induna.

Completing the swoop round Tattenham Corner, Monterey shot for home in the straight and quickly opened up a useful-looking lead. Rae Johnstone always had Lavandin placed in a beautiful position, and picking up the leader with real class, the favourite stamped his authority on the race two-and-a-half furlongs out.

It looked as though Lavandin would coast home, so routinely had he seized the lead from Monterey, but with 200 yards to go, Johnstone inexplicably appeared to ease up on the favourite. Coming like lightning with a dramatic late charge was another French colt, the Fred Palmer-ridden Montaval, and by the time the post arrived, Lavandin had triumphed by no more than a neck. Furthermore, Montaval actually stumbled slightly in the dying strides, an error that Palmer considered race-costing. The Irish hope Roistar came home in third with the top home-trained runner being Hornbeam in fourth, one place ahead of The Queen's horse, Atlas, a colt that was involved in a lot of jostling during the race.

He may have been slightly fortunate in the end, but the favourite Lavandin had prevailed and had given his owner, Pierre Wertheimer – also the colt's breeder – a first Derby success. Wertheimer's first English Classic winner had arrived courtesy of Mesa in the 1,000 Guineas of 1935, and the owner had been the one to give winning jockey Rae Johnstone his first ride in Europe back in 1932, with Johnstone riding off and on for Wertheimer ever since. Johnstone had now gathered a total of thirty Classics in England, Ireland and France.

Lavandin's dam, Lavande, was almost put down before giving foal to Lavandin, as she was considered to be totally sterile. However, allowed one more chance to save grace, a 1952 mating with Verso II resulted in the 1956 Derby winner.

It developed into a remarkable season for French-trained horses. They finished 1-2-3 in the Oaks – won by Sicarelle – and also won the St Leger, Coronation Cup and Eclipse Stakes. Without a doubt though, the shining moment in a glorious catalogue of results was the victory of Lavandin in the greatest Classic of all, the Epsom Derby.

## 1956 DERBY RESULT

| FATE / HORSE | WEIGHT | JOCKEY | ODDS |
|---|---|---|---|
| **1st – Lavandin** | 9-0 | W.R. Johnstone | 7/1* |
| **2nd – Montaval** | 9-0 | F. Palmer | 40/1 |
| **3rd – Roistar** | 9-0 | Jas Eddery | 22/1 |
| 4th – Hornbeam | 9-0 | J. Mercer | 33/1 |
| 5th – Atlas | 9-0 | W.H. Carr | 50/1 |
| 6th – Monterey | 9-0 | W. Snaith | 50/1 |
| 7th – Tenareze | 9-0 | L. Flavien | 20/1 |
| 8th – Cash And Courage | 9-0 | W. Rickaby | 18/1 |
| 9th – Pearl Orama | 9-0 | A. Breasley | 50/1 |
| 10th – Induna | 9-0 | C. Smirke | 9/1 |
| 11th – Articulate | 9-0 | D. Smith | 10/1 |
| 12th – Sacre Bleu | 9-0 | R. Fawdon | 33/1 |
| 13th – Birso Boy | 9-0 | H. Sprague | 100/1 |
| 14th – Al-Mojannah | 9-0 | T.M. Burns | 100/1 |
| 15th – Pirate King | 9-0 | G. Littlewood | 9/1 |
| 16th – Full Measure | 9-0 | E. Smith | 100/7 |
| 17th – Buisson Ardent | 9-0 | R. Poincelet | 100/7 |
| 18th – Royal Splendour | 9-0 | E.J. Cracknell | 100/1 |
| 19th – Stephanotis | 9-0 | K. Gethin | 33/1 |
| 20th – Idle Rocks | 9-0 | S. Clayton | 50/1 |
| 21st – Thunderbolt | 9-0 | F. Durr | 100/1 |
| 22nd – Gilles De Retz | 9-0 | F. Barlow | 28/1 |
| 23rd – Chilham | 9-0 | G. Lewis | 100/1 |
| 24th – Affiliation Order | 9-0 | L. Piggott | 33/1 |
| 25th – Nimrod IV | 9-0 | J. Doyasbere | 100/1 |
| 26th – King David II | 9-0 | J. Massard | 20/1 |
| 27th – Stoney Ley | 9-0 | E. Mercer | 100/1 |

6 June 1956
Going – Firm
Winner – £17,282 10s
Time – 2 mins 36 ⅖ secs
Favourite – Lavandin
27 Ran

| Lavandin | Bay colt by Verso II – Lavande |
|---|---|
| Montaval | Bay colt by Norseman – Ballynash |
| Roistar | Bay colt by Arctic Star – Roisin |

Winner bred by Owner (Pierre Wertheimer) in France
Winner trained by A. Head in France

# CREPELLO

The crop of three-year-olds in 1957 seemed a cut above the generations of recent years. As a result, there was a strong field for the 1957 Derby, and this edition of the race featured a favourite whose reputation already compared most favourably with the very best horses of the era.

Crepello, trained at Newmarket by the great Noel Murless, was a big, handsome, chestnut son of Donatello II, a sire who was himself a son of the 1930 Derby winner Blenheim. For a horse bred to stay the two-and-a-half miles of an Ascot Gold Cup, Crepello exhibited breathtaking speed on the racecourse, winning over five furlongs as a two-year-old before rounding off his juvenile campaign with a win in Newmarket's prestigious Dewhurst Stakes. As a three-year-old, Crepello destroyed a hot field in the 2,000 Guineas, leading all the way to win, untroubled, by four lengths. It was a performance of rare dominance, and was made even more striking considering it was the first time in a number of years that a staying-bred horse had won the Guineas. Not surprisingly, Crepello was installed as a red-hot favourite for Epsom and only heightened his glowing reputation with a sensational, power-packed gallop, watched by the ecstatic eye of Murless a week before the race. Sir Victor Sassoon, whose colours had been carried to victory by Pinza in 1953, owned Crepello and the horse was partnered by Lester Piggott, the boy-genius winner aboard Never Say Die in 1954. Despite negative whispers that surfaced at Sandown Park in the build-up to the Derby, Crepello was reported to be in terrific form prior to his bid for Epsom glory.

The Queen's horse, Doutelle, was one of a host of worthy challengers that Crepello faced on the day. Trained by Captain Boyd-Rochfort, the colt had proven his stamina when narrowly winning the Lingfield Derby Trial from fellow Epsom contender Alcastus, and was out of a mare that was a Cesarewitch winner. Doutelle was unbeaten as a three-year-old and was accompanied to Epsom by stablemate Tempest, a talented if temperamental sort.

Trying to make it a hat-trick of French-trained Derby winners, following the recent successes of Phil Drake and Lavandin, were the more-than-useful pair of Prince Taj and Apostol. The two happened to be the representatives of the previous two winning trainers, with Apostol saddled by Francois Mathet and Prince Taj by Alec Head. In fact, Prince Taj came in for some serious support due to the brilliant form of the Head stable – who had recorded a treble at Longchamp just days before the Derby. A win for Prince Taj would have rewarded the Aga Khan with a sixth victory in the race.

Among those with live chances were Pipe Of Peace, London Cry and Ballymoss. Pipe Of Peace was trained by the twenty-six-times Champion Jockey Sir Gordon Richards and had been a leading two-year-old, beating the heralded Crepello in the Middle Park Stakes. London Cry was the representative of Norman Bertie, and the chestnut colt had only run twice in his life, both as a three-year-old, winning on each occasion. Ballymoss, also a chestnut, was a fairly unconsidered raider from Ireland, trained by Vincent O'Brien – more notably, at the time, a master trainer of National Hunt horses. Ballymoss' price of 33/1 reflected his previous form, but it was to be what the colt achieved after this running of the Derby that was so memorable.

After The Queen had inspected her colt Doutelle – partnered by Harry Carr – in the paddock, where Crepello had stood head and shoulders above the rest of the runners, the field cantered down to the start. At the second attempt, the twenty-two-strong group were on their way, although Prince Taj forfeited six early lengths after being blocked and anchored as the field charged off.

The 100/1 shot Mystic Prince was the first to show, leading from Eudaemon, Bois de Miel, Chippendale II, Crepello and Doutelle, with Pipe Of Peace not too far away.

At the seven-furlong gate, the often hectic, aggressive nature of Derby runnings began to come to the fore. Eudaemon had taken the lead while jockey Frankie Durr had sent Palor right up from the back into a challenging position, but Tempest was the first to find trouble, being jostled back out of the leading group, while worse befell his stablemate Doutelle, as the Royal colt got badly bumped around, practically ruining his chances.

As Eudaemon glided round Tattenham Corner in the lead from his stablemate Brioche, Palor, Ballymoss and Crepello, more rough and tumble took place. The fancied pair of Pipe Of Peace and London Cry were badly hampered, with the jockeys of both accusing the French raider Chippendale II and his pilot, Rae Johnstone, of causing the trouble.

Crepello comes home ahead of Ballymoss and Pipe Of Peace in 1957.

Oblivious to the scrimmaging, Piggott was riding a race of sheer confidence on Crepello, with the favourite never being outside the leading six. Galloping with the utmost ease under tight restraint, Piggott pulled Crepello off the rails in the straight and sent him for home, unimpeded by traffic. The response Piggott got was instant, and Crepello picked off the leaders, including Brioche and Ballymoss, with the innate style of a magnificent horse. By the time the post arrived, Crepello held an advantage of a length-and-a-half to Ballymoss in second, although the jockey of the runner-up, T.P. Burns, suggested Crepello could have won by a far wider margin, so powerfully had he been travelling. Considering the interference he suffered, Pipe Of Peace did remarkably well to finish third under Scobie Breasley.

Crepello's win was a shot in the arm for England, following the Derby's recent foreign victors, and it presented Murless with his first Derby winner. It would not be the last time this special trainer would taste glory in the Blue Riband, and the tribute he paid to Crepello was heart-warming, stating his colt had a marvellous, unflappable temperament. It had been a second Derby success for Piggott, and on this occasion, the beautiful skills that made him a master at Epsom were there for all to see, as he impeccably steered Crepello to an authoritative triumph.

The runner-up, Ballymoss, had impressed many with his bold run, and after Epsom, the chestnut's career ascended into a blitz of brilliance. Ballymoss went on to win the Irish Derby and the St Leger as a three-year-old, and as an older horse, claimed the Coronation Cup at Epsom, the Eclipse Stakes at Sandown, the King George VI and Queen Elizabeth Stakes at Ascot and the jewel in the crown, the Prix de l'Arc de Triomphe at Longchamp. He also proved brilliant at stud where one of his sons was the Derby winner of 1967, Royal Palace.

If it had not been for Crepello, Ballymoss would perhaps be considered one of the top two or three horses of the twentieth century. But the fact was Crepello was an outstanding animal and most likely would have gone on to further glories had injury not cut short his sparkling career. All through his racing life, Crepello operated on suspect tendons that were always bandaged after his races. After the Derby, he was withdrawn from the King George because of heavy ground. Then, preparing for the St Leger, Crepello went lame. His tendons had been stretched in exercise to such an extent that his career was sadly brought to a close. Crepello was held in the highest regard by Murless and Piggott, both of whom were adamant that the colt would have continued to dominate his opponents. At stud, his major successes included a King George winner in Busted, as well as Classic-winning fillies Caergwrle and Mysterious, while he was also responsible for the 1971 Derby runner-up Linden Tree. Without a doubt, the majestic Crepello goes down as one of the finest winners of the great Epsom Derby.

## 1957 DERBY RESULT

| FATE / HORSE | WEIGHT | JOCKEY | ODDS |
| --- | --- | --- | --- |
| **1st – Crepello** | 9-0 | L. Piggott | 6/4* |
| **2nd – Ballymoss** | 9-0 | T.P. Burns | 33/1 |
| **3rd – Pipe Of Peace** | 9-0 | A. Breasley | 100/8 |
| 4th – Tempest | 9-0 | W. Rickaby | 28/1 |
| 5th – Royaumont | 9-0 | J. Deforge | 100/9 |
| 6th – Messmate | 9-0 | E. Mercer | 25/1 |
| 7th – Apostol | 9-0 | J. Doyasbere | 18/1 |
| 8th – Albergo | 9-0 | J. Mercer | 45/1 |
| 9th – Prince Taj | 9-0 | J. Massard | 10/1 |
| 10th – Doutelle | 9-0 | W.H. Carr | 100/6 |
| 11th – Brioche | 9-0 | E. Hide | 50/1 |
| 12th – Barred Rock | 9-0 | D. Ryan | 100/1 |
| 13th – Alcastus | 9-0 | C. Smirke | 33/1 |
| 14th – Palor | 9-0 | F. Durr | 33/1 |
| 15th – Eudaemon | 9-0 | E. Britt | 45/1 |
| 16th – Lightehran | 9-0 | W. Snaith | 50/1 |
| 17th – Chevastrid | 9-0 | Jas Eddery | 50/1 |
| 18th – Hedonist | 9-0 | K. Gethin | 100/1 |
| 19th – London Cry | 9-0 | D. Smith | 18/1 |
| 20th – Chippendale II | 9-0 | W.R. Johnstone | 100/7 |
| 21st – Mystic Prince | 9-0 | B. Swift | 100/1 |
| Last – Bois De Miel | 9-0 | E.J. Cracknell | 100/1 |

5 June 1957
Going – Firm
Winner – £18,659 10s
Time – 2 mins 35 ⅖ secs
Favourite – Crepello
22 Ran

| | |
| --- | --- |
| Crepello | Chestnut colt by Donatello II – Crepuscule |
| Ballymoss | Chestnut colt by Mossborough – Indian Call |
| Pipe Of Peace | Brown colt by Supreme Court – Red Briar |

Winner bred by Eve Stud Ltd
Winner trained by C.F.N. Murless at Newmarket

Charlie Smirke won four Derbys. The second was achieved in record time on the then Aga Khan's Mahmoud (above) in 1936.

# HARD RIDDEN

In what was considered a sub-par field for the 1958 Derby, the real shame was that Alcide – potentially the best three-year-old of his generation – would be missing from the line-up. Alcide had leapt to being favourite for the race at the end of May, having run by far the most convincing Derby trial of the season. Destroying the 2,000 Guineas fifth Paresa by an amazing twelve lengths, Alcide looked breathtaking in winning the respected Lingfield Derby Trial. However, a week before the Epsom Classic, Alcide was found injured in his box, and was discovered to have torn stomach muscles. In subsequent workouts, Alcide proved distinctly average, and the sad decision was taken to scratch him from the Derby field. After he recovered, Alcide proved what a fine colt he was by winning the St Leger and the following season's King George VI and Queen Elizabeth Stakes.

With Alcide sidelined, trainer Captain Boyd-Rochfort turned to two of his other stable stars to represent him at Epsom: Miner's Lamp and Bald Eagle. Miner's Lamp was owned by The Queen and at one time had headed the Derby betting market. However, the horse was passed over for Epsom by Boyd-Rochfort's stable jockey, Harry Carr, in favour of Bald Eagle, an American-bred colt that had been sparkling in work during the build-up to the race. Bald Eagle was a beautiful mover on the racecourse, although he had disappointed bitterly when favourite for the 2,000 Guineas. However, the colt redeemed himself when winning the first-ever running of York's Dante Stakes – a race that would develop into a key trial for Derby contenders in future years – over a distance of one mile and two-and-a-half furlongs, albeit in a slow time.

Continuing the trend of previous years, there was a strong-looking challenge from France. Four of them made the journey to Epsom, with the two most fancied being Noelor II and the horse that would eventually start as favourite, Wallaby II. The two had met each other in the very first race of their lives earlier in the season in the Prix Juigne, with the Francois Mathet-trained Noelor II beating his compatriot – trained by Percy Carter – into third. Noelor II went on to win the Prix Noailles while Wallaby II caught the eye significantly when winning the second of his two races after his debut in the Prix Juigne, showing real staying power in the Prix la Rochette at Longchamp – the same race that Phil Drake had won prior to his Derby victory of 1955. Wallaby II had a stayer's pedigree and was sent to Epsom with the full confidence of his trainer.

Among the other interesting contenders for the 1958 Derby were Boccaccio, Nagami and Hard Ridden. Boccaccio, an almost-black colt, was the representative of 1957's winning combination, Noel Murless and Lester Piggott, and thus the horse carried professional respect with him. However, the truth was that Boccaccio had looked anything but another Crepello when

Smirke returned to the Derby winner's circle aboard Hard Ridden in 1958.

flopping badly in the Dante Stakes. Nagami was a tough chestnut by the 1949 Derby winner Nimbus and was trained by Harry Wragg, twice a Derby winner as a jockey aboard Blenheim in 1930 and Watling Street in 1942. A battling type, Nagami had been third in the 2,000 Guineas. Ireland had experienced lean times in recent Derbys; indeed, their last winner of the race had come courtesy of the Dr Fred MacCabe-trained Orby, way back in 1907, and the chances of their current hope, Hard Ridden, initially appeared slim. Hard

Ridden, a bay colt, was not expected to stay according to his breeding as he was by a sire, Hard Sauce, that was a pure sprinter. However, the horse's young trainer, Mick Rogers, had Hard Ridden in excellent shape for Epsom as the horse took the Irish 2,000 Guineas at The Curragh prior to the Derby. Hard Ridden had an Epsom master to aid his cause, as he was partnered by fifty-one-year-old Charles Smirke, who had won the first of his three Derbys in 1934 on Windsor Lad.

Both The Queen and The Queen Mother were present at Epsom on Derby day. The sun was shining and the going was perfect, and as the twenty runners began their journey, it was evident that there was no real pace in the early stages. An outsider in Midlander took them along at a sedate gallop from the Newmarket Stakes winner Guersillus, Bald Eagle and the French pair, Noelor II and Wallaby II.

As in the year before, there was trouble at the seven-furlong marker. The favourite, Wallaby II, and Miner's Lamp were the two that suffered most from the scrimmaging. Wallaby II was hampered to such an extent that his race had been ruined and it subsequently transpired that he had cut his near-fore.

Hard Ridden was placed no better than tenth coming down the hill, but once in the straight – as the race leaders Guersillus and Amerigo dropped back together with the tiring Bald Eagle – Smirke sent his mount on and they soon went clear with two furlongs to run.

A second Irish horse, the totally unconsidered Paddy's Point, came out of the clouds to chase the leader, but Hard Ridden had broken free and quickened away off the slow pace in commanding style to become a very easy winner of the race by five lengths. Paddy's Point surprised everyone by coming second and the bay colt was ridden by a young Willie Robinson, a jockey who had fallen at the second fence from Longmead in the year's Grand National at Aintree. Robinson would go on to become a top National Hunt jockey, winning the 1963 Cheltenham Gold Cup on Mill House. As he had in the 2,000 Guineas, the game Nagami took third place at Epsom. It had been a tough Derby, and as well as the misfortune of Wallaby II, the other French hope, Noelor II, also found trouble, being well placed for the first mile before stumbling and almost falling coming down the hill.

It was a glorious, fourth Derby win for Smirke and a third for owner Sir Victor Sassoon – previously triumphant with Pinza and Crepello. But much of the post-race praise fell on the shoulders of Rogers. The trainer had not been in his profession long and Hard Ridden was his first runner in an English Classic. Previously, Rogers had sent over Stephanotis to win the 1957 Cambridgeshire.

Hard Ridden had defied the odds and become the first son of a recognised sprinter to win the Derby since Sunstar in 1911. The general opinion was that it was a poor Derby, a theory backed up by the tediously slow winning time and the fact that Hard Ridden was then well beaten in his next race behind the 1957 Derby runner-up, Ballymoss, in the King George VI and Queen Elizabeth Stakes at Ascot. But on the day, Hard Ridden had proven himself King of Epsom, and in doing so, delivered some long-awaited Derby success to Ireland.

## 1958 DERBY RESULT

| FATE / HORSE | WEIGHT | JOCKEY | ODDS |
|---|---|---|---|
| 1st – Hard Ridden | 9-0 | C. Smirke | 18/1 |
| 2nd – Paddy's Point | 9-0 | G.W. Robinson | 100/1 |
| 3rd – Nagami | 9-0 | J. Mercer | 10/1 |
| 4th – Baroco II | 9-0 | A. Breasley | 40/1 |
| 5th – Guersillus | 9-0 | E. Hide | 9/1 |
| 6th – Miner's Lamp | 9-0 | W. Rickaby | 100/6 |
| 7th – Alberta Blue | 9-0 | J. Longden | 18/1 |
| 8th – Noelor II | 9-0 | M. Garcia | 7/1 |
| 9th – Currito | 9-0 | R. Poincelet | 33/1 |
| 10th – Amerigo | 9-0 | E. Smith | 100/7 |
| 11th – Mahu | 9-0 | G. Thiboeuf | 33/1 |
| 12th – Bald Eagle | 9-0 | W.H. Carr | 7/1 |
| 13th – Alberta Pride | 9-0 | W. Swinburn | 100/1 |
| 14th – Elisha | 9-0 | E. Mercer | 100/1 |
| 15th – Trimmer | 9-0 | S. Clayton | 100/1 |
| 16th – Crystal Bay | 9-0 | J. Lindley | 100/1 |
| 17th – Arctic Gittell | 9-0 | D. Ryan | 50/1 |
| 18th – Wallaby II | 9-0 | F. Palmer | 4/1* |
| 19th – Boccaccio | 9-0 | L. Piggott | 20/1 |
| Last – Midlander | 9-0 | A.C. Rawlinson | 100/1 |

4 June 1958
Going – Good
Winner – £20,036 10s
Time – 2 mins 41 ⅕ secs
Favourite – Wallaby II
20 Ran

| | |
|---|---|
| Hard Ridden | Bay colt by Hard Sauce – Toute Belle II |
| Paddy's Point | Bay colt by Mieuxce – Birthday Wood |
| Nagami | Chestnut colt by Nimbus – Jennifer |

Winner bred by Sir Oliver Lambert
Winner trained by M. Rogers in Ireland

1959

# PARTHIA

It takes a lot for a horse to win the Epsom Derby. It is the most sought-after Classic of all, and therefore the very nature of the race is ultra-competitive. The unique structure of the course presents a formidable challenge to horse and rider, and the winning horse must possess stamina, toughness and a touch of class. Another element often overlooked in Derby runnings is luck. It has happened in Derbys gone by and will certainly happen in Derbys of the future, where one horse's misfortune is another's golden benefit. The Derby of 1959 certainly had a feel of 'what might have been' attached to it after the dust had settled.

As had now become the norm, the French colts dominated the top of the betting market for the Derby. Among their chief participants in 1959 were Saint Crespin III, Princillon and Shantung. Saint Crespin III was trained by Alec Head and had long been considered a major player for the Derby, having enjoyed a fabulous two-year-old campaign. The colt had been favourite for the Derby as late as May, but had relinquished that position having been beaten on his latest start as a three-year-old. Taking his place at the top of the market – albeit temporarily – was his stablemate Princillon, the mount of Australian George Moore. Princillon had finished runner-up twice in the current campaign, including over a mile-and-a-half in the Prix Hocquart, showing the staying side of his pedigree. However, displacing both of the Head-trained runners on the day was Shantung, owned by Baron Guy de Rothschild and trained by Geoffrey Watson. An athletic bay specimen, Shantung was partnered at Epsom by Fred Palmer, the winning jockey aboard Phil Drake in 1955 and runner-up a year later on Montaval.

The home challenge was lead by Carnoustie and Parthia. Carnoustie was a top-class two-year-old by the 1945 Derby winner Dante. Trained by Noel Murless and ridden by Lester Piggott, Carnoustie had finished third in the 2,000 Guineas, having previously won the Classic Trial at Thirsk over the distance of a mile. Parthia was a talented (if somewhat underrated) bay colt by a Classic sire in Persian Gulf. Captain Boyd-Rochfort, a man who had been trying for thirty-five years to win the Derby, trained the horse at Newmarket. It was surprising not to see Parthia shorter in price on Derby day, as he had won the Dee Stakes at Chester before giving his trainer an eighth win in the Lingfield Derby Trial, albeit in an unimpressive time. Partnering the colt at Epsom was a veteran of Derby rides, Harry Carr, whose best performance in the race had come when runner-up aboard Aureole in 1953.

Others with definite prospects in a competitive field included Fidalgo and Thymus. The Harry Wragg-trained Fidalgo was a certain stayer, having won the Chester Vase over a mile-and-a-half, while Charles Smirke's twenty-fourth Derby mount, Thymus, although bred to stay, had exhibited more speed than stamina when beating the English 2,000 Guineas winner Taboun in the French equivalent at Longchamp.

It was an extremely hot afternoon on Derby day and The Queen was cheered in the paddock after inspecting her runner Above Suspicion. There was a large crowd in attendance, and they roared their approval as the twenty runners were sent on their way on very firm ground.

The pace was fairly slow early on as the French colt Saint Crespin III took them along. As one French challenger led, another was about to meet disaster after just three furlongs. In a cruel twist of fate, Princillon was bustled by other horses and was sent crashing into the path of the unsuspecting Shantung. Fearing Shantung had been badly injured in the accident – perhaps suffering a broken leg – Palmer quickly pulled-up the favourite. However, swiftly recovering his balance, the horse proceeded to gallop on again. The real shame was that Shantung was now five lengths adrift of an already strung-out field and any chance of winning had surely been obliterated in those few, unfortunate moments.

As the race progressed round Tattenham Corner, it was one of the rank outsiders, Rousseau's Dream, that now led from Saint Crespin III, but once the field straightened for home, the race developed in to a battle between Fidalgo and Parthia. Parthia had always been well positioned throughout the race, and at the two-furlong marker, Carr drove him on and into a commanding lead. Despite the best efforts of Carr's son-in-law, Joe Mercer, to try and rally Fidalgo, Parthia was just too strong and went on to win by a length-and-a-half. Having still been three lengths behind the second-last horse rounding Tattenham Corner, Shantung then made up an incredible twenty-five lengths

Parthia and veteran jockey Harry Carr return victorious in 1959.

## 1959 DERBY RESULT

| FATE / HORSE | WEIGHT | JOCKEY | ODDS |
| --- | --- | --- | --- |
| **1st – Parthia** | 9-0 | W.H. Carr | 10/1 |
| **2nd – Fidalgo** | 9-0 | J. Mercer | 10/1 |
| **3rd – Shantung** | 9-0 | F. Palmer | 11/2* |
| 4th – Saint Crespin III | 9-0 | A. Breasley | 10/1 |
| 5th – Above Suspicion | 9-0 | D. Smith | 100/6 |
| 6th – Carnoustie | 9-0 | L. Piggott | 10/1 |
| 7th – Amourrou | 9-0 | E. Mercer | 25/1 |
| 8th – Princillon | 9-0 | G. Moore | 7/1 |
| 9th – Regent II | 9-0 | M. Garcia | 20/1 |
| 10th – Dan Cupid | 9-0 | R. Poincelet | 18/1 |
| 11th – Rousseau's Dream | 9-0 | G. Lewis | 100/1 |
| 12th – Josephus | 9-0 | W. Rickaby | 40/1 |
| 13th – Lindrick | 9-0 | S. Clayton | 66/1 |
| 14th – Reactor | 9-0 | G. Littlewood | 33/1 |
| 15th – New Brig | 9-0 | R. Fawdon | 28/1 |
| 16th – Beau Tudor | 9-0 | S. Smith | 100/1 |
| 17th – Arvak | 9-0 | J. Lindley | 40/1 |
| 18th – Thymus | 9-0 | C. Smirke | 10/1 |
| 19th – Barbary Pirate | 9-0 | E. Hide | 100/1 |
| Last – Casque | 9-0 | E.J. Cracknell | 33/1 |

3 June 1959
Going – Firm
Winner – £36,078
Time – 2 mins 36 secs
Favourite – Shantung
20 Ran

| | |
| --- | --- |
| Parthia | Bay colt by Persian Gulf – Lightning |
| Fidalgo | Bay colt by Arctic Star – Miss France |
| Shantung | Bay colt by Sicambre – Barley Corn |

Winner bred by Owner (Sir H. De Trafford)
Winner trained by Capt. C. Boyd-Rochfort at Newmarket

in the straight to catch Saint Crespin III and take third place close to home. Such was the manner in which he finished that Palmer stated that Shantung was the unluckiest Derby loser of all time. Unlucky and brave, as it transpired after the race that Shantung had finished lame. Of the remainder, Carnoustie and Princillon had held every chance at Tattenham Corner but had simply not lasted home, while Thymus was unable to ever land a blow.

It was a romantic, heart-warming win for the veteran jockey Carr and the trainer Boyd-Rochfort. The Derby was the only Classic the latter had failed to win during a distinguished career. Parthia's win made up for Alcide missing out on the chance to win the 1958 Derby. Alcide, like Parthia, was owned by Sir Humphrey de Trafford and had been red-hot favourite for the previous year's Derby before injury had ruled him out.

As for Parthia, it looked like he was an above-average winner of the Derby on initial opinion. However, the remainder of the colt's career proved disappointing, and he failed to win anything of consequence the year after his finest moment.

# ST PADDY

If a home-trained colt was going to win the 1960 Derby, the horse was going to have to fight off a fierce-looking foreign invasion. Four of the top five in the betting market on Derby day were trained in either France or Ireland.

The sizzling-hot favourite for the race was a beautiful-looking colt called Angers, trained in France by George Bridgland. Angers had clearly been the best two-year-old in France the season before, taking the important and respected Grand Criterium. The colt was unbeaten at three, and had outclassed some strong opposition when winning over the full Derby distance at Longchamp on his latest start. The one worry about Angers was that he was a recognised front-runner, and the last horse to win the Derby having led the majority of the way was Nimbus in 1949, so it was a style that rarely brought success in the Blue Riband.

The challenge from Ireland appeared particularly strong on this occasion, as they searched for their second win in three years following the success of Hard Ridden in 1958. As a son of the 1954 winner Never Say Die, Die Hard certainly appeared to have strong credentials for the Derby, and the tough colt had been impeccable when winning all three of his races in his native land during the season, races that happened to be the first three of his life. Initially, he had beaten the subsequent 2,000 Guineas winner Martial, while his latest winning venture had come over the Derby distance at Leopardstown. However, it was not all good news in the Die Hard camp, as on the eve of the race, the hot fancy's stablemate and fellow contender, Exchange Student, broke a near-fore fetlock when exercising on the course and sadly had to be put down. It would not be the last tragedy surrounding this edition of the Derby.

Irish trainer Paddy Prendergast had been enjoying a wonderful season, having already captured the 2,000 Guineas at Newmarket with Martial and the Irish equivalent with Kythnos. Although Martial was an absentee at Epsom, Kythnos was allowed to take his chance, and it was a chance that Prendergast felt sure would turn into a winning one, such was the trainer's confidence in the bay colt. As well as Kythnos, Prendergast also saddled the useful Alcaeus.

Before the Dante Stakes at York, there had not been so much as a trace of an English-trained challenger in the Derby betting, but that all changed courtesy of a horse named St Paddy. The bay challenger, a winner of the Royal Lodge Stakes as a two-year-old, had finished unplaced in the 2,000 Guineas, apparently not quite having the speed to threaten the principals in that race, of which third-placed Auroy and fourth-placed Tulyartos reopposed at Epsom. But at York, over a longer distance, St Paddy came into his own, putting up a breathtaking winning performance after toying with his rivals. St Paddy was a genuine, no-nonsense type of horse that went about his task with the minimum of fuss, and was by the 1953 runner-up Aureole, a stallion that had sired the previous year's fourth, Saint Crespin III, who in turn was the subsequent winner of the Eclipse Stakes and Prix de l'Arc de Triomphe. St Paddy had identical connections to the triumphant Crepello team of 1957; owned by Sir Victor Sassoon, trained by Noel Murless and ridden by the genial Lester Piggott.

It was to prove to be a Derby of mixed emotions, run on very fast ground, and after a good start, it was the initially reluctant Tudor Period, ridden by Bill Rickaby, that showed the way.

Tudor Period was joined by Die Hard, and these two continued to bowl along to the top of the hill, albeit at a conservative pace. Halfway into the descent to Tattenham Corner, Tudor Period shaped awkwardly, quickly dropping back through the pack, interfering with Alcaeus as he did so. This incident was totally independent of the cruel fate that awaited the favourite, Angers. The classy colt was well down the field and out of trouble when, out of the blue, his near-fore leg snapped. It was later revealed that Angers had also shattered his pastern and fetlock joints, and mercifully, a vet was on hand instantly to put the poor colt out of his misery. It was a tragedy, but a pure accident, and Angers' jockey, Gerard Thiboeuf, attributed no blame to anyone for the incident. Angers became the first fatality in the race since Marsyad had broken a leg in 1952, and the favourite's demise left a dark shadow hanging over the race.

Rounding Tattenham Corner, it was Auroy and Die Hard that led from Tulyartos, followed by a group including Marengo, Kythnos and St Paddy – always held in a beautiful position by Piggott.

St Paddy comes home a very easy winner in 1960.

St Paddy and connections.

**1960 DERBY RESULT**

| FATE / HORSE | WEIGHT | JOCKEY | ODDS |
| --- | --- | --- | --- |
| **1st – St Paddy** | 9-0 | L. Piggott | 7/1 |
| **2nd – Alcaeus** | 9-0 | A. Breasley | 10/1 |
| **3rd – Kythnos** | 9-0 | R. Hutchinson | 7/1 |
| 4th – Auroy | 9-0 | G. Lewis | 33/1 |
| 5th – Proud Chieftain | 9-0 | S. Clayton | 66/1 |
| 6th – Die Hard | 9-0 | G. Bougoure | 9/2 |
| 7th – Oak Ridge | 9-0 | E. Hide | 66/1 |
| 8th – Lustrous Hope | 9-0 | G. Moore | 28/1 |
| 9th – Marengo | 9-0 | R. Fawdon | 9/1 |
| 10th – Chrysler II | 9-0 | J. Mercer | 45/1 |
| 11th – Tudor Period | 9-0 | W. Rickaby | 66/1 |
| 12th – Ides Of March | 9-0 | E. Eldin | 50/1 |
| 13th – Mr Higgins | 9-0 | D. Smith | 50/1 |
| 14th – Tulyartos | 9-0 | W. Williamson | 7/1 |
| 15th – Port St Anne | 9-0 | S. Millbanks | 200/1 |
| Last – Picture Goer | 9-0 | W. Elliott | 200/1 |
| Broke Down – Angers | 9-0 | G. Thiboeuf | 2/1* |

1 June 1960
Going – Firm
Winner – £33,052
Time – 2 mins 35 ⅘ secs
Favourite – Angers
17 Ran

| St Paddy | Bay colt by Aureole – Edie Kelly |
| --- | --- |
| Alcaeus | Chestnut colt by Alycidon – Marteline |
| Kythnos | Bay colt by Nearula – Capital Issue |

Winner bred by The Eve Stud Ltd
Winner trained by C.F.N. Murless at Newmarket

Irish roars went up as Die Hard turned for home in control, as Marengo and Tulyartos faded away timidly. But those same roars soon petered out to a whimper as, confident as could be, Piggott brought St Paddy through with consummate ease with a quarter-of-a-mile to travel, passing first Die Hard, then the gritty Auroy. Though he never flashed exuberance, St Paddy ran out a very comfortable winner by three lengths. Kythnos had been the one to chase him home, but he was ultimately pipped for second place by his fast-finishing stablemate, Alcaeus.

It was the fourth time in seven years the famous peacock-blue and old-gold hoops of Sir Victor Sassoon had been carried to Derby glory, and on recording his third win in the race, Piggott was now acclaimed as a true master of Epsom.

Though not as physically imposing or naturally athletic as the likes of Crepello, St Paddy had repelled the strong foreign challenge in a professional manner, prompting Piggott to state the colt was the easiest of his three Derby heroes. St Paddy went on to prove his class again by winning the St Leger before retiring to a decent career at stud, getting, among others, the talented 1968 Derby runner-up Connaught.

The Newmarket gallops where Psidium was trained by Harry Wragg.

# PSIDIUM

Sir Victor Sassoon had undoubtedly been the leading owner when it came to Derby runners in the race's recent history. Beginning with Pinza in 1953, the owner had taken four of the previous eight Derbys. In 1961, it would have taken an extremely brave man to bet against his supremely talented colt Pinturischio becoming winner number five. But in a field lacking true star quality, further weakened by the absence of the 2,000 Guineas winner Rockavon, the race was dealt a bitter blow when the Noel Murless-trained horse was ruled out of the contest with a recurrence of the stomach problem that had already seen him miss the Dante Stakes at York.

It was a huge and extremely open-looking field that did make it to Epsom for the Blue Riband. Turning to a French colt once more, punters latched on to the George Bridgland-trained Montiers as Pinturischio's successor at the top of the betting market. Few would have begrudged Bridgland a Derby triumph after what had happened to Angers the year before, and on paper, Montiers appeared to have as good a chance as any. In his Derby warm-up, Montiers had taken the Prix Hocquart at Longchamp, beating fellow Epsom contender Aliosha.

Another interesting raider from France was the bay colt Dicta Drake, a son of the 1955 Derby winner Phil Drake. Not unlike his father in appearance, Dicta Drake was owned and trained by the same 1955 combination of Madame Leon Volterra and Francois Mathet, and had won the Grand Prix de Printemps the week prior to Epsom.

While Ireland was represented by the 2,000 Guineas third Time Greine – a soft-ground performer trained by Seamus McGrath – the top English hopes seemed to lie with Just Great, Pardao and Sovrango. Just Great had taken the Royal Stakes at Sandown in April and had then solidified his place in the Derby field by winning the Brighton Derby Trial. The interesting aspect of Just Great's bid was that the colt was actually trained at Epsom by S. Ingham, and no locally-trained horse had triumphed in the Derby since April The Fifth in 1932. The chestnut colt Pardao was one of the most progressive horses in the field. Trained by Captain Boyd-Rochfort, Pardao had won the Lingfield Derby Trial in his build-up, beating another Epsom hopeful, the Sir Gordon Richards-trained Nicomedus, a son of the 1949 Derby winner Nimbus. The biggest horse in the field was the Harry Wragg-trained Sovrango, a colt well over sixteen hands high. Sovrango was unbeaten in his two runs as a three-year-old and had won a useful trial in the Chester Vase. As well as the fancied Sovrango, Wragg also saddled the outsider Psidium. Totally unconsidered come Derby day, Psidium had been slaughtered by Montiers over ten furlongs in France in April before making a similarly nondescript impression in the 2,000 Guineas at Newmarket. Frenchman Roger Poincelet took the mount on the 66/1 shot.

Psidium shocks the field to win at 66/1.

The ground was extremely fast for this particular running of the Derby, and as the horses broke away, Pardao and Montiers were quickly to the head of affairs, although as the field settled in to a racing pattern after two furlongs, outsiders Patrick's Choice and Pinzon dictated proceedings.

As the field began their descent, chief French challengers Montiers and Dicta Drake were placed in mid-division, and here the Irish hope Time Greine – going well at the time – was baulked by jostling horses and dropped back out of contention. Time Greine aside, there were few that could blame ill-luck in running, as this was, despite the big field, a far from aggressive edition of the Derby.

Coming down the hill, Patrick's Choice still held the lead from Supreme Verdict and Pinzon, but once the runners came to the home straight, a plethora of challengers gobbled up the leaders and set sail for glory. Sweeping past the brief leader Supreme Verdict, there were now six with exceptionally strong chances, and they were Cipriani, Sovrango, Latin Lover, Pardao, Dicta

Drake and Psidium. Of the group, Psidium had been dead last at the mile marker, and was still in a lowly position rounding Tattenham Corner.

With two furlongs to run, Cipriani and Sovrango were duelling for supremacy, but their private battle only served in the cutting of each other's throats, as in behind, the remainder of the leading bunch were about to pounce. With 100 yards to go, Harry Carr drove the fancied Pardao into the lead, but no sooner had he done so when Dicta Drake arrived on the scene with the same finishing burst that had seen his father swallow up Panaslipper six years previously. Just as the French were preparing to celebrate their third Derby victory in seven years, Psidium delivered one final burst of speed to get up under Poincelet and win by two lengths in stunning style. Dicta Drake held Pardao by a length for second with Sovrango fourth. The disappointing favourite, Montiers, had been prominent early on but his challenge proved to be a timid one, as the colt faded to finish twenty-fifth of the twenty-eight that

Psidium led in by his owner Mrs Plesch.

| FATE / HORSE | WEIGHT | JOCKEY | ODDS |
| --- | --- | --- | --- |
| **1st – Psidium** | 9-0 | R. Poincelet | 66/1 |
| **2nd – Dicta Drake** | 9-0 | M. Garcia | 100/8 |
| **3rd – Pardao** | 9-0 | W.H. Carr | 13/2 |
| 4th – Sovrango | 9-0 | G. Moore | 100/7 |
| 5th – Cipriani | 9-0 | R. Hutchinson | 66/1 |
| 6th – Latin Lover | 9-0 | D. Smith | 20/1 |
| 7th – Just Great | 9-0 | N. Sellwood | 9/1 |
| 8th – Bounteous | 9-0 | J. Sime | 50/1 |
| 9th – Nicomedus | 9-0 | A. Breasley | 25/1 |
| 10th – Hot Brandy | 9-0 | T. Gosling | 66/1 |
| 11th – Aliosha | 9-0 | L. Flavien | 30/1 |
| 12th – Belliqueux II | 9-0 | F. Palmer | 25/1 |
| 13th – Scatter | 9-0 | J. Mercer | 50/1 |
| 14th – Supreme Verdict | 9-0 | P. Powell | 40/1 |
| 15th – Oakville | 9-0 | E. Hide | 66/1 |
| 16th – Fontana Di Trevi | 9-0 | B. Swift | 66/1 |
| 17th – Polyktor | 9-0 | D. Keith | 66/1 |
| 18th – Patrick's Choice | 9-0 | J. Uttley | 66/1 |
| 19th – Gallant Knight | 9-0 | E. Smith | 50/1 |
| 20th – Owen Davis | 9-0 | S. Smith | 50/1 |
| 21st – Neanderthal | 9-0 | G. Bougoure | 20/1 |
| 22nd – Time Greine | 9-0 | W. Williamson | 100/9 |
| 23rd – Perfect Knight | 9-0 | G. Lewis | 33/1 |
| 24th – Pinzon | 9-0 | E. Larkin | 66/1 |
| 25th – Montiers | 9-0 | G. Thiboeuf | 5/1* |
| 26th – Dual | 9-0 | J. Lindley | 100/8 |
| 27th – Prince Tudor | 9-0 | W. Rickaby | 66/1 |
| 28th – Ploermel | 9-0 | J. Massard | 66/1 |

31 May 1961
Going – Firm
Winner – £34,548
Time – 2 mins 36 ⅖ secs
Favourite – Montiers
28 Ran

| | |
| --- | --- |
| Psidium | Chestnut colt by Pardal – Dinarella |
| Dicta Drake | Bay colt by Phil Drake – Dictature |
| Pardao | Chestnut colt by Pardal – Three Weeks |

Winner bred by Owner (Mrs A. Plesch)
Winner trained by H. Wragg at Newmarket

started, increasing the recent Derby gloom for his trainer Bridgland and jockey Gerard Thiboeuf.

Psidium's win, exciting and dashing as it was, came as a total shock. The horse had shown nothing in his warm-up races and his return to the winner's enclosure was greeted with stunned silence. Indeed, Aboyeur at 100/1 in 1913 had been the last true shock in the Derby and that horse was only awarded the race after the 'original' winner, the 6/4 favourite Craganour, was disqualified for bumping others.

But on this Derby day at Epsom, Psidium proved that a position at the top of the betting market does not always translate to a place at the top of the finishing order, and the way that Poincelet guided the colt from last to first was certainly impressive. It was a first Derby win for Harry Wragg as a trainer, with his Sovrango coming home well in fourth, while the winning owner, Mrs Arpad Plesch, had bred Psidium in Ireland out of an Italian mare called Dinarella. For Psidium's sire, Pardal, the 1961 Derby proved something of a crowning moment, as the stallion was also responsible for the third-placed Pardao.

The Derby of 1961 proved to be a very open contest, and it was certainly hard to gauge where Psidium ranked among modern winners of the race, obviously because of his poor form prior to Epsom. This problem was heightened further when Psidium injured a tendon after the Derby. He never raced again, but his place in the record books was already assured.

# LARKSPUR

It is like no other Flat race. The undulations, tight swings and corners of Epsom Downs make it the most unique course of all. The Derby is not always about the best horse; it can often be about survival. With the Derby often comes rough and tumble. One of the fiercest of all Derbys arrived in 1962 and would be unlike any that had gone before it, or indeed any that have graced Epsom since.

Favourite for the 1962 Derby was Hethersett, a superbly balanced, relaxed sort of horse that was considered an ideal Epsom type. Hethersett had been a leading two-year-old and had leapt to Derby favouritism at three by winning the Brighton Derby Trial in an authoritative manner. Trained by Dick Hern and ridden by the veteran Harry Carr, the worry over Hethersett was his ability to stay, although the fast ground on Derby day gave his followers every reason for optimism.

One trainer beginning to establish himself on the Flat scene, following a spectacular career training National Hunt horses, was the County Tipperary-based Vincent O'Brien. In his time training jumpers, O'Brien had saddled winners of four Cheltenham Gold Cups, three Champion Hurdles and three Grand Nationals. Among his successes prior to the 1962 Blue Riband of Flat racing were winners of two Irish Derbys, a St Leger and a Prix de l'Arc de Triomphe. On this occasion, the Irish trainer saddled Sebring and Larkspur. Sebring, the self-selected mount of jockey Pat Glennon, had at one time been extremely well fancied for the Derby, but had slipped somewhat in the betting following a disappointing sixth in the Irish 2,000 Guineas. Larkspur was more of a dark-horse challenger, and was a son of the 1954 winner Never Say Die.

Larkspur had sufficient stamina in his pedigree – through not only his Derby-winning father, but also his dam, Skylarking. A chestnut, like his father, Larkspur had won his previous outing at Leopardstown and was ridden by Australian Neville Sellwood.

As in the year before, the 1962 Derby appeared very open, with the trials failing to unveil a definitive gap in superiority between many of the runners. In a field where many could be given chances, Silver Cloud, Pindaric, Miralgo, High Noon and Le Cantilien stood out. Silver Cloud, trained by Jack Jarvis, had won the Chester Vase, while Pindaric – a son of the 1953 hero Pinza – had won the Lingfield Derby Trial, beating Bill Williamson's Derby mount Miralgo, a horse that had previously won the Timeform Gold Cup. High Noon, partnered by Edward Hide, had won the Craven Stakes at Newmarket before finishing fifth in the 2,000 Guineas, while Le Cantilien, trained by Francois Mathet, was the top hope of France. A firm-ground lover, the bay colt Le Cantilien had previously been runner-up in the Prix Lupin.

Scobie Breasley's mount, Prince d'Amour, delayed the start for a while having been kicked, but once the runners were on their way, it was an outsider in Romancero that shot into a commanding lead.

As the horses started coming down the hill, those on the outside of the big field of twenty-six began drifting inwards to gain a better position. From that moment, chaos broke out. What happened next resulted in one of the most sensational Derbys of all time. As a number of horses were jostled back, the trailing pair of Romulus and Crossen collided with the heels of the backpedallers, and fell. With the stricken pair on the turf, those behind were given no chance and, in a huge melee, Hethersett, Pindaric, Changing Times, Persian Fantasy and King Canute II also fell, meaning that seven in total had been eliminated from the race, and the sight of loose horses galloping round Tattenham Corner set a scene more reminiscent of the Grand National than the Derby.

Leaving behind the brutal incidents, the blinkered Valentine led the remainder round Tattenham Corner, closely followed by River Chanter, Escort, Sebring and Le Cantilien, but the fancied Miralgo began to drop away tamely.

River Chanter, under Jimmy Lindley, took over in the straight, but going best of all now was the Irish raider Larkspur, and once the chestnut colt hit the front two furlongs out, the result was never in danger. Showing superb acceleration, the smallish but particularly neat Larkspur flew home to record a distinctly more comfortable success than the two-length winning margin over Arcor indicated. The French horse Le Cantilien filled third place.

Not surprisingly, Larkspur did not receive the most robust applause as he crossed the winning line, with many of the spectators transfixed on the array of scattered jockeys and loose horses still on the course. Of the fallen horses, poor

Larkspur leads home the 1962 Derby field having survived the mid-race carnage.

King Canute II had received injuries so severe he had to be put down, while Pindaric and Hethersett suffered cuts and Romulus returned back lame and bleeding. Some of the jockeys too had been badly affected. Carr suffered a concussion, Wally Swinburn injured a neck in his fall from Romulus and Stan Smith came out worst of all, breaking a leg after parting company with Persian Fantasy. It was a sad end to a tough race, and although no blame was attached to a particular horse or rider, the steward's inquest stated that too many of the horses did not belong in a race like the Derby, and that many were dropping back too early, causing interference. Of those that failed to complete, Hethersett proved himself a fine horse by winning the St Leger later in the season, while at stud was responsible for the 1969 Derby winner Blakeney.

The unhappy episodes aside, Larkspur had proved far superior to the horses that had completed the race, and he too had almost been brought down by the fall of Hethersett, possibly resulting in the slightly below average time. Even so, Larkspur – the first winner to be sired by a former Derby winner since Mahmoud in 1936 – must have been a fine horse, for the colt had suffered an interrupted preparation and was only a week removed from having heat in a hock. For a horse that was at one time thought to be a doubtful runner, his courage and toughness surely must be recognised, as should the feat of being able to get Larkspur to Epsom that O'Brien achieved.

O'Brien had bought Larkspur as a yearling for 12,200 guineas at the Dublin Sales on behalf of American owner Mr Raymond Guest. It was a dream of Mr Guest to win the Derby, the Cheltenham Gold Cup and the Grand National. The latter two races would come his way in time, courtesy of the legendary Irish jumper L'Escargot, while there was yet more Derby success laying in wait for Guest in the not-too-distant future. For O'Brien, little Larkspur's triumphant day was just the beginning. The future for him would deliver a catalogue of glorious Derby days on Epsom's famous Downs.

## 1962 DERBY RESULT

| FATE / HORSE | WEIGHT | JOCKEY | ODDS |
|---|---|---|---|
| **1st – Larkspur** | 9-0 | N. Sellwood | 22/1 |
| **2nd – Arcor** | 9-0 | R. Poincelet | 40/1 |
| **3rd – Le Cantilien** | 9-0 | Y. Saint-Martin | 8/1 |
| 4th – Escort | 9-0 | J. Mercer | 20/1 |
| 5th – Sebring | 9-0 | T.P. Glennon | 100/6 |
| 6th – Prince D'Amour | 9-0 | A. Breasley | 22/1 |
| 7th – Triborough | 9-0 | E. Smith | 28/1 |
| 8th – River Chanter | 9-0 | J. Lindley | 22/1 |
| 9th – High Noon | 9-0 | E. Hide | 100/7 |
| 10th – Spartan General | 9-0 | G. Ramshaw | 100/1 |
| 11th – Miralgo | 9-0 | W. Williamson | 8/1 |
| 12th – Pavot | 9-0 | G. Bougoure | 100/1 |
| 13th – Tannhills | 9-0 | W. Rickaby | 100/1 |
| 14th – Romancero | 9-0 | D. Keith | 100/1 |
| 15th – Valentine | 9-0 | D. Smith | 20/1 |
| 16th – Ribobo | 9-0 | D. Ryan | 100/1 |
| 17th – Son Of Pan | 9-0 | T. Masters | 100/1 |
| 18th – Young Lochinvar | 9-0 | W. Snaith | 28/1 |
| Last – Silver Cloud | 9-0 | R. Hutchinson | 100/7 |
| Fell – Pindaric | 9-0 | R.P. Elliott | 100/6 |
| Fell – Romulus | 9-0 | W. Swinburn | 50/1 |
| Fell – King Canute II | 9-0 | G. Lewis | 100/1 |
| Fell – Changing Times | 9-0 | T. Gosling | 100/1 |
| Fell – Hethersett | 9-0 | W.H. Carr | 9/2* |
| Fell – Persian Fantasy | 9-0 | S. Smith | 100/1 |
| Fell – Crossen | 9-0 | M. Larraun | 22/1 |

6 June 1962
Going – Firm
Winner – £34,786
Time – 2 mins 37 ⅗ sces
Favourite – Hethersett
26 Ran

| | |
|---|---|
| Larkspur | Chestnut colt by Never Say Die – Skylarking |
| Arcor | Bay colt by Arbar – Corejada |
| Le Cantilien | Bay colt by Norseman – La Perie |

Winner bred by Messrs Philip A. Love Ltd
Winner trained by M.V. O'Brien at Cashel, Co. Tipperary, Ireland

Relko thrashes the 1963 Derby field.

# RELKO

Just because a horse has outstanding speed does not necessarily mean it will win the Derby. The normally fierce gallop round Epsom's dips and twists will often blunt what stamina the speed merchants have before they reach the final stages. Every so often though, there comes an exception: a horse with blazing pace coupled with the class and toughness to see out the Derby distance. Certainly in recent Derbys before 1963, Crepello had illustrated an incredible turn of foot over shorter distances, together with powerful stamina over longer trips. Even though the field for the 1963 race was considered sub-standard, one horse possessed the special qualities of a fine Derby winner.

Trained in France by Francois Mathet, Relko had simply been an electric two-year-old, winning twice over five furlongs. At three, Relko had set himself up for Epsom by winning the French 2,000 Guineas, again displaying top-class speed. However, with stamina a question mark, there were rumours in the build-up to the race that Relko would bypass Epsom in favour of a tilt at the French equivalent. Even though Relko had never raced over the Derby distance in his life, the rumours were soon quashed by Mathet, and Relko eventually lined-up for the big race as a warm favourite, partnered by one of the better French jockeys to have graced the Derby scene, Yves Saint-Martin.

The field that opposed Relko was deep in size but lacked the overall class associated with the Derby. As one of the few English challengers at the top of the betting market, the John Oxley-trained chestnut, Merchant Venturer, seemed to possess sound claims. The colt had shown true battling qualities when landing the Dante Stakes at York, and was a son of Hornbeam, fourth in Lavandin's Derby.

Relko and jockey Yves Saint-Martin are led in by Mme Dupre.

The Brighton Derby Trial winner Portofino, the 2,000 Guineas third Corpora – the mount of Lester Piggott – and Deep Gulf, the Irish runner representing 1962's winning trainer Vincent O'Brien, all held respectable chances, while one horse had leapt from relative obscurity to eventually start as second-favourite. The horse in question was Duplation, trained by Captain Boyd-Rochfort. Duplation had won the Lingfield Derby Trial in fine style and, as such, his Derby odds had tumbled from 100/1 to 20/1 and then again to a final starting price of 6/1. Even so, there were many who considered the prospect of Duplation winning the Derby hard to believe; such was his quick rise from seemingly nowhere.

The 100/1 outsider Hullabaloo caused a five-minute delay at the start of the race with a display of stubbornness, and this act seemed to get the better of the well-fancied pair Duplation and Portofino, both of whom began sweating alarmingly. Eventually the race began, although the troublesome Hullabaloo was left rooted at the start, extinguishing his already hopeless chance.

Unlike some of the previous Derbys, the early pace was strong and fast, and coupled with the softer going, one trait the 1963 Derby winner would have to possess was stamina.

Iron Peg, under Harry Carr, set the gallop together with one of the long shots, Hyacinthe. The favourite Relko was kept tucked in nicely behind the leaders by Saint-Martin.

At the top of the hill, Hyacinthe began to drop away as Billy Snaith drove an Irish raider, Tarqogan, in to a challenging position – one that he maintained rounding Tattenham Corner followed by Iron Peg, Happy Omen and Credo. Relko was absolutely cruising at this stage, with Merchant Venturer and Portofino just behind.

Early on in the straight, Tarqogan held a slight advantage from Merchant Venturer and the Piggott-ridden Corpora, but with two-and-a-half furlongs to run, Relko's overall class began to tell in stunning fashion. As Saint-Martin skilfully allowed the bay colt to lengthen his stride, Relko's response was breathtaking, and the horse instantly left his opponents for dead. Bursting clear, Relko perhaps could have won by more than the six lengths that he did, if his jockey had been harder on him. However, that was not necessary, as Relko had proved that he harnessed the stamina to go with his blatantly brilliant speed and the horse became one of the easiest and most routine Derby winners for many a year. Merchant Venturer, admirably ridden by Greville Starkey on his first Derby ride, had been tracking Relko for much of the way, and had attempted to match the favourite's burst in the straight, but quite simply, Merchant Venturer could not live with the French colt, and eventually settled for second in front of the Irish runner Ragusa, a horse trained by Paddy Prendergast and one that would pay a large compliment to

Relko by later winning the Irish Derby and the St Leger, as well as, after retiring to stud, siring the 1973 Derby winner Morston. The well-backed Duplation had clearly been bothered by the preliminaries and the delay at the start and as such never ran any sort of race, eventually finishing a disappointing thirteenth.

It was a second Derby triumph for Mathet following Phil Drake's victory in 1955, while for Saint-Martin, his status would rise dramatically after winning the Derby on only his second attempt at the race, having previously been third in 1962 aboard Le Cantilien. Both Mathet and Saint-Martin were delighted for Relko's owner and breeder, Francois Dupre, who was sadly an invalid. Dupre had previously owned the 1952 Derby third Fanbourg II.

Relko had been one of the classiest Derby winners of the era, and he became the sixth French-trained winner of the race, and the third in a nine-year period. After the race though, there was some cause for concern, as Relko failed a dope test. However, the horse was cleared of any illegalities, and was finally confirmed the winner of the 1963 Derby a few months after the actual race. Among the French flyer's successes at stud were the 1973 Derby third Freefoot and the 1976 Derby second Relkino, each narrowly failing to match their father's finest achievement of marrying wonderful speed with relentless staying power.

**1963 DERBY RESULT**

| FATE / HORSE | WEIGHT | JOCKEY | ODDS |
|---|---|---|---|
| **1st – Relko** | 9-0 | Y. Saint-Martin | 5/1* |
| **2nd – Merchant Venturer** | 9-0 | G. Starkey | 18/1 |
| **3rd – Ragusa** | 9-0 | G. Bougoure | 25/1 |
| 4th – Tarqogan | 9-0 | W. Snaith | 100/1 |
| 5th – Corpora | 9-0 | L. Piggott | 100/8 |
| 6th – Portofino | 9-0 | W. Rickaby | 100/6 |
| 7th – Fighting Ship | 9-0 | S. Smith | 8/1 |
| 8th – Coliseum | 9-0 | E. Hide | 100/1 |
| 9th – Happy Omen | 9-0 | F. Durr | 100/6 |
| 10th – Doudance | 9-0 | J. Mercer | 50/1 |
| 11th – Singer | 9-0 | J. Uttley | 100/1 |
| 12th – Deep Gulf | 9-0 | T.P. Glennon | 33/1 |
| 13th – Duplation | 9-0 | J. Lindley | 6/1 |
| 14th – Fern | 9-0 | A. Breasley | 100/6 |
| 15th – Credo | 9-0 | P. Matthews | 66/1 |
| 16th – Iron Peg | 9-0 | W.H. Carr | 30/1 |
| 17th – Neverlone | 9-0 | D. Keith | 50/1 |
| 18th – Count Albany | 9-0 | F. Palmer | 100/1 |
| 19th – African Drum | 9-0 | D. Smith | 28/1 |
| 20th – Hanassi | 9-0 | R.P. Elliott | 100/1 |
| 21st – Vakil-Ul-Mulk | 9-0 | A. Harrison | 100/1 |
| 22nd – Hyacinthe | 9-0 | S. Clayton | 100/1 |
| 23rd – The Willies | 9-0 | R. Hutchinson | 66/1 |
| 24th – Final Move | 9-0 | W. Williamson | 100/7 |
| Last – Fair Decision | 9-0 | W. Swinburn | 66/1 |
| Left – Hullabaloo | 9-0 | E. Smith | 100/1 |

29 May 1963
Going – Good to Soft
Winner – £35,338 10s
Time – 2 mins 39 ⅗ secs
Favourite – Relko
26 Ran

| | |
|---|---|
| Relko | Bay colt by Tanerko – Relance III |
| Merchant Venturer | Chestnut colt by Hornbeam – Martinhoe |
| Ragusa | Bay colt by Ribot – Fantan II |

Winner bred by Owner (M.F. Dupre)
Winner trained by F. Mathet at Chantilly, France

## SANTA CLAUS

The prize money for the 1964 Derby was by far the richest yet. The £72,067 on offer to the winning horse was double the amount that Parthia earned when collecting the previous biggest prize in 1959. It was perhaps surprising then that, given the high numbers of runners in recent years, only seventeen horses faced the starter, matching St Paddy's year of 1960 as the smallest Derby field since fifteen lined up in 1947. It may have been the softer-than-normal going, but more likely the presence in the field of a scintillating-looking individual had done enough to scare off many would-be opponents.

As a two-year-old, Santa Claus had won Ireland's most important juvenile race, the National Stakes at The Curragh, subsequently becoming winter favourite for the Derby. Santa Claus made his reappearance at three in the Irish 2,000 Guineas at the same course, and his performance there was quite simply breathtaking. Never once being shown the whip by jockey Billy Burke, the horse crushed his rivals with ease and arrogance and was installed as the hottest favourite for Epsom since Crepello. Trained in Ireland by Mick Rogers, Santa Claus would be having just his fourth ever run come the Derby, and had never competed at further than a mile. Even so, the impression that Santa Claus had made at The Curragh was so strong that he was expected to take the extra distance in his stride, and being by a former St Leger winner in Chamossaire, the optimism seemed justified. For the Derby, the well-tempered, bay favourite was partnered by Scobie Breasley in place of Burke, while the soft conditions were expected to be of no detriment whatsoever.

The most likely threats to Santa Claus seemed set to come from the French-trained pair of Baldric II and Corah IV, Sweet Moss and the impressive-looking

The 1964 Derby gets underway.

Oncidium. The challenge for Baldric II – a fine-actioned colt – was to conquer the curse that had plagued recent 2,000 Guineas winners in the Derby, as no victor at Newmarket had followed up at Epsom since Crepello in 1957. The Guineas winner's compatriot, Corah IV, had been pleasing connections, including trainer Geoffrey Watson, immensely in the build-up to the race and had been the subject of much ante-post activity in the betting market as rumours of his impressive work spread. Second on both his starts during the season, Corah VI was a son of Shantung, bitterly unlucky in Parthia's Derby. Sweet Moss, representing Noel Murless and Lester Piggott, had opened eyes with a stylish win in the Dante Stakes at York, but the strongest home challenge appeared to lie with the Jack Waugh-trained Oncidium. A medium-sized, well-balanced horse with an ultra-competitive heart, Oncidium had advertised fine Epsom credentials when handling the ups and downs of

The brilliant Santa Claus gave jockey
Scobie Breasley his first of two Derby triumphs.

Lingfield in his Derby trial. The colt was very impressive in his win; crushing his opposition, including fellow Epsom rival Lionhearted. Oncidium was owned and bred by the senior steward, Lord Howard de Walden, and had a jockey in Eph Smith who had won the 1939 Derby on Blue Peter. Like Santa Claus, Oncidium was also sired by a St Leger winner, the excellent Alcide, and with the going on the soft side, Oncidium's relentless galloping style was expected to give the colt a major chance.

Indeed, as the field broke away, Oncidium seemed determined to make the race a thorough test of stamina as he shot into an early lead, followed by Hotroy, Balustrade and Baldric II. It was noticeable that, even at halfway, Breasley was keeping Santa Claus under a tight hold at the back of the field, either conserving the colt's energy on the decidedly sticky ground or simply showing the utmost confidence in his partner's ability.

Once the field reached Tattenham Corner, the whole nature of the race changed. Fading dramatically out of contention, Oncidium was overhauled by Indiana, and that horse then led into the straight from the big outsider Dilettante II and Baldric II. Even rounding the famous corner, Santa Claus was only eighth and still had much to do with just three furlongs to run. But inside the final two furlongs, the tactics of Breasley became apparent. Moving the favourite to the centre of the track, Santa Claus came gracefully and unhurried with his run, and though his acceleration was not as smooth or as devastating as it had been at The Curragh, he picked up Indiana with seventy yards to run – to the delight of the crowd – and seemed to laugh at those who had doubted him moments earlier, as he held total control of the race as he crossed the line a length winner. Behind the runner-up Indiana came Dilettante II, a mighty effort given it was only the bay's second lifetime race, while among the finishing positions of the more fancied horses were Baldric II in fifth and the most disappointing Oncidium in eighth. The second French fancy, Corah VI, was never a factor, finishing third from last.

True, Santa Claus had not delivered a performance of mind-blowing proportions, and the time was distinctly slow, albeit on sticky ground, but the horse had demonstrated his class, doing all that was necessary, giving the impression he could have won by further if driven harder. Additionally, Santa Claus met with some in-race interference at the six-furlong marker.

Scobie Breasley had been tactically perfect on Santa Claus, showing patience and true faith in his mount. It was the jockey's first win in the Derby at the thirteenth attempt, and at fifty, Breasley was one of the oldest riders to win the race. Breasley had ridden his first winner at Werribee in his native Australia at the age of fourteen. He hailed from Wagga Wagga, a small town between Melbourne and Sydney, and had previously ridden Ki Ming to victory in the 1951 2,000 Guineas.

Santa Claus became the third Irish winner in seven years, and gave Mick Rogers his second Derby success after Hard Ridden in 1958. More was to follow, as Santa Claus became the first Derby winner for fifty-seven years to follow up his Epsom win with victory in the Irish Derby at The Curragh, where he won in a far more electrifying style under Billy Burke. Sadly, the high-class Santa Claus died of thrombosis in 1970 before he truly had a chance to make his mark at stud.

## 1964 DERBY RESULT

| FATE / HORSE | WEIGHT | JOCKEY | ODDS |
| --- | --- | --- | --- |
| 1st – Santa Claus | 9-0 | A. Breasley | 15/8* |
| 2nd – Indiana | 9-0 | J. Lindley | 30/1 |
| 3rd – Dilettante II | 9-0 | P. Matthews | 100/1 |
| 4th – Anselmo | 9-0 | P. Cook | 100/1 |
| 5th – Baldric II | 9-0 | W. Pyers | 9/1 |
| 6th – Crete | 9-0 | G. Bougoure | 22/1 |
| 7th – Penny Stall | 9-0 | R. Poincelet | 40/1 |
| 8th – Oncidium | 9-0 | E. Smith | 9/2 |
| 9th – Balustrade | 9-0 | W. Williamson | 25/1 |
| 10th – Sweet Moss | 9-0 | L. Piggott | 100/8 |
| 11th – Hotroy | 9-0 | G. Lewis | 33/1 |
| 12th – Cold Slipper | 9-0 | J. Roe | 50/1 |
| 13th – Con Brio | 9-0 | R. Hutchinson | 40/1 |
| 14th – Roquefeuil | 9-0 | D. Ryan | 100/1 |
| 15th – Corah IV | 9-0 | J. Deforge | 9/1 |
| 16th – Dromoland | 9-0 | J. Mercer | 100/1 |
| Last – Lionhearted | 9-0 | W.H. Carr | 18/1 |

3 June 1964
Going – Good to Soft
Winner – £72,067
Time – 2 mins 41.98 secs
Favourite – Santa Claus
17 Ran

| Santa Claus | Bay colt by Chamossaire – Aunt Clara |
| --- | --- |
| Indiana | Bay colt by Sayajirao – Willow Ann |
| Dilettante II | Bay colt by Sicambre – Barbizonnette |

Winner bred by Dr F.A. Smorfitt
Winner trained by M. Rogers at The Curragh, Co. Kildare, Ireland

The awesome Sea Bird II.

# SEA BIRD II

When the Derby winners of modern times are assessed to determine the very best winners of the race, it is fair to say that every critic will have their own opinion of a 'pecking order'. Crepello was undoubtedly a wonderful horse, full of versatility and power. The 1970s were treated to the flair of Nijinsky while the '80s had the devastating Shergar. But, in general opinion, the 1965 Derby produced, quite possibly, the finest winner of them all.

Sea Bird II was an imposing-looking chestnut colt, over sixteen hands high, and was easy to identify on the racecourse because of a white streak on his face and white socks on his back legs. Like many of the fancied Derby runners in the preceding years, he was trained in France, this time by Etienne Pollet. As a two-year-old, Sea Bird II had won two of his three races, with his sole defeat coming in the Grand Criterium. But it was his progression as a three-year-old that had most people salivating. After winning the Prix Greffulhe on his seasonal debut, Sea Bird II delivered a performance of tantalising promise over ten-and-a-half furlongs in the Prix Lupin at Longchamp, demonstrating the acceleration that would become his trademark; winning as he liked. Subsequently, and with a bid for the French Derby refuted in favour of Epsom, he was made the red-hot favourite. Franco-American bred by his owner Jean Ternynck, Sea Bird's detractors reasoned he had never raced left-handed, and that his temperament had been somewhat suspect in the past – two traits most horses have trouble overcoming at Epsom – but the colt's awesome power and potential were impossible to ignore. Having arrived in England the day before the race, and with a gentle, orientating spin on the course taken on the eve of the big day, Sea Bird II would start a 7/4 favourite for the Derby, and as an

indication of his status in relation to the rest of the field, the next horse in the betting came in at 10/1.

That next horse happened to be another foreign invader, the Irish colt Meadow Court, trained by Paddy Prendergast. Originally, Prendergast had hoped to run the well-fancied Hardicanute, but when that horse fell victim to a bout of coughing, Meadow Court – runner-up in the Dante Stakes – took over as the stable's main hope. As Derby day approached, it was revealed that Lester Piggott had been booked to ride the chestnut colt, and being the reigning Champion Jockey, as well as having won three previous Derbys, Meadow Court's price consequently fell dramatically.

The English-based trials had proved bitterly disappointing, with no horse establishing themselves as a legitimate threat to win the Derby. Look Sharp had won the Dee Stakes at Chester but had since run miserably, Ballymarais had won an inconclusive Dante, while Bill Williamson's mount Solstice had captured a tight Lingfield Derby Trial – yet his price of 40/1 was a fair reflection of his true chance. Therefore, the two colts considered the most likely to give Sea Bird II a real challenge were Gulf Pearl and Niksar. Gulf Pearl had won the Chester Vase and was by a sire in Persian Gulf that had got the 1959 Derby hero Parthia. Niksar was thought to be the top English colt, having led all the way in

The field at Tattenham Corner in 1965. Sea Bird II, dark jockey silks and cap, lies poised in sixth.

the 2,000 Guineas. Trained by Walter Nightingall, Niksar was bred to stay, and his recent homework had given connections reasons to be optimistic for Epsom.

Even in the parade, it was evident that Sea Bird II was a cut above his competitors, as he strode around the ring covered in muscle and looking as strong as an ox.

From the off, the outsiders Sunacelli and Bam Royal were the first to show from I Say and Meadow Court, while the favourite was nicely settled by jockey Pat Glennon, just in behind the leaders in the early stages.

At the top of the hill, Bam Royal's run began to hit a retreat and it was the Guineas hero Niksar, travelling smoothly, that came through to join Sunacelli in leading from I Say, Meadow Court and the improving Gulf Pearl.

Despite hanging slightly left on his first run on such a course, Sea Bird II was moving like a champion, and rounding Tattenham Corner he appeared to be relishing the contest.

The one surprising aspect of the 1965 Derby was that the pace was nothing more than sedate. This puzzled many people, who believed the English colts would try and examine Sea Bird's stamina with a brutally fast gallop. However, the cut-throat chase never materialized, and as the leaders turned in to the straight, and with Gulf Pearl now weakening badly, it was I Say that shot clear from his stablemate Niksar and quickly opened up a three-length lead.

However, the race was about to witness a stunning explosion of class and power. From being two-and-a-half lengths down as the leaders approached the two-furlong marker, the devastating acceleration that Sea Bird II possessed now came in to play, as the favourite burst through, stamping his authority firmly over the rest of the field. As soon as he got to the front, the race was over. Sea Bird II was not even extended in winning, and he crossed the line on the bridle, an extremely impressive two-length winner. Meadow Court – a subsequent winner of the Irish Derby and the King George – could not live with him, although he stayed on bravely for second, with the Nightingall-trained pair of I Say and Niksar next to finish.

Sea Bird II had won in the style of a true champion and had proved himself as a horse that had everything: speed, power, blistering acceleration and, above all, class. He was a racehorse that gave off a feeling of invincibility, such was his stature. His owner had been breeding horses since before the Second World War, including the 1,000 Guineas heroine of 1950, Camaree, and had turned down an offer of some $200,000 after Sea Bird's defeat in the previous season's Grand Criterium – a race where he would suffer his only ever loss.

It was another fine triumph for France and gave Etienne Pollet a first Derby winner, although the trainer had won an Irish Derby three years previously courtesy of the smart Tambourine. It was also a first Derby win for Australian Pat Glennon, who amazingly had not fancied Sea Bird's chances as much as when he had ridden the Vincent O'Brien-trained Sebring in Larkspur's Derby.

As brilliant as Sea Bird's Derby success had been, there was better still to come. Later that year, the colt headed for Longchamp and the Prix de l'Arc de Triomphe. In what is still considered one of the finest fields ever assembled for the race, there were countless horses ready to wrestle Sea Bird's proud mantle from him. In a star-studded field were the unbeaten French Derby winner Reliance II, Meadow Court, the Kentucky Derby winner from America Tom Rolfe, the exciting Russian champion Anilin and the Coronation Cup winner Oncidium. After coming clear of the majority of the field with his compatriot Reliance II, Sea Bird II simply went to another level, raising his game to new heights and crushing his opponents in a runaway six-length victory from Reliance II. It was his destructive performance in the Arc coupled with his graceful, effortless success at Epsom that determines Sea Bird II as perhaps the finest Derby winner of all time.

His offspring included another huge, talented chestnut Derby contender in Gyr and a horse that would develop in to a dual Champion Hurdle winner in Sea Pigeon. Those two aside, Sea Bird II was nothing extraordinary at stud. On the racecourse, however, he was a champion. Good enough to be labelled the best.

## 1965 DERBY RESULT

| FATE / HORSE | WEIGHT | JOCKEY | ODDS |
|---|---|---|---|
| **1st – Sea Bird II** | 9-0 | T.P. Glennon | 7/4* |
| **2nd – Meadow Court** | 9-0 | L. Piggott | 10/1 |
| **3rd – I Say** | 9-0 | R. Poincelet | 28/1 |
| 4th – Niksar | 9-0 | W. Rickaby | 100/8 |
| 5th – Convamore | 9-0 | E. Hide | 40/1 |
| 6th – Cambridge | 9-0 | A. Breasley | 25/1 |
| 7th – Ballymarais | 9-0 | W. Pyers | 25/1 |
| 8th – Vleuten | 9-0 | J. Deforge | 25/1 |
| 9th – Solstice | 9-0 | W. Williamson | 40/1 |
| 10th – Look Sharp | 9-0 | J. Roe | 25/1 |
| 11th – Alcade | 9-0 | D. Smith | 25/1 |
| 12th – Gulf Pearl | 9-0 | J. Lindley | 100/8 |
| 13th – Silly Season | 9-0 | G. Lewis | 50/1 |
| 14th – Billionaire | 9-0 | G. Bougoure | 66/1 |
| 15th – King Log | 9-0 | G. Hutchinson | 50/1 |
| 16th – Bucentaur | 9-0 | S. Smith | 50/1 |
| 17th – Sunacelli | 9-0 | B. Connorton | 66/1 |
| 18th – Foothill | 9-0 | J. Mercer | 20/1 |
| 19th – Bam Royal | 9-0 | P. Matthews | 66/1 |
| 20th – Creosote | 9-0 | P. Robinson | 66/1 |
| 21st – As Before | 9-0 | G. Starkey | 33/1 |
| Last – Sovereign Edition | 9-0 | R. Maddock | 66/1 |

2 June 1965
Going – Good
Winner – £65,301
Time – 2 mins 38.41 secs
Favourite – Sea Bird II
22 Ran

| | |
|---|---|
| Sea Bird II | Chestnut colt by Dan Cupid – Sicalade |
| Meadow Court | Chestnut colt by Court Harwell – Meadow Music |
| I Say | Brown colt by Sayajirao – Isetta |

Winner bred by Owner (M.J. Ternynck)
Winner trained by E. Pollet in France

1966

# CHARLOTTOWN

Beginning from the middle of May 1966, the Minister of Agriculture had placed a ban on Continental horses entering the country. This was because of the threat of swamp fever – an infectious equine anaemia. Therefore, no French horses would be attempting to follow-up Sea Bird's memorable win of the year before. It also meant that the chances of a home-trained runner becoming the first to win since Psidium in 1961 rose dramatically.

Also unlike the year before, the competition at the top of the betting market was strong. The race featured a meeting of the top two-year-olds of the season before, the home-trained pair of Charlottown and Pretendre. Charlottown had been unbeaten in three starts at two, and had marked himself down as a colt of real potential. However, under the guidance of first-year public trainer Gordon Smyth, the bay horse was forced to miss his intended reappearance at three in the Brighton Derby Trial after being found lame in his box. Consequently, Charlottown made his seasonal debut in the Lingfield Derby Trial, and perhaps not at his peak, despite finishing fast, was beaten, although the race was run at a slow pace and the horse hung to his left. Possibly for this reason, Charlottown was not placed at the very top of the market for Epsom, with this honour going partly to Pretendre. The chestnut Pretendre had ranked right alongside Charlottown at two, and was trained by Jack Jarvis, who had twice trained Derby winners: Blue Peter in 1939 and Ocean Swell in 1944. Pretendre was a big, well-built colt with a giant stride, and had possessed sufficient speed to win the shorter-distanced Dewhurst Stakes and Observer Gold Cup as a juvenile. Additionally, Pretendre had previously won at Epsom, but had disappointed when only eighth when favourite for the 2,000 Guineas.

Sharing 9/2 favouritism with Pretendre was one of three Derby contenders trained by Vincent O'Brien, Right Noble. A beautifully-actioned brown horse,

Right Noble had won his only race of the season impressively over a mile-and-a-half at Ascot and was to be ridden by Lester Piggott. The jockey had broken from his long-standing partnership with Noel Murless earlier in the season, after a disagreement regarding riding plans. Piggott had ridden two Derby winners for Murless, but he would now focus on what would become an awesome combination with O'Brien, one that would dominate the Derby scene until the late 1970s. In 1966, O'Brien also saddled Grey Moss – a horse that had won Chester's Dee Stakes by an amazing twenty lengths – and the 2,000 Guineas fifth, Ambericos.

Other notable contenders for the 1966 Derby were Hermes, Sodium and Black Prince II. In eight runnings of York's Dante Stakes, only St Paddy had won and gone on to win the Derby, yet Hermes appeared to have a decent-enough chance of emulating the 1960 hero, having also won the Thirsk Classic Trial. Hermes was a lazy individual, trained by John Oxley and ridden by Greville Starkey. Sodium, the mount of Frankie Durr, was a son of the 1961 winner Psidium and had won Brighton's Derby Trial earlier in the season, but perhaps the most interesting of those just outside the most favoured group was the Jack Watts-trained Black Prince II. True to his name, the colt was pure black in colour, but despite winning the Lingfield Derby Trial – beating Charlottown in the process – the horse seemed virtually friendless in the betting market, starting at a rather generous 20/1.

Rain had graced the build-up to the race and it continued as the runners prepared to line-up. Charlottown held up the start when he had to be replated after losing a shoe in the paddock. When the field finally got away to a good even start, it was St Puckle – a son of St Paddy – that jumped in to the lead from Allenheads, One For You, Mehari and Drevno.

With a mile to run and with both Pretendre and Charlottown some way back, tragedy struck as Northern Union broke a fetlock and sadly had to be destroyed.

St Puckle and Right Noble had delivered a solid, fast-paced gallop up front and while Pretendre and Charlottown definitely picked up strongly coming down the hill, they were still well adrift of the lead, with Scobie Breasley aboard Charlottown having to work tirelessly to get his colt interested.

Bill Rickaby on St Puckle and Piggott on Right Noble still held command entering the straight, but a plethora of talented challengers were poised to pounce on the leaders. First, Durr moved Sodium into a threatening position before Black Prince II stormed through to take what appeared to be a decisive grip on proceedings.

Black Prince II was really moving like a winner under Jimmy Lindley, but soon, the class of the two-year-old crop were about to confirm their superiority. First, Pretendre battled his way to the head of affairs and then Charlottown – squashed against the rails going round Tattenham Corner – glided through a crack on the inside and settled down for a battle with Pretendre.

Clearly the best two colts in the 1966 field, Charlottown gets the better of Pretendre.

Scobie Breasley is all smiles as he comes back on Charlottown
with trainer Gordon Smyth (top hat).

**1966 DERBY RESULT**

| FATE / HORSE | WEIGHT | JOCKEY | ODDS |
|---|---|---|---|
| **1st – Charlottown** | 9-0 | A. Breasley | 5/1 |
| **2nd – Pretendre** | 9-0 | P. Cook | 9/2* |
| **3rd – Black Prince II** | 9-0 | J. Lindley | 20/1 |
| 4th – Sodium | 9-0 | F. Durr | 13/1 |
| 5th – Crisp And Even | 9-0 | G. Bougoure | 66/1 |
| 6th – Ambericos | 9-0 | J. Mercer | 18/1 |
| 7th – Khalekan | 9-0 | D. Lake | 20/1 |
| 8th – Radbrook | 9-0 | W. Williamson | 50/1 |
| 9th – Right Noble | 9-0 | L. Piggott | 9/2* |
| 10th – St Puckle | 9-0 | W. Rickaby | 40/1 |
| 11th – Allenheads | 9-0 | E. Hide | 50/1 |
| 12th – Bermondsey | 9-0 | R. Maddock | 100/1 |
| 13th – Hermes | 9-0 | G. Starkey | 100/8 |
| 14th – One For You | 9-0 | G. Lewis | 100/1 |
| 15th – Nous Esperons | 9-0 | E. Eldin | 100/1 |
| 16th – Borodino | 9-0 | S. Clayton | 100/1 |
| 17th – Dream Man | 9-0 | B. Taylor | 100/1 |
| 18th – Splice The Mainbrace | 9-0 | R. Hutchinson | 66/1 |
| 19th – Baylanx | 9-0 | P. Sullivan | 100/1 |
| 20th – Mehari | 9-0 | D. Smith | 33/1 |
| 21st – Drevno | 9-0 | B. Raymond | 100/1 |
| 22nd – Raket II | 9-0 | D. Keith | 50/1 |
| 23rd – Permit | 9-0 | G. Cadwaladr | 100/1 |
| Last – Grey Moss | 9-0 | L. Ward | 8/1 |
| Pulled-Up – Northern Union | 9-0 | J. Roe | 33/1 |

25 May 1966
Going – Good
Winner – £74,489 10s
Time – 2 mins 37.63 secs
Joint Favourites – Pretendre & Right Noble
25 Ran

| Charlottown | Bay colt by Charlottesville – Meld |
|---|---|
| Pretendre | Chestnut colt by Doutelle – Limicola |
| Black Prince II | Black colt by Arctic Prince – Rose II |

Winner bred by The Someries Stud
Winner trained by G. Smyth at Lewes, Sussex

The pair tore right away from the shell-shocked Black Prince II and Sodium, and endured their own mighty struggle. Neither would give in, and even though Charlottown hung again to his left and had to be urged on by Breasley, it was he that got up on the line to deny Pretendre by a neck in a scintillating finish – one of the closest and most exciting of modern times. Black Prince II had battled on arduously further back to claim third ahead of Sodium. The other joint favourite, Right Noble, faded to eventually finish ninth.

So Charlottown had won the Derby, and unlike Breasley's previous Derby win aboard Santa Claus, he had been made to work extremely hard on his equine partner to get the better of the ultra-game Pretendre – given a fine ride by youngster Paul Cook.

The owners of Charlottown, Sir Harold and Lady Zia Wernher, had long been racing and breeding horses of their own, but this was their first Derby win. Charlottown certainly had a Classic pedigree, as his dam, Meld, had won the 1955 fillies Triple Crown of the 1,000 Guineas, Oaks and St Leger.

The 1966 Derby was a particularly pleasing result for the 'home team' and had been dominated by two almost inseparable colts that had delivered in most satisfying style upon their two-year-old form, and were undeniably the best two horses in the field. It was also a result where the form had played out, with the third and fourth-placed horses having won recognised Derby Trials. Ultimately, it was the powerful and resilient Charlottown that had won the day and become the newest hero of the Epsom Derby.

horse was still a maiden. Dominion Day was sired by Charlottesville, the stallion responsible for the previous year's hero, Charlottown. Dominion Day's most impressive performance of the season had come at Leopardstown where he was beaten a short head by another Derby contender, Royal Sword, in early May. That same Leopardstown trial had caught the eye of many pundits, and prompted a gamble that saw Royal Sword promoted to Derby second-favourite. The horse was trained by Mick Rogers, who was looking for his third Derby win following the glories of Hard Ridden and Santa Claus, and Royal Sword was partnered by Jimmy Lindley.

The Irish contingent aside, Dart Board – trained by Sir Gordon Richards – made most appeal from the home team. A chestnut colt, Dart Board was a son of the 1954 Derby third Darius, and had been a very easy winner of the Brighton Derby Trial earlier in the season. Dart Board had progressed well from his two-year-old campaign, one that had seen him win the Dewhurst Stakes, and the horse had the Derby's top jockey of recent years, Scobie Breasley, to guide him round.

1967 was the first Derby where starting stalls were used, and as the twenty-two-strong field broke away to the delight of the crowd, it was Kiss Of Life – a son of the 1954 hero Never Say Die – and the Paul Cook-ridden El Mighty, that rose to early prominence.

Although the big outsider Kiss Of Life rapidly began to fade away before the halfway stage, El Mighty continued to travel strongly in front and, after a mile, he was still right there. Royal Palace was travelling extremely well, and as the field descended into Tattenham Corner, the favourite had coasted through from a midfield position to be on the heels of the leaders.

Swooping round in thunderous, transfixing style, El Mighty was clinging onto supremacy from Belted – a son of the 1958 winner Hard Ridden – outsiders Privy Seal and Persian Genius and the favourite Royal Palace. The fancied Irish stablemates, Great Host and Dominion Day, were struggling at this point, with the latter clearly not acting on the course, while it emerged later that Great Host had endured a miserable passage, being knocked about during the race.

Halfway up the straight, and the spectators rose to their feet as Royal Palace made his bid for glory. Leaving behind El Mighty and the rest with sheer arrogance, Royal Palace surged clear with two furlongs to run and although Lester Piggott on Ribocco came from out of the pack to challenge on the extreme outside, Moore simply asked his partner for a turn of foot and received an instant response, as the favourite went away again, meeting the rising ground and flying home like a bird.

Ribocco had come from some eight lengths back from Royal Palace at one stage, yet he had no answer to the favourite's acceleration and raw power and

# ROYAL PALACE

As had happened in 1965, one horse in particular would dominate the betting market for the Derby. Trained by Noel Murless, Royal Palace was similar in make-up to the handler's 1957 winner Crepello in that he was a big, robust colt with plenty of speed and power. As a two-year-old, the bay Royal Palace had emerged as a genuine Classic contender with two wins from three starts, including a win in the Royal Lodge Stakes – where he had been left twelve lengths behind at the start. Indeed, the colt's only defeat as a juvenile had arrived when he was an awkward, backward youngster in Ascot's Coventry Stakes. Already a big favourite for the imminent Derby, Royal Palace began his three-year-old campaign with a short-head victory over the highly regarded French colt Taj Dewan in the 2,000 Guineas, cementing his place at the top of the Epsom market. Like Crepello, Royal Palace was bred to stay and he was widely recognised as the class horse in the 1967 field. Working tremendously well prior to the race, Royal Palace started a hot 7/4 favourite, partnered by Australian George Moore, whose previous best Derby performance had come aboard Sovrango in 1961.

The main challenge to Royal Palace was thought to come from the Irish horses. Paddy Prendergast and Mick Rogers both had contenders that were considered threats to Murless' colt. Prendergast trained Great Host and Dominion Day as he attempted to capture his first Derby win. Great Host had won both his races as a three-year-old, including a defeat of one-time Derby hopeful Sun Rock – another Murless-trained colt, one that just happened to be related to Royal Palace – in convincing style in the Chester Vase. Even more fancied than his stablemate was Dominion Day – surprising, considering the

El Mighty is the leader rounding Tattenham Corner.

had to be content with second place, the second time in three years that Piggott had claimed such a position. Dart Board came home in third with Royal Sword the best of the ultimately tame Irish raid in fourth.

Royal Palace's win had given his owner Mr Jim Joel a realisation of a long-standing dream of winning the Derby. Mr Joel had bred Royal Palace, having taken over the Childwick Bury Stud on the death of his father some forty-five years previously. Twenty years after Royal Palace's Derby win, Joel's scarlet and black colours would be carried to victory by Maori Venture in the Grand National.

It was a third Derby win for Noel Murless, yet the trainer refused to admit whether Royal Palace ranked higher in his opinion than Crepello or St Paddy. Murless, who would end his career with nine Champion Trainer titles to his name, would later receive a much-deserved knighthood, and is regarded as one of the finest trainers of the twentieth century.

George Moore became the fifth Australian jockey to win the Derby in recent years, following the successes of Rae Johnstone, Neville Sellwood, Scobie Breasley and Pat Glennon. Moore reported Royal Palace to have been at optimum temperament throughout the race, never giving a moment's worry

Jockey George Moore is greeted by daughter Michelle having won the 1967 race aboard Royal Palace.

**1967 DERBY RESULT**

| FATE / HORSE | WEIGHT | JOCKEY | ODDS |
|---|---|---|---|
| **1st – Royal Palace** | 9-0 | G. Moore | 7/4* |
| **2nd – Ribocco** | 9-0 | L. Piggott | 22/1 |
| **3rd – Dart Board** | 9-0 | A. Breasley | 10/1 |
| 4th – Royal Sword | 9-0 | J. Lindley | 15/2 |
| 5th – Helluvafella | 9-0 | A. Barclay | 200/1 |
| 6th – Landigou | 9-0 | C. Barends | 200/1 |
| 7th – Sloop | 9-0 | G. Starkey | 33/1 |
| 8th – Dancing Moss | 9-0 | P. Boothman | 100/1 |
| 9th – Starry Halo | 9-0 | F. Durr | 22/1 |
| 10th – Hang On | 9-0 | G. Cadwaladr | 150/1 |
| 11th – Dominion Day | 9-0 | D. Lake | 8/1 |
| 12th – Hambleden | 9-0 | J. Mercer | 66/1 |
| 13th – Great Host | 9-0 | Y. Saint-Martin | 100/9 |
| 14th – Acroplier | 9-0 | D. Keith | 66/1 |
| 15th – Belted | 9-0 | A. Murray | 200/1 |
| 16th – Persian Genius | 9-0 | E. Eldin | 200/1 |
| 17th – El Mighty | 9-0 | P. Cook | 22/1 |
| 18th – Kiss Of Life | 9-0 | E. Larkin | 200/1 |
| 19th – Privy Seal | 9-0 | B. Raymond | 200/1 |
| 20th – Scottish Sinbad | 9-0 | V. Faggotter | 200/1 |
| 21st – Tapis Rose | 9-0 | R. Hutchinson | 28/1 |
| Last – Great Pleasure | 9-0 | G. Lewis | 66/1 |

7 June 1967
Going – Good
Winner – £61,918
Time – 2 mins 38.36 secs
Favourite – Royal Palace
22 Ran

| | |
|---|---|
| Royal Palace | Bay colt by Ballymoss – Crystal Palace |
| Ribocco | Bay colt by Ribot – Libra |
| Dart Board | Chestnut colt by Darius – Shrubswood |

Winner bred by owner (Mr H.J. Joel)
Winner trained by C.F.N. Murless at Newmarket

in the new starting stalls, and the jockey also suggested the horse could have gone on to win by further than he did, such was his awesome cruising speed during the contest. For Moore, his greatest moment would also turn out to be his final Derby ride, as he was soon to leave the country amid controversial circumstances.

There was no doubting that the best horse had won the 1967 Derby, and Royal Palace became the first Derby winner for the excellent sire Ballymoss, while also becoming the thirty-third horse to complete the 2,000 Guineas/Derby double. Although he did not go on to win the Triple Crown as had been hoped, Royal Palace confirmed his powers as an older horse by winning the King George in 1968.

# SIR IVOR

The 1968 Derby began the trend that saw a new breed of racehorse consistently appear on the Epsom scene. With North American stock becoming increasingly influential in the top European races, more and more of the finest young horses from across the Atlantic were finding their way to British trainers. Half of the Derby winners between 1968 and 1989 were North American-bred, with a magnificent, all-conquering stallion named Northern Dancer proving himself time and time again to be the most important sire of runners in the Derby – and countless other races – to emerge in the twentieth century.

Sir Ivor was just one of these 'new breed' of champions bred in North America, and fittingly, he started the 1968 Derby as one of the hottest favourites for years. Sir Ivor was a tall, bay colt, with his main weapon a deadly turn of foot that he would unleash with explosiveness at the end of his races. Owned by Mr Raymond Guest of Larkspur fame, Sir Ivor was trained in Ireland by Vincent O'Brien and the colt had been that country's top two-year-old the year before. He had won his last three races at two, including the top juvenile contest in France, the Grand Criterium. Because of a lack of stamina in his pedigree, Sir Ivor had to be ridden in a certain way, where he was held up for long periods before being allowed to deliver his electric finishes. These tactics were on display to full effect in his two runs at three prior to the Derby, where he first won at Ascot and then, in a superb exhibition of raw speed, in winning the 2,000 Guineas, thrashing the previously unbeaten Petingo. His performance in the Guineas had prompted O'Brien to reveal that Sir Ivor was the best horse he had trained – even superior to Larkspur and Ballymoss – and

Tall and athletic, Sir Ivor possessed a demonesque turn of foot that won him the 1968 Derby.

it was an opinion shared by Lester Piggott, who had ridden Sir Ivor in the Guineas and would again be on board at Epsom. Despite the fact that the colt had never even galloped further than a mile-and-a-quarter, Piggott considered Sir Ivor a certainty for the Derby.

Sir Ivor's frightening performance at Newmarket had apparently scared off many potential Derby rivals. It did not help the spectacle when the Guineas runner-up Petingo proceeded to flop badly in the Prix Lupin at Longchamp, ruling him out of Epsom, while another Derby prospect, the talented but

Sir Ivor shoots past long-time leader Connaught to win the 1968 Derby.

infuriatingly inconsistent Candy Cane, also bypassed the Derby having failed miserably in the Irish 2,000 Guineas at The Curragh. Ribero – a full brother to the 1967 Derby runner-up Ribocco – was also scratched from the line-up after disappointing his trainer, Fulke Johnson-Houghton, in work just days before the race.

Of the twelve that did oppose Sir Ivor, however, the big, bay colt Connaught was thought to have a fair chance of emerging from what was considered a poor bunch of challengers to the favourite. A son of the 1960 Derby winner, St Paddy, Connaught was trained by Noel Murless and carried the same colours as the 1967 hero Royal Palace for owner Jim Joel. Although he had only been runner-up in the Chester Vase, Connaught possessed no small amount of power and drive, and had been sparkling in his homework. Connaught was partnered by Sandy Barclay, the man who had succeeded Piggott when the Champion Jockey had split from Murless.

Of the remainder, only Remand and Laureate made any kind of appeal to racegoers. The unbeaten Remand – a son of the excellent Alcide – had won the Chester Vase earlier in the season, while Laureate would be a first Derby ride for the twenty-five-year-old Willie Carson, a Scot who would develop into one of Epsom's finest sons. Laureate had won two useful Derby trials: the Dee Stakes at Chester and the Lingfield Derby Trial, on the latter occasion beating fellow Epsom raider Torpid.

The early leader in the race was the 150/1 outsider Benroy, but this running of the Derby would be, as they say in football, a game of two halves. The first half kicked off with intent when Connaught picked up the running coming down the hill. For a large, long-striding horse, Connaught was handling the twists and turns of Epsom admirably. As he led the field vigorously round Tattenham Corner, he appeared to be travelling ominously well, with Society and Remand his closest pursuers. Looking back for the favourite, Piggott could be seen tight against the inside rail, radiating confidence aboard Sir Ivor, who was simply cruising in an almost casual manner.

Cruising the favourite may have been, but at the three-furlong marker, Barclay drove Connaught on again, and the bay quickly opened up a four-length lead – a lead that he held well in to the straight.

Just as it looked as though a shock may be on the cards, Piggott, with a beautiful 'lack' of effort, sent Sir Ivor forward to deliver his raid, and the speed that the favourite showed was stunning. Quickening like a cheetah with a quarter-of-a-mile to go, Sir Ivor headed Connaught in the last hundred yards, and the moment he passed the leader, he came back on the bit, winning in mesmerising style by a length-and-a-half. Such was the divine speed of Sir Ivor, Piggott never had to use the whip, as the favourite became one of the cosiest and most deliberate of all Derby winners. Connaught had run his heart

Sir Ivor is led in by Mrs Raymond Guest.

out and had come away with great credit in finishing second. His performance would have been good enough to have won a number of Derbys, yet he had met with a horse harnessed with lightning speed.

Piggott considered Sir Ivor to be the best of his four Derby winners, and although the time was on the slow side, the manner in which Sir Ivor quickened off the race gallop marked him down as a horse of exceptional quality. Of his four winners, the ride Piggott gave Sir Ivor was masterful, showing total belief, confidence and judgment in his partner. This was just the first Derby success of a legendary Epsom partnership that Piggott would strike up with O'Brien.

Despite his brilliance, Sir Ivor unquestionably had to be ridden a certain way in order to preserve his still borderline stamina. Curiously, Sir Ivor lost his next four races, including the Irish Derby and the Prix de l'Arc de Triomphe. However, showing the class of a fine Derby winner, Sir Ivor finished his career with wins in the Champion Stakes at Newmarket and finally in the Washington International at Laurel Park in America. The race in America was run on abysmal ground, going that Sir Ivor had never encountered before, yet the horse proved he was a champion by delivering the same acceleration that had made him one of the most exciting Derby winners of recent times, and certainly one of the most enjoyable to watch. Soon after, Sir Ivor was retired to stud, where he would enjoy a highly successful career. Among his offspring that made an impact at Epsom were Cavo Doro – second in the 1973 Derby – and Imperial Prince, runner-up a year later.

**1968 DERBY RESULT**

| FATE / HORSE | WEIGHT | JOCKEY | ODDS |
| --- | --- | --- | --- |
| **1st – Sir Ivor** | 9-0 | L. Piggott | 4/5* |
| **2nd – Connaught** | 9-0 | A. Barclay | 100/9 |
| **3rd – Mount Athos** | 9-0 | R. Hutchinson | 45/1 |
| 4th – Remand | 9-0 | J. Mercer | 4/1 |
| 5th – Society | 9-0 | W. Williamson | 28/1 |
| 6th – Torpid | 9-0 | G. Starkey | 25/1 |
| 7th – Atopolis | 9-0 | J. Lindley | 45/1 |
| 8th – Royal Rocket | 9-0 | F. Durr | 66/1 |
| 9th – Myrtus | 9-0 | A. Murray | 150/1 |
| 10th – Floriana | 9-0 | W. Rickaby | 200/1 |
| 11th – Laureate | 9-0 | W. Carson | 100/8 |
| 12th – Benroy | 9-0 | D. Keith | 150/1 |
| Last – First Rate Pirate | 9-0 | P. Cook | 200/1 |

29 May 1968
Going – Good
Winner – £58,525 10s
Time – 2 mins 38.73 secs
Favourite – Sir Ivor
13 Ran

Sir Ivor        Bay colt by Sir Gaylord – Attica
Connaught       Bay colt by St Paddy – Nagaika
Mount Athos     Bay colt by Sunny Way – Rosie Wings

Winner bred by Mill Ridge Farm, USA
Winner trained by M.V. O'Brien at Cashel, Co. Tipperary, Ireland

# BLAKENEY

Unlike the previous two runnings of the Derby, the 1969 trials had failed to establish a clear-cut favourite for the big race. It did not help that poor weather had claimed a number of fixtures, robbing the season of some important races, like the Chester Vase and Dee Stakes. Possibly more so than in most years, the Derby market focused on the form of horses in their two-year-old campaigns, with many of the runners fancied more on potential than what they had actually achieved on the racecourse.

One horse that definitely fitted in to this category was the Fulke Johnson-Houghton-trained Ribofilio. The colt had been an exceptional juvenile and had been expected to progress at three. But strangely, Ribofilio flopped badly when a searing-hot favourite for the 2,000 Guineas, clouding his status for Epsom. However, in a year where no other colts were making a name for themselves, a decent public workout at Sandown was enough to make Ribofilio favourite for the Derby, although in fairness, he was an extremely speculative one – given that the same workout had failed to impress the horse's Derby jockey, four-time winner Lester Piggott.

Another horse that was well fancied but with precious little experience was Paddy's Progress, a son of the 1960 Derby winner St Paddy. Paddy's Progress – a strong, grand-looking horse – had the same connections as the 1968 runner-up Connaught, and the colt had been pleasing Noel Murless in his homework by training admirably with Connaught. Paddy's Progress had only run twice in his life, and although he had won the Craven Stakes at Newmarket earlier in the season, his intended Derby trial, the Chester Vase, was abandoned, so the horse entered the 1969 battle both unexposed and inexperienced.

Derby victors Blakeney and jockey Ernie Johnson.

One of the trials that did receive a lot of focus on this occasion was the Lingfield Derby Trial. No horse had won at Lingfield and followed up in the Derby since Parthia in 1959. The race was won by The Elk, trained by the Beckhampton-based Jeremy Tree, but the horse that gathered most of the attention was the runner-up Blakeney. A big, bay son of the 1962 Derby favourite Hethersett and out of the 1964 Oaks runner-up Windmill Girl, Blakeney was having his first run of the season at Lingfield after recovering from a bout of equine flu suffered in April. During the race, Blakeney was baulked numerous times but finished like a train, confirming that he was getting stronger all the time. Blakeney was owned and trained by Arthur Budgett in Berkshire and was ridden by a young Derby debutant in Ernie Johnson.

Perhaps the most informative Derby trial on this occasion came from France. The race was the Prix Lupin at Longchamp and the winner was the speedy brown colt Prince Regent. The horse had looked very good in beating, among others, fellow Derby contender Belbury, although many worried that the Etienne Pollet-trained colt would not have sufficient stamina for a race such as the Derby.

With the going perfect, the huge field of twenty-six – twice the number that had lined-up for Sir Ivor's Derby of the year before – set out for what was sure to be one of the most competitive of Derbys in years, and it was Moon Mountain – representing the 1968 winning stable of Vincent O'Brien – that broke out to dictate the early running. Also up with the lead in the opening stages were a quartet of outsiders: Timon, Mitsouko, Ribomar and Sylvalgo.

As the race progressed, it was interesting to note that Paddy's Progress was being kept very wide and out of trouble by Sandy Barclay, perhaps in an attempt to keep the inexperienced colt from encountering any unwanted grief. Unfortunately, that grief would not escape Prince Regent. Coming down the hill, the French raider was impeded by other horses, so much so that he lost his action and was very nearly brought down. The incident had left Prince Regent almost last and extremely wide on the track as the field rounded Tattenham Corner.

The white-faced Moon Mountain still held an advantage swooping round Tattenham Corner, although he was being craftily tracked by Brian Taylor on Shoemaker and Barclay on Paddy's Progress, both of whom appeared ready to threaten for honours – if good enough. Timon and the Geoff Lewis-ridden Agricultore were also in the leading bunch as the race started to get serious. Making progress from further down the field was Blakeney, who had been tucked against the rails, unsighted for most of the way.

As the leaders entered the straight, it became obvious a thrilling finish was on the cards. Moon Mountain led on, but he was being chased frantically

Pictured in 2001, Arthur Budgett trained the 1969 Derby hero Blakeney.

by Shoemaker and Paddy's Progress, but being brilliantly guided through the tiniest of openings by Johnson, it was Blakeney that was finishing the strongest.

Storming up the inside, Blakeney overthrew the leaders inside the final furlong and in, a desperate battle, held off the game Shoemaker – who in turn had overtaken Moon Mountain moments before – to win by a length. Prince Regent, despite his mid-race drama, had contributed to a pulsating finish by making up a tremendous amount of late ground to finish just a length further back in third. Both Prince Regent and his jockey, Jean Deforge, could be considered mightily unlucky, and may well have won the race given better luck in running. Moon Mountain had run a brave race to finish fourth, while the green Paddy's Progress had to settle for seventh. Despite staying on towards the end, the favourite Ribofilio never seriously threatened to win the race, with Piggott claiming the colt had pulled too hard during the contest.

Blakeney had shown real determination to win the 1969 Derby and had landed his trainer a dream result in the process. Budgett had bred Blakeney at his Park Farm Stud in Oxford and had tried to sell the horse as a yearling. However, with a sales reserve of 5,000 guineas, Blakeney only fetched 3,000, so Budgett decided to keep him and train the horse himself. Budgett could also feel proud of his decision to stick with young Ernie Johnson when many had advised him to go with a more experienced rider. Johnson had repaid Budgett's faith with a classy ride reminiscent of Lester Piggott himself, with a vintage display of patience and guidance before exploiting his horse's considerable power and drive.

After the Derby, Blakeney saw his colours lowered in the Irish equivalent, beaten into fourth by the unlucky Epsom third Prince Regent. Blakeney trained on at four and, despite running in some very important races, including a match-up with his Epsom successor, Nijinsky (who beat Blakeney resoundingly), in the 1970 King George, he never quite hit the heights of his finest hour in the 1969 Epsom Derby.

## 1969 DERBY RESULT

| FATE / HORSE | WEIGHT | JOCKEY | ODDS |
| --- | --- | --- | --- |
| **1st – Blakeney** | 9-0 | E. Johnson | 15/2 |
| **2nd – Shoemaker** | 9-0 | B. Taylor | 25/1 |
| **3rd – Prince Regent** | 9-0 | J. Deforge | 13/2 |
| 4th – Moon Mountain | 9-0 | Y. Saint-Martin | 28/1 |
| 5th – Ribofilio | 9-0 | L. Piggott | 7/2* |
| 6th – Tantivy | 9-0 | J. Seagrave | 100/1 |
| 7th – Paddy's Progress | 9-0 | A. Barclay | 11/2 |
| 8th – Intermezzo | 9-0 | R. Hutchinson | 15/1 |
| 9th – Belbury | 9-0 | R. Poincelet | 100/9 |
| 10th – Hard Slipper | 9-0 | G. Starkey | 200/1 |
| 11th – Stoned | 9-0 | D. Keith | 18/1 |
| 12th – Dutch Bells | 9-0 | A. Murray | 100/1 |
| 13th – Chadwick Stone | 9-0 | B. Jago | 200/1 |
| 14th – Pardigras | 9-0 | D. Ryan | 50/1 |
| 15th – Backing Britain | 9-0 | W. Carson | 100/1 |
| 16th – Sylvalgo | 9-0 | W. Bentley | 50/1 |
| 17th – Ribomar | 9-0 | J. Mercer | 50/1 |
| 18th – Soroco | 9-0 | E. Eldin | 100/1 |
| 19th – Agricutore | 9-0 | G. Lewis | 18/1 |
| 20th – Santamoss | 9-0 | E. Hide | 75/1 |
| 21st – Agustus | 9-0 | W. Williamson | 25/1 |
| 22nd – Dieudonne | 9-0 | D. Yates | 200/1 |
| 23rd – Timon | 9-0 | J. Gorton | 50/1 |
| 24th – The Elk | 9-0 | J. Lindley | 100/9 |
| 25th – Silence D'Or | 9-0 | T.P. Burns | 200/1 |
| Last – Mitsouko | 9-0 | D. Richardson | 200/1 |

4 June 1969
Going – Good
Winner – £63,108 6s
Time – 2 mins 40.30 secs
Favourite – Ribofilio
26 Ran

| | |
| --- | --- |
| Blakeney | Bay colt by Hethersett – Windmill Girl |
| Shoemaker | Chestnut colt by Saint Crespin III – Whipcord |
| Prince Regent | Brown colt by Right Royal V – Noduleuse |

Winner bred by Park Farm Stud
Winner trained by Owner (Mr A.M. Budgett) at Whatcombe, Berkshire

The imposing Nijinsky and the Derby's finest-ever jockey, Lester Piggott.

# NIJINSKY

Every so often, a horse emerges on the racing scene that is taken to the hearts of the professionals and public alike. These horses capture the imagination and set the adrenalin flowing in sheer anticipation of their presence. For every so-called 'great' racehorse that meets merely half the expectation placed upon them, there are countless others that fail to live up to the hype, seemingly falling by the wayside. In 1970, there emerged a true champion, a racehorse that had the ability to draw crowds to the racecourse in their thousands. Here was a horse that would become a modern-day giant of the game.

Bred in Canada and owned by Mr Charles Engelhard, Nijinsky was a big, strong, handsome bay colt with a magnificent-looking head and was the star of the County Tipperary stables of Vincent O'Brien. Nijinsky had been a truly exceptional two-year-old, winning all five of his races, including the important Dewhurst Stakes at Newmarket. Like another O'Brien Derby legend, Sir Ivor, Nijinsky was blessed with a devastating blitz of speed, but there was more to him than the 1968 hero, both on and off the racecourse. Very temperamental, Nijinsky was an extremely difficult horse to handle and O'Brien had to exert the utmost patience in preparing him for his races. However, the patience appeared to be being rewarded mightily, as Nijinsky won both of his opening two races at three, including the 2,000 Guineas, to take his seven-race unbeaten streak to Epsom. Nijinsky's sire was the superb American stallion Northern Dancer. At the time of the 1970 Derby, Northern Dancer was barely known as a stallion in Europe, but over time, he would prove to be perhaps the greatest sire of racehorses of all time. Northern Dancer had been the American three-year-old Champion of 1964, having won the first two legs of the American Triple Crown – the Preakness Stakes at Baltimore, Maryland and the Kentucky Derby – but had failed to stay in the final leg, the mile-and-a-half Belmont Stakes in New York. With this in mind, coupled with the fact that Nijinsky had never raced over the Derby distance, some questioned Nijinsky's stamina, although both O'Brien and Lester Piggott were adamant the horse would stay.

With eleven horses going to post for the 1970 Derby, it was the smallest field since ten lined-up in 1916, but this was a quality collection of individuals, and even though Nijinsky was heavily fancied to win, there was no shortage of worthwhile challengers.

France sent over a particularly strong raid on this occasion, with both Gyr and Stintino extremely talented colts. The most intriguing of the pair was Gyr. Although he was an awkward, lanky colt, he was an absolutely massive chestnut with an abundance of raw power. Gyr's breeding too was impeccable for the Derby, being by the great 1965 winner Sea Bird II and out of a St Leger-winning dam in Feria, while his trainer, Etienne Pollet, had delayed his own retirement by a year because of the presence of Gyr in his yard. There were plenty of people that believed Gyr's somewhat clumsy, bumbling style to be unsuited to Epsom,

Nijinsky crushes Gyr to win in 1970.

however, and the horse had also failed to convince many with his latest performance, a win in the Prix Hocquart at Longchamp. Even so, Gyr remained a potential threat to Nijinsky, and he was joined in his raid across the Channel by the Francois Boutin-trained Stintino. A talented and unbeaten bay colt, Stintino had put in an electric finish to win the Prix Lupin at Longchamp most recently, impressing massively as he beat all the top French three-year-olds, with the exception of Gyr who was absent. A win for either Gyr or Stintino would give the French their eighth post-war Derby victory.

With the representatives from Ireland and France dominating the betting market, the chances of a home-trained winner looked remote. There were, however, a number of useful colts, including Cry Baby and Approval. Trained by Noel Murless, Cry Baby was a son of Crepello and had impressed when

winning the Royal Stakes at Ascot in April, while Approval was the entry of promising young trainer Henry Cecil, and the horse had beaten, among others, Cry Baby in the Dante Stakes at York.

Despite his suspect temperament, Nijinsky was very calm and composed during the pre-race preliminaries and, as the field broke away on ground on the firm side of good, it was Sandy Barclay aboard Cry Baby that set out to make the running.

The pattern of the race was settled as the field made their descent into Tattenham Corner; Cry Baby still led from Long Till, Mon Plaisir, Meadowville, Gyr and Nijinsky, with the lattermost travelling very comfortably under Piggott.

One of the main talking points before the race was the issue of how Gyr would handle the unique Epsom track. As he came down the hill on the heels of the leaders, the answer was that the colt had adapted better than expected. In spite of his style and action, Gyr moved round Tattenham Corner in grand style and when he overtook Long Till for the lead at the three-furlong marker in the straight, it became obvious just why Pollet held the horse in the highest regard.

With the other French horse, Stintino, not far off the lead, Gyr – his striking white face shining in the June sun – took command in the straight under Bill Williamson, moving beautifully with surprising balance and grace. But just as it looked as though the big chestnut had taken a winning hold on the race, Piggott began a charge on Nijinsky. Coming on the outside of the leaders at the furlong marker, the elegant acceleration that Nijinsky displayed was lethal, and the race was simply settled in a matter of seconds as soon as he hit the front. Nijinsky's finish had arrived in blistering fashion, with an irresistible combination of speed and power that quickly separated him from the French horses. At the line, Nijinsky had won the Derby by two-and-a-half lengths from Gyr and Stintino, and there were no excuses for the beaten horses.

It was the first time that Mr Engelhard had seen his horse run, and joining him as a guest to watch the race was the widow of the famous dancer the horse had been named after.

Once again, Lester Piggott had displayed his craft at Epsom to perfection, timing Nijinsky's run immaculately, dispelling in an instant any fears that the horse would not stay. It was Piggott's fifth win in the race, his second riding for O'Brien, who himself had now trained a trio of Derby winners following the victories of Larkspur and Sir Ivor.

The manner in which he stalked a fine horse like Gyr before delivering his awesome finish ranks Nijinsky as one of the best ever winners of the Derby – the sixth to be trained in Ireland. As if to prove his imperious position (and now with a huge public following), Nijinsky then sauntered home in the Irish Derby before slaughtering the best of the older generation in the King George at Ascot, totally outclassing the 1969 Derby winner Blakeney in the process. Then came the icing on the cake as Nijinsky won the St Leger at Doncaster later in the season, gloriously becoming the first horse to win the Triple Crown since Bahram in 1935, and securing a place among the all-time great racehorses. As a stallion, Nijinsky remained outstanding, and the impact he had on subsequent Derbys was huge. Passing on the proud traits he possessed as a racehorse, including his superior, powerful head, he became responsible for three future Derby winners in Golden Fleece, Shahrastani and Lammtarra, as well as a horse who himself would sire a Derby winner, Caerleon.

Nijinsky was the first son of Northern Dancer to truly impact the Derby scene. He would by no means be the last, as in future years, the likes of The Minstrel, Northern Baby, Secreto and El Grand Senor would each have their chance of matching the famous Epsom win of the legendary Irish-trained wonder, Nijinsky.

## 1970 DERBY RESULT

| FATE / HORSE | WEIGHT | JOCKEY | ODDS |
|---|---|---|---|
| **1st – Nijinsky** | 9-0 | L. Piggott | 11/8* |
| **2nd – Gyr** | 9-0 | W. Williamson | 100/30 |
| **3rd – Stintino** | 9-0 | G. Thibeouf | 7/1 |
| 4th – Great Wall | 9-0 | J. Mercer | 80/1 |
| 5th – Meadowville | 9-0 | G. Lewis | 22/1 |
| 6th – The Swell | 9-0 | Ron Hutchinson | 50/1 |
| 7th – Approval | 9-0 | G. Starkey | 13/2 |
| 8th – Long Till | 9-0 | D. Keith | 80/1 |
| 9th – Cry Baby | 9-0 | A. Barclay | 40/1 |
| 10th – Tambourine Man | 9-0 | A. Murray | 200/1 |
| Last – Mon Plaisir | 9-0 | J. Lindley | 33/1 |

3 June 1970
Going – Good to Firm
Winner – £62,311
Time – 2 mins 34.68 secs
Favourite – Nijinsky
11 Ran

| | |
|---|---|
| Nijinsky | Bay colt by Northern Dancer – Flaming Page |
| Gyr | Chestnut colt by Sea Bird II – Feria |
| Stintino | Bay colt by Sheshoon – Cynara |

Winner bred by E.P. Taylor in Canada
Winner trained by M.V. O'Brien at Cashel, Co. Tipperary, Ireland

# MILL REEF

The early 1970s was a golden era for Flat racing. At every turn, there seemed to be one superstar after another ready to rise to the top of the tree. The 1970 season had seen the great Nijinsky carry all before him; the 1971 season was to throw forward a further two horses that would gain legendary status. The first was Brigadier Gerard, a three-year-old that would perhaps go down as the best horse of the twentieth century at a distance of a mile – although he did triumph in the one-mile-four-furlong King George VI and Queen Elizabeth Stakes at Ascot in 1972. Brigadier Gerard would run fifteen times in his career, with his only defeat coming in the 1972 season to that year's gritty Derby winner, Roberto, in the Benson & Hedges Gold Cup at York.

Despite his sky-high status, Brigadier Gerard did not run in the 1971 Derby, but the horse he had beaten when winning the 2,000 Guineas at Newmarket, Mill Reef, did. Mill Reef had been an outstanding two-year-old, winning five of his six races, including the Dewhurst Stakes. On his reappearance at three, he had won the Greenham Stakes at Newbury before running a race of vast potential behind Brigadier Gerard at Newmarket. Mill Reef was a smallish bay colt bred in Virginia, USA by American art connoisseur Mr Paul Mellon, his owner, and he was trained by a young Ian Balding at Kingsclere Stables in Berkshire. The jockey of Mill Reef was Geoff Lewis, who had injured his neck at the Guineas meeting and had only just returned to the saddle, but both he and Balding were ultra-confident the horse would improve again for his showing at Newmarket, such was the brilliance Mill Reef had been showing in his homework. Considering that, Mill Reef was made the 100/30 favourite for the Derby.

Ian Balding and son Andrew at Kingsclere Stables.

Ragusa, third in the 1963 Derby behind Relko, was a horse that was making a significant mark as a stallion. In the 1971 Derby, he was responsible for four of the twenty-one runners: Frascati, Homeric, Juggernaught and Lombardo. Like his father, Homeric was considered to be a late-developing colt and had come into the Derby picture when beating Alderney – a half brother to the 1969 Derby hero Blakeney – in the Lingfield Derby Trial. Lombardo was thought to be the top hope from Ireland, having conquered the Italian Derby winner Ortis in the Player-Wills Stakes at Leopardstown in May. While Juggernaught was seen as a big outsider, Frascati was one of two horses pleasing his trainer, Noel Murless, in work prior to the big day, the other being the Dante Stakes runner-up, The Parson, the mount of Lester Piggott.

Mill Reef beats Linden Tree in the 1971 Derby.

Owner Paul Mellon leads in Mill Reef and jockey Geoff Lewis.

Other interesting challengers for the 1971 Derby were Bourbon, Millenium and Linden Tree. The temperamental Bourbon – a son of a French Derby winner in Le Fabuleux – was one of two fancied raiders from France. Bourbon was trained by Alec Head and ridden by his son, Freddie, and the horse had warmed-up for Epsom with a win in the Prix Hocquart at Longchamp. Millenium too had his supporters, having booked his place in the Derby field by winning the Prix de la Force at Longchamp in late May, one of his two wins at that course in his three-year-old campaign. Trained by Jack Cunnington Jnr, Millenium was ridden at Epsom by race debutant Maurice Philipperon. Sired by the 1957 hero Crepello, Linden Tree was perhaps the dark–horse of the 1971 Derby field, being less fancied than his French rivals. Trained by Peter Walwyn, the chestnut had impressed many when winning the Chester Vase earlier in the season.

Once again showing his mulish side, Bourbon held up proceedings by becoming troublesome in the parade, then bluntly refusing to canter down to the start. In the end, Freddie Head was forced to dismount the quarrelsome animal to get the colt to co-operate.

From an even break, it was Linden Tree that made the running from Credit Man and the big outsiders Beaming Lee and Meaden, and having reached the top of the hill, Linden Tree still held pole position under Duncan Keith, with Lombardo and Homeric now moving up to track him, while the favourite Mill Reef glided through nonchalantly to hold fourth place.

Entering the straight, the gutsy Linden Tree attempted to make a final push for glory, but the classy Mill Reef was moving sweetly on the outside. With a quarter-of-a-mile to run, the favourite – having handled Tattenham Corner with admirable fluentness – coasted into the lead, and staying-on strongly, with his sheepskin noseband making him easy to identify, he outclassed the brave Linden Tree by two-and-a-half lengths. Irish Ball finished like a train, having been well back at Tattenham Corner, to claim third from Lombardo. The French horses had disappointed on this occasion. Millenium had been stuck at the back of the field early on and had failed to strike a meaningful blow, while Bourbon had fared even worse, his antics at the start clearly wreaking havoc with his mindset, and he eventually came home thirteenth. Indeed, Alec Head stated that he would have withdrawn Bourbon had it been any race other than the Derby.

Mill Reef's size and nimbleness had proved ideally suited to Epsom and he had ultimately outpointed his rivals in convincing style. His was a popular win, coming for a dedicated supporter of racing on both sides of the Atlantic in Paul Mellon and a thirty-two-year-old trainer in Balding. Mr Mellon had named Mill Reef after an Antiguan coastline where he held a winter residence, while the 1971 Derby was the first Classic success for Balding. The trainer was part of a talented racing family. His brother Toby also trained with great success, particularly on the National Hunt side – where he trained two Grand National winners. Ian's son, Andrew, would eventually take over from his father at Kingsclere in 2002, and quickly gained his first Classic win courtesy of Casual Look in the 2003 Oaks, while Ian's daughter, Clare, became the nation's most recognisable racing presenter when she took over the top job at the BBC in the late 1990s.

It was also a first Derby win for jockey Geoff Lewis, although he had one previous Classic to his name, the 2,000 Guineas of 1969 with Right Track. The 1971 Epsom Derby meeting would become Lewis' personal moment of stardom. He also took the Oaks with Altesse Royale and, in between the two Classics, became the first jockey in history to pull off a famous Epsom treble in one season as he won the Coronation Cup aboard the 1970 Oaks heroine, Lupe.

As for Mill Reef, he simply went from strength to strength after the Derby, confirming his status as one of the finest winners of the twentieth century. He would win Sandown's Eclipse Stakes, the King George VI and Queen Elizabeth Stakes and then the Prix de l'Arc de Triomphe. With his last reversal coming when beaten into second by Brigadier Gerard in the 2,000 Guineas of 1971, Mill Reef carried over his winning streak into his four-year-old season until disaster struck when a near-fatal leg injury cut short his career. The beautifully relaxed, intelligent Mill Reef proved to be a model patient as masterful surgery was performed on his leg to save him. As if to say 'thank you', Mill Reef then proceeded to have an equally triumphant career at stud, getting two Derby winners in the 1978 hero Shirley Heights and the 1987 winner Reference Point. Mill Reef had finished his racing career, having won twelve of fourteen races, and the magnificent Derby winner of 1971 was also Champion Sire twice, in 1978 and 1987. He passed away in 1986, aged eighteen.

**1971 DERBY RESULT**

| FATE / HORSE | WEIGHT | JOCKEY | ODDS |
| --- | --- | --- | --- |
| **1st – Mill Reef** | 9-0 | G. Lewis | 100/30* |
| **2nd – Linden Tree** | 9-0 | D. Keith | 12/1 |
| **3rd – Irish Ball** | 9-0 | A. Gibert | 25/1 |
| 4th – Lombardo | 9-0 | W. Williamson | 25/1 |
| 5th – Athens Wood | 9-0 | G. Starkey | 14/1 |
| 6th – The Parson | 9-0 | L. Piggott | 16/1 |
| 7th – Homeric | 9-0 | J. Mercer | 25/1 |
| 8th – Zug | 9-0 | J.C. Desaint | 20/1 |
| 9th – Meaden | 9-0 | W. Carson | 100/1 |
| 10th – Millenium | 9-0 | M. Philipperon | 10/1 |
| 11th – L'Apache | 9-0 | E. Eldin | 25/1 |
| 12th – Frascati | 9-0 | A. Murray | 25/1 |
| 13th – Bourbon | 9-0 | F. Head | 8/1 |
| 14th – Juggernaught | 9-0 | B. Taylor | 66/1 |
| 15th – Beaming Lee | 9-0 | T. Ives | 100/1 |
| 16th – Tucan | 9-0 | G. Ramshaw | 100/1 |
| 17th – Seaepic | 9-0 | E. Hide | 30/1 |
| 18th – Coffee Royal | 9-0 | D. Maitiand | 100/1 |
| 19th – Dapper Dan | 9-0 | B. Jago | 80/1 |
| 20th – Joe's Dream | 9-0 | J. Lynch | 100/1 |
| Last – Credit Man | 9-0 | Y. Saint-Martin | 25/1 |

2 June 1971
Going – Good
Winner – £61,125 25p
Time – 2 mins 37.14 secs
Favourite – Mill Reef
21 Ran

| | |
| --- | --- |
| Mill Reef | Bay colt by Never Bend – Milan Mill |
| Linden Tree | Chestnut colt by Crepello – Verbena |
| Irish Ball | Bay colt by Baldric II – Irish Lass |

Winner bred by Owner (Mr P. Mellon) in the USA
Winner trained by I. Balding at Kingsclere, Berkshire

Barry Hills would train an agonising four Derby seconds, the first being Rheingold in 1972.

# ROBERTO

There is absolutely no doubt that Lester Piggott was the outstanding jockey of his generation, and perhaps the greatest of all time. He had everything that made up a great champion: strength in the saddle, an unrivalled tactical brain, an immense knowledge of his own equine partners – and those of his competitors – and behind a quiet, almost sombre public personality, a powerful determination to be the best. When it came to the Derby, there was simply no better man to have on board than Piggott. Only Jem Robinson between 1817 and 1836 and Steve Donoghue between 1915 and 1925 had won more Derbys (six) than Piggott's current total of five going into the 1972 event. However, as incomparably brilliant as he was, Piggott was certainly no stranger to controversy. He had already gone through a split with his previous retainer, Noel Murless, in the 1960s, and days before the 1972 Derby, a further incident occurred, although in fairness to Piggott, this episode was more of a result of his priceless talent rather than any wrongdoing.

Initially, Piggott had been scheduled to ride the Vincent O'Brien-trained outsider Manitoulin in the Derby, with the big-race favourite Roberto partnered by Australian Bill Williamson. The horses were stablemates and were both owned by Mr and Mrs John Galbreath. The drama had started the week before the Derby, when Williamson had fallen heavily at Kempton. Even though he was eventually passed fit for Epsom, a meeting involving O'Brien, Mr Galbreath and the two jockeys resulted in the champion Piggott being named as Roberto's jockey in the Derby, with Williamson to be reinstated in the future. Although it was agreed that Williamson would receive an equal share of the prize money should Roberto win, the whole situation left Williamson naturally disappointed and with his pride somewhat dented.

As for the favourite, he was a tough, not over-big, bay colt, and had been bred in America. Roberto was an exceptional two-year-old, winning three of his four races – his only setback coming in the Grand Criterium at Longchamp. Prior to the Derby, Roberto had finished runner-up in the 2,000 Guineas at Newmarket, where he had been ridden by Williamson, and O'Brien reported his colt to be working fantastically at home.

Having won the 1956 Derby with Lavandin, trainer Alec Head had high hopes of adding a second victory on this occasion courtesy of Lyphard – partnered by his son Freddie. Lyphard was sired by Northern Dancer and had won his first two races of the campaign at the French tracks Maisons-Laffitte and Longchamp. He had then been well beaten in the Prix Lupin, although that race had been run on very heavy ground, while at Epsom on Derby day the good going was far more to Lyphard's liking.

Perhaps the most intriguing horse in the 1972 Derby field was a colt that had not yet appeared at three. Trainer Noel Murless made no secret of the fact that he rated his Yaroslav very highly, possibly among the top five he had ever trained, and considering Murless had trained three previous Derby winners in Crepello, St Paddy and Royal Palace, that was extremely high praise for the inexperienced Yaroslav. An athletic-looking chestnut, Yaroslav had won both his races as a juvenile, including the Royal Lodge Stakes at Ascot, but had been denied a run at three – including an intended outing in the 2,000 Guineas – because of a virus. Obviously, his lack of experience made Yaroslav a risky betting proposition, and the last horse to win the Derby on his first run of the season was Grande Parade in 1919, yet the Derby certainly appeared tailor-made for him, with his sire being the 1964 winner Santa Claus, while Yaroslav was also a half-brother to the 1971 Oaks winner Altesse Royale. With news that Yaroslav had been working tremendously well at home, he quickly became the top English hope and was made the 4/1 joint-second favourite with Lyphard.

Pentland Firth leads the twenty-two-strong field round Tattenham Corner. The arrow indicates the position of Roberto.

Along with Harry Wragg's Chester Vase winner Ormindo and the two-time Derby winning jockey-turned-trainer Scobie Breasley's charge, Steel Pulse – fourth in the 2,000 Guineas – Rheingold was an interesting contender. Rheingold, a big, bay colt, had not acted on the Epsom course in the Blue Riband Trial but had since been very impressive when winning the Dante Stakes at York, causing some to re-evaluate his Derby prospects. Rheingold was trained by Barry Hills and owned by Austrian Henry Zeisel.

It was the French horse Sukawa under Yves Saint-Martin that broke away to lead, and there he stayed for the first few furlongs until the outsider Pentland Firth took over. Pentland Firth was a son of Crepello and he was a first Derby ride for the twenty-year-old apprentice Pat Eddery. Pat's father, Jas, had been runner-up aboard Panaslipper in 1953 and third a year later on Roistar.

Pentland Firth continued to lead as the field hurtled round Tattenham Corner. Next came Willie Carson on Meadow Mint, followed by Ormindo, Manitoulin, Roberto and Mercia Boy. It was now that the French raider Lyphard took a bizarre course, drifting hopelessly wide on the track, losing yards of ground and ruining any chance he had of winning.

There were plenty of horses with winning chances as they came in to the straight, with Pentland Firth bravely keeping up his unexpected bid for glory. The chestnut Yaroslav could be seen making headway towards the outside of the leaders as the race really got going. Sadly for the Yaroslav team, it was progress that was all too brief as he could not quicken with the main players and was soon beaten.

Rheingold had been some way back at Tattenham Corner, but as jockey Ernie Johnson sent his powerful and game mount down the middle of the track, he began to make up a tremendous amount of ground, and with a quarter-of-a-mile to run, he was joined on his inside by Roberto. The pair then swallowed up Pentland Firth and commenced their own private war to the line.

The closing stages developed into a brutal fight – a situation that would become a trademark of Roberto's future races – and there was no small amount of jostling in the charge to the line. Locked together, neither horse giving an inch, it was a sight to behold, but at the line, it was Roberto that had emerged victorious by a short head, having simply refused to be beaten under a momentous drive by Piggott. Pentland Firth had stayed on admirably to take third ahead of another Barry Hills-trained horse, Our Mirage.

It was no surprise that a steward's enquiry was announced shortly after the finish. Roberto and Rheingold had appeared to clash inside the final furlong, although Rheingold was the one that seemed to be causing more interference. After an agonising wait of twenty-two minutes, it was announced that the places remained unaltered and that Roberto had won the Derby. Rheingold had given his all, but his second place would be a position that cursed his

Roberto (nearest rails) edges Rheingold in a Derby thriller.

trainer for the rest of his career, with Hills frustratingly saddling three more Derby runner-ups in the future and unfortunately – to date – failing to win. Rheingold did have a fine career after the Derby, the dark-bay's starring moment arriving when he won France's most prestigious race, the Prix de l'Arc de Triomphe.

Piggott did not receive the warmest of receptions when he brought Roberto – his record-equalling sixth Derby win – into the winner's enclosure, with many of the crowd siding with the unlucky Williamson in light of the latter being 'jocked-off'. In stark contrast, Williamson received a booming reception after he won the next race on the card, the Woodcote Stakes.

None of this though was the fault of Roberto, and the horse had shown himself to be a true fighter with enormous heart in his Derby win. There was no doubt that Piggott had extracted the most from Roberto's ability and the jockey had always had the favourite positioned near the lead Roberto was a horse that did not appreciate being held up in his races, unlike a previous O'Brien Derby winner, Sir Ivor.

Roberto had been bred by his owners, the Galbreaths, at their Derby Dan Farm in Kentucky, USA, and the horse had been named after the legendary baseball player Roberto Clemente. Mr Galbreath also happened to be the owner of Major League Baseball's Pittsburgh Pirates.

Roberto was badly beaten in his next race, the Irish Derby, but in August 1972, ridden by the top rider in American racing, Braulio Baeza, Roberto claimed a major scalp when inflicting the only ever defeat on the magnificent Brigadier Gerard at York, showing the toughness that had earned him a Derby victory. For this fact alone, Roberto will be remembered as one of the hardest, most unforgiving of Derby winners, and he went on to have a fine career at stud, coming close to siring the Derby winner of 1982, when he was responsible for runner-up Touching Wood and third-placed Silver Hawk.

**1972 DERBY RESULT**

| FATE / HORSE | WEIGHT | JOCKEY | ODDS |
| --- | --- | --- | --- |
| **1st – Roberto** | 9-0 | L. Piggott | 3/1* |
| **2nd – Rheingold** | 9-0 | E. Johnson | 22/1 |
| **3rd – Pentland Firth** | 9-0 | P. Eddery | 50/1 |
| 4th – Our Mirage | 9-0 | F. Durr | 100/1 |
| 5th – Gombos | 9-0 | C. Roche | 50/1 |
| 6th – Scottish Rifle | 9-0 | Ron Hutchinson | 22/1 |
| 7th – Ormindo | 9-0 | B. Taylor | 20/1 |
| 8th – Steel Pulse | 9-0 | W. Pyers | 9/1 |
| 9th – Moulton | 9-0 | E. Hide | 40/1 |
| 10th – Meadow Mint | 9-0 | W. Carson | 50/1 |
| 11th – Manitoulin | 9-0 | W. Swinburn | 66/1 |
| 12th – Charling | 9-0 | J. Lindley | 28/1 |
| 13th – Sukawa | 9-0 | Y. Saint-Martin | 66/1 |
| 14th – Palladium | 9-0 | J. Higgins | 66/1 |
| 15th – Lyphard | 9-0 | F. Head | 4/1 |
| 16th – Mercia Boy | 9-0 | R. Marshall | 200/1 |
| 17th – Yaroslav | 9-0 | G. Lewis | 4/1 |
| 18th – Paper Cap | 9-0 | J. Gorton | 200/1 |
| 19th – Donello | 9-0 | J. Mercer | 200/1 |
| 20th – Young Arthur | 9-0 | A. Murray | 200/1 |
| 21st – Mezzanine | 9-0 | P. Waldron | 200/1 |
| Last – Neptunium | 9-0 | A. Barclay | 35/1 |

7 June 1972
Going – Good
Winner – £63,735 75p
Time – 2 mins 36.09 secs
Favourite – Roberto
22 Ran

| | |
| --- | --- |
| Roberto | Bay colt by Hail To Reason – Bramalea |
| Rheingold | Bay colt by Faberge II – Athene |
| Pentland Firth | Bay colt by Crepello – Free For All |

Winner bred by Owner (Mr J.W. Galbreath) in the USA
Winner trained by M.V. O'Brien at Cashel, Co. Tipperary, Ireland

# 1973

# MORSTON

The beginning of the 1973 race.

In recent years, the Derby had tended to be dominated by one horse in both the build-up and the race itself. Indeed, eight of the previous ten Derbys had been won by the favourite, and some of those winners, such as Sea Bird II, Sir Ivor, Nijinsky and Mill Reef, had won with consummate ease. Even the other two horses that had won the Derby in that period without starting as favourite, Charlottown and Blakeney, had been extremely well fancied. However, the twenty-six runners that made up the 1973 Derby field contributed to one of the most open-looking Derbys of recent years, and the race appeared primed for a surprise result.

Favourite on this occasion was Ksar, a colt trained by Bernard Van Custem. Ksar had won both of his races as a three-year-old, including displaying excellent stamina when capturing the Lingfield Derby Trial. Van Custem had always been confident that Ksar would develop in to an exciting three-year-old having initially been a backward, slow-maturing horse, and Ksar had begun to sparkle in his work prior to the Derby. Also pleasing Van Custem was Ksar's stablemate, Noble Decree, a horse that had finished runner-up in the 2,000 Guineas. However, that Newmarket race had been run on soft ground, going considered ideal for Noble Decree, and at Epsom in 1973, the ground was very firm. Also against Noble Decree was the fact that he was passed over by both Willie Carson – who opted to ride Ksar – and Lester Piggott, who partnered Vincent O'Brien's charge Cavo Doro, a dual winner at The Curragh during the season. Noble Decree was eventually paired with Brian Taylor.

The winner of that 2,000 Guineas, Mons Fils, was also in the Derby field. Though he was undoubtedly a surprise winner at Newmarket, Mons Fils possessed a staying pedigree, although in the Guineas he had illustrated no shortage of speed. Trained by Richard Hannon, Mons Fils was another reported to be in super shape in the run-up to Derby day.

The French raiding party from Alec Head's stable was headed this time by Satingo, who would be partnered by Freddie Head. Even though Satingo was not among the leading horses in the betting market, the Head stable arrived at Epsom in blistering form and full of confidence after their Roi Lear had recently taken the French Derby – the Prix du Jockey Club at Chantilly.

Without a doubt, the ultimate dark–horse in an incredibly open race was the Arthur Budgett-trained Morston. Budgett had trained Blakeney to win the Derby in 1969, and Morston was a half-brother to that horse as they shared the same dam in Windmill Girl. A tall, athletic chestnut, Morston had frightfully little experience to take with him to Epsom. He had not run as a two-year-old, and his only run at three had come at Lingfield in May. On that occasion, the horse had displayed plenty of scope and potential in winning, but the last horse to win the Derby having had just one previous lifetime run had been Bois Roussel in 1938, so Morston was tentatively priced at 25/1.

The inexperienced Morston gets the better of Cavo Doro.

Underneath baking sun on rock-hard ground, it was Mons Fils and the 200/1 outsider Romoke that duelled for the early lead, with the French runners Satingo and Balompie close behind.

This edition of the Derby would transpire to be fairly clean running, and racing down the hill, the same two leaders held command until Mons Fils surged round Tattenham Corner on the inside to give himself a clear advantage heading into the straight.

Passing the three-furlong marker, Mons Fils went on, but his blaze of glory was about to be rudely interrupted, as ready to shoot him down were the favourite Ksar and the Pat Eddery-ridden Freefoot, and these two arrived sharply on the scene like vultures at a kill.

Ksar had been well back early on, but the progression in the horse that Van Custem had raved about was now in full evidence, as the favourite went into overdrive and apparently a winning position. However, Ksar and his jockey Carson had not accounted for the late finishers, and from positions in the middle of the pack, first Edward Hide on Morston and then the charging Cavo Doro under Piggott, got to Ksar and swallowed him alive.

For a moment, it looked as though Piggott would drive Cavo Doro home to register a record seventh Derby win, but it was not to be on this occasion as Morston was strong and resilient, and with Hide asking the chestnut for a little extra, it was Morston that prevailed in a thrilling finish by half-a-length. Freefoot had stayed on two-and-a-half lengths back in third with Ksar in fourth. After leading the field in the straight, the challenge of Mons Fils had petered out tamely and he could only finish eighteenth, with his jockey Frank Durr saying that the horse had detested the going and had almost fallen coming down the hill. One that had faired even more miserably was Noble Decree, and the Guineas runner-up was never sighted in the heat of the battle, finishing next to last. One notable finisher was Sea Pigeon, who finished creditably in seventh but would go on to become one of the finest hurdlers of his generation, winning Cheltenham's Champion Hurdle in 1980 and 1981.

The win marked the second time in five years that Arthur Budgett had won the Derby. When Blakeney had won in 1969, Budgett had sold a share of the horse prior to the race, but on this occasion, the Derby winner belonged totally to him. Originally, Budgett had planned a crack at the St Leger with Morston, but despite thinking that the colt may lack the necessary experience, he elected to let him run at Epsom. Despite the surprise win, Budgett was delighted with Morston's performance, as were the bookmakers, who reported their first winning Derby result in years on a horse that wore number thirteen – unlucky for some – during the race. Thirteen was certainly not unlucky for jockey Hide however: it was his thirteenth ride in the Derby.

Morston became the first Derby winner for the excellent sire Ragusa, who had sadly died shortly before the race, as had the winning dam Windmill Girl. The latter had been put down after fracturing her skull in a fall prior to an imminent visit from the prolific Mill Reef.

The manner of Morston's win suggested he had not yet reached his full potential, and the chestnut certainly appeared open to further improvement, with races such as the King George and St Leger now looking inviting. However, due to a succession of setbacks, the Derby winner of 1973 never raced again, and Morston was soon retired to stud with an unbeaten record.

Morston and jockey Eddie Hide come back victorious.

**1973 DERBY RESULT**

| FATE / HORSE | WEIGHT | JOCKEY | ODDS |
|---|---|---|---|
| **1st – Morston** | 9-0 | E. Hide | 25/1 |
| **2nd – Cavo Doro** | 9-0 | L. Piggott | 12/1 |
| **3rd – Freefoot** | 9-0 | P. Eddery | 33/1 |
| 4th – Ksar | 9-0 | W. Carson | 5/1* |
| 5th – Ragapan | 9-0 | W. Williamson | 28/1 |
| 6th – Relay Race | 9-0 | G. Starkey | 20/1 |
| 7th – Sea Pigeon | 9-0 | A. Murray | 50/1 |
| 8th – Honey Crepe | 9-0 | P. Cook | 200/1 |
| 9th – Knock Out | 9-0 | A. Barclay | 33/1 |
| 10th – Balompie | 9-0 | J. Cruguet | 50/1 |
| 11th – Natsun | 9-0 | G. Lewis | 11/1 |
| 12th – Projector | 9-0 | G. Baxter | 28/1 |
| 13th – Solar Wind | 9-0 | T. Murphy | 66/1 |
| 14th – Bally Game | 9-0 | Y. Saint-Martin | 10/1 |
| 15th – Draw The Line | 9-0 | P. Waldron | 45/1 |
| 16th – Duke Of Ragusa | 9-0 | J. Gorton | 25/1 |
| 17th – Proverb | 9-0 | E. Johnson | 40/1 |
| 18th – Mons Fils | 9-0 | F. Durr | 11/2 |
| 19th – Club House | 9-0 | J. Mercer | 22/1 |
| 20th – Flintstone | 9-0 | R.F. Parnell | 100/1 |
| 21st – Princely Review | 9-0 | G. Moore | 200/1 |
| 22nd – Proboscis | 9-0 | E. Eldin | 200/1 |
| 23rd – Romoke | 9-0 | M.L. Thomas | 200/1 |
| 24th – Noble Decree | 9-0 | B. Taylor | 9/1 |
| Last – Satingo | 9-0 | F. Head | 22/1 |

6 June 1973
Going – Firm
Winner – £66,348 75p
Time – 2 mins 35.92 secs
Favourite – Ksar
25 Ran

| Morston | Chestnut colt by Ragusa – Windmill Girl |
|---|---|
| Cavo Doro | Bay colt by Sir Ivor – Limuru |
| Freefoot | Bay colt by Relko – Close Up |

Winner bred by Owner (Mr A.M. Budgett)
Winner trained by Mr A.M. Budgett at Whatcombe, Berkshire

# SNOW KNIGHT

The most important trial in terms of the make-up of the 1974 Derby had been the 2,000 Guineas at Newmarket. Quite often, horses that win that particular race have too much speed and insufficient stamina to triumph at Epsom. However, in recent Derbys, Royal Palace, Sir Ivor and Nijinsky had proved it was well within the realms of possibility to achieve success in both races. The top two horses in the betting market for the 1974 Derby had finished first and second in the Guineas, and their respective camps had total confidence that their particular colt could follow-up in the big race.

The winner of the Guineas was the beautiful French colt Nonoalco, trained by Francois Boutin. Nonoalco had been an excellent two-year-old, losing just once, and had carried his fine form over to his three-year-old season. He had won at Newmarket in eye-catching style, illustrating his exceptional acceleration to win smoothly on his first start in England. Nonoalco was trying to continue the recent streak that had seen North American-bred horses Sir Ivor, Nijinsky, Mill Reef and Roberto win the Derby, as he too had been bred on the other side of the Atlantic, and his first gallop on the Downs two days prior to the Derby had connections dreaming of joining that fine group as Nonoalco simply shone in his workout. The fact that he was bereft of a stayer's pedigree seemed to matter less, as his style of racing was so relaxed, and he started the race as a hot 9/4 favourite.

If Boutin and his team were optimistic over Nonoalco's Derby chance, then the Ryan Price team were literally brimming with confidence over the prospects of their candidate, Giacometti. Both trainer Price and owner Charles St George had total faith in their chestnut, who had won all three of his races

Francois Boutin (pictured in 1991), trainer of Nonoalco.

at two before finishing runner-up to Nonoalco in the Guineas. Partnered at Epsom by Tony Murray, Giacometti appeared to have the necessary stamina for the Derby, as his sire, Faberge II, had been responsible for the excellent 1972 runner-up Rheingold.

There were some huge outsiders in the field, with four horses listed at 200/1, but the remainder of the eighteen-strong line-up appeared to have fair prospects at least. Among the interesting runners were Northern Taste, Imperial Prince, Bustino and Snow Knight. Northern Taste, trained in France by Jack Cunnington, had run on really strongly to finish fourth in the 2,000 Guineas and was expected to appreciate the longer distance of the Derby, while Noel Murless' charge, Imperial Prince, was a son of the 1968 hero Sir Ivor. Bustino, trained by Dick Hern, had enhanced his Derby claims when taking the Lingfield Derby Trial, while one of the horses he beat in that race, Snow Knight – trained in Berkshire by Peter Nelson – had impressed many with a strong workout at Epsom just days before the race.

Snow Knight steals first run on Imperial Prince in the 1974 Derby.

In the parade before the race, Nonoalco showed just why he was held in such high regard, oozing superiority and walking like a champion, his striking white face standing out. In total contrast, Snow Knight had appeared to scupper his hopes with a display of misbehaviour, playing up to the boisterous nature of the occasion, and at one point, he unshipped his jockey, Brian Taylor.

However, once the race got under way, Taylor quickly settled Snow Knight into a smooth rhythm behind the early leader Grand Orient, with Grey Thunder, Giacometti, Imperial Prince, Charlie Bubbles and Nonoalco in close attention.

Grey Thunder, a huge outsider like Grand Orient, took over with seven furlongs to run, but it was noticeable in behind that Snow Knight was being specifically ridden by Taylor with the intention of making the race a thorough test of stamina, perhaps hoping to blunt the speed of the Guineas horses, and it was no surprise when he took over a furlong later, chased frantically by Giacometti and Imperial Prince as they came down the hill. One horse that was visibly struggling as the race progressed was the favourite Nonoalco. As the field raced round Tattenham Corner, he seemed in real trouble. Later it emerged that he had, most unluckily, swallowed his tongue, and from then on, his cause was hopeless.

As the race headed into the home straight, Taylor asked Snow Knight to maintain his relentless gallop, and the response the chestnut gave was strong and direct, as he continued powerfully towards the finish. Despite Imperial Prince and Giacometti battling to get back in to contention, Snow Knight – somewhat surprisingly – kept finding extra and always seemed to be in control of the race. The tactics of making the contest a thorough test of stamina had worked to perfection, and at the line, Snow Knight had won by two lengths from Imperial Prince with Giacometti – who according to Murray had struggled to cope with Epsom's undulations – a length further back in third. Bustino had finished like a train to take fourth in the style of a horse that yearned for greater success, and these four were some way clear of the next group, headed by Northern Taste. The beleaguered favourite came home in seventh place.

The victorious Snow Knight had been purchased for a measly 5,200 guineas for his owner, Mrs Sharon Phillips – the wife of a Montreal solicitor – and the horse had won the most lucrative running of the Derby, worth some £15,000 more than the previous richest in 1966. Snow Knight was Mrs Phillips' first Derby runner, and the race had been the sole objective for her horse ever since he had been purchased.

Peter Nelson had begun training back in 1948, and the 1974 Derby was his first Classic victory, as it was for jockey Brian Taylor. Snow Knight had won two of his five races as a juvenile, with his most notable effort coming in Doncaster's Champagne Stakes, where he was second to Giacometti. Nelson had also trained the horse's sire, Firestreak.

At first glance, the surprise 50/1 win of Snow Knight could translate in to the 1974 Derby being deemed a poor contest. But Snow Knight had loved the fast ground, had acted magnificently on the course and had recorded a very quick time. The result was backed up by the fact that horses such as Imperial Prince, Giacometti, Mistigri, Nonoalco and Bustino all won good races after the Derby, with Bustino taking the St Leger. In his career at stud, Snow Knight would become the grandsire to the 1989 Oaks winner Snow Bride, a horse that in turn became the dam of the 1995 Derby winner, Lammtarra.

## 1974 DERBY RESULT

| FATE / HORSE | WEIGHT | JOCKEY | ODDS |
|---|---|---|---|
| **1st – Snow Knight** | 9-0 | B. Taylor | 50/1 |
| **2nd – Imperial Prince** | 9-0 | G. Lewis | 20/1 |
| **3rd – Giacometti** | 9-0 | A. Murray | 5/2 |
| 4th – Bustino | 9-0 | J. Mercer | 8/1 |
| 5th – Northern Taste | 9-0 | J.C. Desaint | 8/1 |
| 6th – Mistigri | 9-0 | C. Roche | 40/1 |
| 7th – Nonoalco | 9-0 | Y. Saint-Martin | 9/4* |
| 8th – Radical | 9-0 | M. Goreham | 100/1 |
| 9th – Court Dancer | 9-0 | W. Carson | 25/1 |
| 10th – Regular Guy | 9-0 | W. Pyers | 66/1 |
| 11th – Sin Y Sin | 9-0 | E. Eldin | 33/1 |
| 12th – Arthurian | 9-0 | L. Piggott | 28/1 |
| 13th – Charlie Bubbles | 9-0 | P. Eddery | 25/1 |
| 14th – Live Arrow | 9-0 | R. Marshall | 50/1 |
| 15th – Grey Thunder | 9-0 | Ron Hutchinson | 200/1 |
| 16th – Barbarie Corsaire | 9-0 | R. Edmondson | 200/1 |
| 17th – Hope Of Holland | 9-0 | G. Starkey | 200/1 |
| Last – Grand Orient | 9-0 | G. Ramshaw | 200/1 |

5 June 1974
Going – Good to Firm
Winner – £89,229 25p
Time – 2 mins 35.04 secs
Favourite – Nonoalco
18 Ran

| | |
|---|---|
| Snow Knight | Chestnut colt by Firestreak – Snow Blossom |
| Imperial Prince | Bay colt by Sir Ivor – Bleu Azur |
| Giacometti | Chestnut colt by Faberge II – Naujwan |

Winner bred by J.A.C Lilley
Winner trained by P. Nelson at Upper Lambourn, Berkshire

Freddie Head partnered the favourite, Green Dancer, in 1975.

# GRUNDY

The clear favourite for the 1975 Derby was trained in France by Alec Head. The horse was Green Dancer, a striking bay colt with a distinctive white star on his forehead. The main trait of Green Dancer was his remarkable speed, a weapon he had used decisively in winning four of his five lifetime races, including both at three – the French 2,000 Guineas and the Prix Lupin at Longchamp. Impressively, his three-year-old wins had come on contrasting grounds, firm and soft. Green Dancer was to become – together with the big outsider Tanzor – the first offspring of the great Nijinsky to run in the Derby, so he understandably attracted a lot of pre-race interest and excitement. Indeed, Green Dancer's only previous visit to England had come in his juvenile campaign when he won Doncaster's Observer Gold Cup, although no horse had ever won that race and the Derby the following year. Those that opposed Green Dancer reasoned that his jockey, Freddie Head, was a poor tactician around Epsom, with his three former rides in the Derby ending in dismal failure aboard fancied runners. Even so, Green Dancer started the race a very warm 6/4 favourite.

On paper, the only horse that appeared ready to threaten Green Dancer's bid for glory was the Peter Walwyn-trained Grundy. A flaxen-maned chestnut, Grundy had clearly been the best of the English colts as a two-year-old, having won all four of his races, including the Champagne Stakes at Doncaster and the Dewhurst Stakes at Newmarket. In the current campaign, Grundy, a tough, hard-nosed individual, had been forced to miss vital preparation for the 2,000 Guineas at Newmarket after being kicked in the head at home by a stablemate, but he still ran respectably behind Bolkonski, a horse not present at Epsom. Next, Walwyn's charge headed for The Curragh, where he was impressive in winning the Irish 2,000 Guineas. In contrast to the electric speed of Green Dancer, Grundy demonstrated superb galloping ability as he was finishing relentlessly at The Curragh, and it was his performance in Ireland that had his jockey, Pat Eddery, convinced that Grundy would see out the trip at Epsom.

Pat Eddery won the first of three Derbys on the powerful chestnut Grundy.

Grundy (blue and yellow colours) beats Bustino in the 'Race of the Century'.

After the top two in the market, the race appeared open, and among the interesting contenders were Sea Break, Bruni, Dominion and Nobiliary. Sea Break, a son of the 1965 winner Sea Bird II, was the main hope of Ireland, where he was trained by Stuart Murless. Sea Break had been a fine two-year-old, yet had run poorly in the 2,000 Guineas, while Lester Piggott's mount, Bruni, was the best of four challengers from the yard of Ryan Price. Dominion had finished third in the Guineas and he would be a first Derby ride for twenty-year-old Ian Johnson, while the French runner Nobiliary – trained by Maurice Zilber – was the first filly to run in the race since Gainsborough Lass in 1937, although Garden Path had taken part in the war-time substitute race at Newmarket in 1944.

For the second consecutive year, the race was by far the richest-ever running of the Derby, and as the crowd settled down to watch the battle, it was Grundy's much less-heralded stablemate Red Regent – a son of the vastly unlucky 1969 third Prince Regent – that took the field along for the opening few furlongs, followed by Anne's Pretender, Carolus, Hobnob and another Irish raider in the form of Nuthatch, and this group stayed together as they made the journey to the top of the hill, with the second-favourite Grundy not too far off the lead.

The excitement grew as the runners ploughed down the hill and round Tattenham Corner, with plenty of the eighteen-strong field still in contention. It was Tony Murray on Anne's Pretender that held a slight advantage now from

Red Regent, Nuthatch, Whip It Quick and Grundy, but as they entered the straight, the race was about to change dramatically.

In the perfect position, Eddery decided the time was right to burst for daylight on Grundy and, as he reached the two-furlong marker, the horse began to display the deep finishing drive that had come to light in the Irish 2,000 Guineas, and he began to draw clear of the pack. Devouring the ground in the closing stages, Grundy galloped home relentlessly, staying the trip convincingly to run out a three-length winner. In second place came another chestnut in the filly Nobiliary, with the 50/1 outsider Hunza Dancer another three lengths back in third under Frank Durr. Next came two generally unconsidered horses in Anne's Pretender and Whip It Quick, with the favourite Green Dancer sixth and the Irish challengers Nuthatch and Sea Break a disappointing tenth and thirteenth respectively. Green Dancer had given real reason for optimism after working delightfully on the course just days before the big race and he had travelled well for a long time in the race itself, but when the contest had hit serious levels in the straight, he had found no answer, and was generally considered not to have stayed.

Under an inspirational and confident ride from Eddery, Grundy had proved himself both tough and durable and provided trainer Walwyn with his first Derby winner, having been runner-up with Shoemaker in 1969 and Linden Tree in 1971. It was Walwyn's fourth Classic success, having won an Irish Derby, the 1,000 Guineas of 1970 and the previous year's Oaks. Grundy's Derby win came for his owner, the Milan-based Dr Carlos Vittadini.

Grundy had proved a very comfortable winner of the Derby and the sires of Grundy, Nobiliary and Hunza Dancer would all prove excellent stallions in terms of future Derby horses. Grundy's sire, Great Nephew, got a second Derby winner in the phenomenal 1981 hero Shergar; Nobiliary's sire, Vaguely Noble, would be responsible for the 1976 victor Empery; while Hunza Dancer's sire, Hawaii, would get the 1978 runner-up Hawaiian Sound and the 1980 winner Henbit.

As for Grundy, he went on to win the Irish Derby before capturing the race that would become known as the 'Race Of The Century' when he beat the 1974 Derby fourth and St Leger winner Bustino in a thrilling, all-the-way-to-the-line battle in the renamed King George VI and Queen Elizabeth Diamond Stakes at Ascot, again displaying the tenacity and attitude that had seen him crowned the Derby hero of 1975.

## 1975 DERBY RESULT

| FATE / HORSE | WEIGHT | JOCKEY | ODDS |
|---|---|---|---|
| **1st – Grundy** | 9-0 | P. Eddery | 5/1 |
| **2nd – Nobiliary** | 8-9 | Y. Saint-Martin | 20/1 |
| **3rd – Hunza Dancer** | 9-0 | F. Durr | 50/1 |
| 4th – Anne's Pretender | 9-0 | A. Murray | 33/1 |
| 5th – Whip It Quick | 9-0 | P. Waldron | 66/1 |
| 6th – Green Dancer | 9-0 | F. Head | 6/4* |
| 7th – Royal Manacle | 9-0 | W. Carson | 16/1 |
| 8th – Fidion | 9-0 | J.C. Desaint | 18/1 |
| 9th – Dominion | 9-0 | I. Johnson | 28/1 |
| 10th – Nuthatch | 9-0 | W. Swinburn | 20/1 |
| 11th – Romper | 9-0 | F. Morby | 66/1 |
| 12th – Red Regent | 9-0 | B. Taylor | 40/1 |
| 13th – Sea Break | 9-0 | J. Roe | 11/1 |
| 14th – Bruni | 9-0 | L. Piggott | 16/1 |
| 15th – No Alimony | 9-0 | J. Mercer | 25/1 |
| 16th – Hobnob | 9-0 | G. Lewis | 20/1 |
| 17th – Carolus | 9-0 | E. Hide | 66/1 |
| Last – Tanzor | 9-0 | G. Starkey | 66/1 |

4 June 1975
Going – Good to Firm
Winner – £106,465 50p
Time – 2 mins 35.35 secs
Favourite – Green Dancer
18 Ran

| | |
|---|---|
| Grundy | Chestnut colt by Great Nephew – Word From Lundy |
| Nobiliary | Chestnut filly by Vaguely Noble – Goofed |
| Hunza Dancer | Bay colt by Hawaii – Omagh |

Winner bred by Overbury Stud
Winner trained by P. Walwyn at Lambourn, Berkshire

# EMPERY

In 196 previous runnings of the Derby, 27 of the favourites had started the race at odds-on. Of those 27, 16 had won; the last being Sir Ivor in 1968. That strike rate of almost sixty per cent indicated that those winning horses carried with them an extreme amount of confidence in to the boiling cauldron of the Derby fight. The favourite for the 1976 Derby would start as the shortest-priced favourite since Sir Ivor, and the horse was seen as being as near to a certainty as one could find for such a race, such was his sparkling reputation.

The colt in question was called Wollow, trained by Henry Cecil. Wollow was unbeaten in six lifetime races, and he had won both his starts in the current campaign, including the 2,000 Guineas, where he had illustrated some exceptional quickness against some of the speediest colts around on fast ground. Wollow was a horse that relaxed well and was able to settle in his races, a trait that boded well for his Epsom venture. On occasions during his career prior to the Derby, he had also displayed raw power and exuberance, yet the worry for his supporters came in two areas – stamina and jockeyship. Wollow had never raced beyond a mile, although his sire, Wolver Hollow, had won an Eclipse Stakes over a mile-and-a-quarter. Wollow's jockey, Gianfranco Dettori, would be having his first Derby ride, having never ridden at Epsom before. On the positive side, Cecil believed that the horse would prove most excellent over the further distance of the Derby and Wollow had been glowing in his homework leading up to the big day, while even though he was an Epsom debutant, Dettori had been Champion Jockey in Italy five times and had ridden all over the world. Come

Derby day, defeat seemed out of the question for Wollow, and he began the race a scorching hot 11/10 favourite.

One of the horses expected to test Wollow's mettle to the maximum was Norfolk Air. Trained by John Dunlop, Norfolk Air had previously won the Lingfield Derby Trial over the Derby distance, and despite a suspect temperament, the horse certainly possessed the stamina that some believed to be bereft in Wollow. Norfolk Air was sired by the 1969 Derby winner Blakeney – a stallion that had already been responsible for the 1975 Oaks winner Juliette Marny. It was an indication of just how highly Wollow was perceived that Norfolk Air, together with Oats and Empery, started next in the betting at 10/1.

Oats and Empery were a pair of honest, reliable bay colts that seemed sure to give positive accounts of themselves in the Derby. Having won the previous year's race with his wonderful chestnut Grundy, trainer Peter Walwyn was represented on this occasion by Oats – like Grundy, partnered by Pat Eddery. Oats had previous experience of Epsom, having won the Blue Riband Trial on the course earlier in the season. Empery was trained in France by Maurice Zilber and the horse was bidding to give Lester Piggott a record-breaking seventh Derby success. Empery had finished third in Longchamp's important Prix Lupin prior to Epsom, and was a horse expected to greatly appreciate the extra distance of the race.

As well as the lightning-quick French raider Vitiges – runner-up in the 2,000 Guineas – the Derby also featured three horses trained by Dick Hern in the Guineas sixth Relkino, Riboboy and Smuggler, as well as two outsiders from Ireland, Whistling Deer and Hawkberry. Whistling Deer had warmed up for Epsom when finishing second in the ten-furlong Nijinsky Stakes in Ireland while Hawkberry – a third Derby ride for Christy Roche – had recently won a maiden race at Phoenix Park.

True to his free-running style, it was Vitiges that set an electric early pace, a stampede that virtually guaranteed a thorough examination of stamina. The French colt was tracked early on by Radetzky, Illustrious Prince and Empery.

It would turn into a fairly rough Derby, and the first horse to feel the brunt of the congestion was the favourite Wollow as he ran in to some interference at the top of the hill. However, his cause was not lost.

Plenty of horses held strong claims as they flew round Tattenham Corner, still led by Vitiges. Relkino had made eyecatching progress to go second at this stage, and close behind came Radetzky, Norfolk Air, Hawkberry, Oats and Illustrious Prince, the lattermost though had been badly hampered coming round Tattenham Corner and, entering the straight, he was soon left for dead.

The action was heating up considerably and, once in the straight, there seemed a plethora of possibilities in regards to the final outcome. Wollow was

Lester Piggott's seventh winning Derby ride, Empery, was – to date – the last French-trained winner of the race.

in touch and appeared to have every chance if he could find the same finishing speed that had landed him the Guineas the month before. Joe Mercer though had other ideas, and snatching first run, he quickly sent Relkino past Vitiges and on for home.

Having always been well placed just behind the leaders, Piggott knew that now was the time to test Empery's staying powers. Reaching Relkino inside the final furlong, Empery began to reveal his true colours – Piggott majestically pushed him out and guided him to the line to win from the game Relkino. The strong early pace set by the trailblazing Vitiges had played directly in to the hands of the strong-staying Empery, and his was a decisive victory from Relkino and the fast-finishing Oats. Hawkberry ran a fine, if somewhat surprising, race to claim fourth ahead of the favourite Wollow. Dettori claimed that Wollow had not given him the same feel as in his previous races. It was possible that Wollow may have not been comfortable on the unusual Epsom track, as Dettori reasoned the horse had not failed through an absence of stamina.

Empery, a son of the 1968 Prix de l'Arc de Triomphe winner Vaguely Noble, was owned by the Dallas-based Mr Bunker Hunt, and had been bred by his owner in North America. Interestingly, Mr Hunt was not present at Epsom to see his horse capture the greatest prize in Flat racing, instead allowing his twenty-one-year-old daughter, Betsy – a student at the University of Alabama – to represent him on the day.

The training achievement of Zilber meant that Empery became the eighth horse since the war to have won the Derby from a French stable, but the really striking note to emerge from the 1976 race was the fact that the genial Lester Piggott had now won seven Derbys, a clear record. As with many of his previous Epsom victories, Piggott had ridden Empery to maximise his ability, having him perfectly placed for long periods before sapping the stamina from his rivals. If it was not already accepted, Piggott was now the greatest Derby jockey of all time, and he was by no means done with the great race yet.

Empery may have not been a great Derby winner – indeed, Piggott still rated Sir Ivor the best of his seven winners – but he was a thorough stayer and came to win the race in genuine style. After the race, Empery went wrong and was never sighted in England again, although Mr Hunt was celebrating further victory four days later when Youth – a horse that would later sire the 1983 Derby winner Teenoso – won the French Derby. Empery failed to make a significant impact at home at stud, and like the 1975 hero Grundy, he was eventually dispatched to stand as a stallion in Japan.

## 1976 DERBY RESULT

| FATE / HORSE | WEIGHT | JOCKEY | ODDS |
|---|---|---|---|
| **1st – Empery** | 9-0 | L. Piggott | 10/1 |
| **2nd – Relkino** | 9-0 | J. Mercer | 25/1 |
| **3rd – Oats** | 9-0 | P. Eddery | 10/1 |
| 4th – Hawkberry | 9-0 | C. Roche | 100/1 |
| 5th – Wollow | 9-0 | G. Dettori | 11/10* |
| 6th – Vitiges | 9-0 | G. Rivases | 16/1 |
| 7th – No Turning | 9-0 | A. Murray | 25/1 |
| 8th – Smuggler | 9-0 | F. Durr | 45/1 |
| 9th – Danestic | 9-0 | E. Hide | 50/1 |
| 10th – Radetzky | 9-0 | M.L. Thomas | 100/1 |
| 11th – Tierra Fugeo | 9-0 | W. Carson | 35/1 |
| 12th – Norfolk Air | 9-0 | Ron Hutchinson | 10/1 |
| 13th – Il Padrone | 9-0 | B. Rouse | 150/1 |
| 14th – Frankie | 9-0 | E. Johnson | 75/1 |
| 15th – Whistling Deer | 9-0 | G. Curran | 75/1 |
| 16th – Coin Of Gold | 9-0 | R. Fox | 150/1 |
| 17th – Loosen Up | 9-0 | G. Starkey | 70/1 |
| 18th – Illustrious Prince | 9-0 | Y. Saint-Martin | 16/1 |
| 19th – Kafue Park | 9-0 | B. Taylor | 100/1 |
| 20th – Phleez | 9-0 | T. Cain | 200/1 |
| 21st – Our Anniversary | 9-0 | E. Eldin | 200/1 |
| 22nd – Black Sabbath | 9-0 | C. Leonard | 100/1 |
| Last – Riboboy | 9-0 | G. Lewis | 33/1 |

2 June 1976
Going – Good
Winner – £111,825 50p
Time – 2 mins 35.69 secs
Favourite – Wollow
23 Ran

| Empery | Bay colt by Vaguely Noble – Pampiona II |
|---|---|
| Relkino | Bay colt by Relko – Pugnacity |
| Oats | Bay colt by Northfields – Arctic Lace |

Winner bred by Owner (Mr N.B. Hunt) in the USA
Winner trained by M. Zilber at Chantilly, France

Robert Sangster, owner of The Minstrel.

# THE MINSTREL

If Lester Piggott had dominated the Derby as a jockey in modern times, then the Irish magician Vincent O'Brien took the honours as the dominant trainer. Since switching from a highly successful training career on the National Hunt side, where his achievements had included winning three Grand Nationals, O'Brien had risen to new, glorious heights. He had already trained four Derby winners, Larkspur being the first in 1962, followed by Sir Ivor, Nijinsky and Roberto, and every runner he ever entered in the Blue Riband commanded severe respect, regardless of the individual's chance. For the 1977 race, O'Brien saddled three of the seven Irish runners in the field, each attracting their fair share of attention.

The three horses O'Brien sent to war were Valinsky, Be My Guest and The Minstrel. Valinsky, the mount of Geoff Lewis, seemed to have exactly the right Derby credentials in terms of pedigree, being by the great Nijinsky out of an Oaks-winning mare in Valoris, while Edward Hide – like Lewis, a previous Derby winner – partnered Be My Guest, a horse that had been running well in Ireland and had been runner-up in the Nijinsky Stakes at Leopardstown in April. But the best horse of the O'Brien trio was undoubtedly the flashy, extremely good-looking chestnut The Minstrel. A stunning, unmistakable individual with a white face and legs, the powerfully-built colt was sired by Northern Dancer and therefore related to Nijinsky. A brilliant two-year-old, he was unbeaten in three races, including Newmarket's Dewhurst Stakes, The Minstrel was pitched against the very best milers at the start of his three-year-old campaign, and responded with brave performances to be third in the 2,000 Guineas at Newmarket and then runner-up to fellow Derby contender

Pampapaul in an extremely rough-and-tumble Irish 2,000 Guineas at The Curragh. After the Irish 2,000 Guineas, O'Brien was caught in two minds as to whether to send The Minstrel to Epsom, reasoning the horse may have had too tough a battle at The Curragh. But on the extreme persuasion of Lester Piggott – who would be partnering him in the Derby – O'Brien decided to let the horse take his chance. Piggott was very familiar with the way The Minstrel ran, and was convinced the colt would be suited to the longer distance at Epsom, where his stamina and definite courage could be used to his advantage. The Minstrel was a horse that tended to get worked up before his races, and having been beaten in both Guineas contests, the horse had to settle for second place in the betting market, as starting a 5/1 chance.

Taking the honour as favourite was a horse with an abundance of class, but one that also harboured strong stamina doubts. The colt was another chestnut, called Blushing Groom, and he was sired by Red God, a horse that did not win beyond seven furlongs. Blushing Groom was trained in France by Francois Mathet and was owned by the Aga Khan. The horse was currently on an incredible winning streak of seven races, stretching back to his juvenile season where he had won the important Grand Criterium. Blushing Groom was partnered by Derby first-timer Henri Sumani, a jockey considered inferior to only Yves Saint-Martin in France, but it was the stamina worries that were giving Blushing Groom fans the most to sweat over. Even so, the classy chestnut started at a short 9/4.

A flashy, tough chestnut, The Minstrel outgunned Hot Grove in the 1977 Derby.

Vincent O'Brien with one of his six Derby winners, The Minstrel.

Among the other leading contenders for the 1977 Derby were Nebbiolo, Hot Grove, Caporello and Lucky Sovereign. Trained by Kevin Prendergast in Ireland, Nebbiolo had ousted the English colts to win the 2,000 Guineas at Newmarket, while Willie Carson's mount, the bay Hot Grove, had been an easy winner of the Chester Vase. The other two main trials in England – the Lingfield Derby Trial and the Dante Stakes – had been claimed by Caporello – a son of Crepello – and Lucky Sovereign respectively. The latter was trained by Harry Wragg and was certainly a fast-improving colt, with the recent fitting of blinkers apparently having revitalised the horse.

It was Greville Starkey on Milliondollarman that got first jump on the twenty-two-strong field and the outsider took them along in a swift, positive manner. Not so positive was the outcome after just a quarter-of-a-mile for Pat Eddery's mount Night Before, as the horse had to be pulled-up, having broken a blood vessel.

Milliondollarman had continued his game run as they thundered down the hill and curled in mesmerising fashion round Tattenham Corner, with Hot Grove, Caporello and the three O'Brien horses, Be My Guest, Valinsky and The Minstrel in pursuit. The lattermost was travelling very well, and was particularly easy to spot with his white features as the field hurtled into the straight.

As they straightened for home, the favourite Blushing Groom held a fantastic chance of winning the race for France. Sumani had dispelled any fears that he would struggle to guide the colt round Epsom, and now it was up to the horse to prove if he was good enough. Surely if he stayed, Blushing Groom would win? He did not stay. Instead, with three furlongs to run, Willie Carson turned up the pressure on his rivals by soaring Hot Grove in to a clear lead, and the further they embarked down the straight, the more that this looked like being a winning move.

However, lurking in the wings as he had done in countless other Derbys, was the great Lester Piggott, and the crowd were about to see why the legend had placed so much faith in The Minstrel. As he came to challenge Hot Grove in the closing stages, The Minstrel put his heart on the line for Piggott, and with sheer guts and a steely determination, the chestnut outbattled the bay in pulsating style, refusing to be beaten and winning by a neck. Carson could not believe it; he had ridden a wonderfully positive race on Hot Grove, but the impeccable timing of the Piggott challenge and The Minstrel's lionhearted nature had been too much. Five lengths back came Blushing Groom, who could have done no more in defeat and had been denied by a pair of prototypical Derby horses. A quartet of French and Irish horses filled the next

The Minstrel followed up his Epsom success by winning the Irish Derby.

**1977 DERBY RESULT**

| FATE / HORSE | WEIGHT | JOCKEY | ODDS |
|---|---|---|---|
| **1st – The Minstrel** | 9-0 | L. Piggott | 5/1 |
| **2nd – Hot Grove** | 9-0 | W. Carson | 15/1 |
| **3rd – Blushing Groom** | 9-0 | H. Samani | 9/4* |
| 4th – Monseigneur | 9-0 | P. Paquet | 20/1 |
| 5th – Lorededaw | 9-0 | Y. Saint-Martin | 40/1 |
| 6th – Nebbiolo | 9-0 | G. Curran | 12/1 |
| 7th – Pampapaul | 9-0 | G. Dettori | 33/1 |
| 8th – Milliondollarman | 9-0 | G. Starkey | 50/1 |
| 9th – Caporello | 9-0 | E. Eldin | 28/1 |
| 10th – Valinsky | 9-0 | G. Lewis | 20/1 |
| 11th – Be My Guest | 9-0 | E. Hide | 22/1 |
| 12th – St Petersburg | 9-0 | P. Waldron | 66/1 |
| 13th – Milverton | 9-0 | C. Roche | 33/1 |
| 14th – In Haste | 9-0 | J. Lowe | 100/1 |
| 15th – Lucky Sovereign | 9-0 | M.L. Thomas | 12/1 |
| 16th – Gairloch | 9-0 | B. Taylor | 33/1 |
| 17th – Baudelaire | 9-0 | F. Durr | 50/1 |
| 18th – Mr Music Man | 9-0 | P. Cook | 150/1 |
| 19th – Sultan's Ruby | 9-0 | E. Johnson | 200/1 |
| 20th – Royal Plume | 9-0 | J. Mercer | 22/1 |
| Last – Noble Venture | 9-0 | R. Fox | 150/1 |
| Pulled-Up – Night Before | 9-0 | P. Eddery | 28/1 |

1 June 1977
Going – Good
Winner – £107,530
Time – 2 mins 36.44 secs
Favourite – Blushing Groom
22 Ran

| | |
|---|---|
| The Minstrel | Chestnut colt by Northern Dancer – Fleur |
| Hot Grove | Bay colt by Hotfoot – Orange Grove |
| Blushing Groom | Chestnut colt by Red God – Runaway Bride |

Winner bred by Mr Edward P. Taylor in Canada
Winner trained by M.V. O'Brien at Cashel, Co. Tipperary, Ireland

group of finishers, with Milliondollarman in eighth being the second English-trained horse home after the Fulke Johnson-Houghton-trained Hot Grove.

Five Derby wins had placed O'Brien among the finest trainers in the great race's long and illustrious history, though this win he owed in no small way to Piggott, for both his insight and jockeyship. It was the fourth time that the combination of O'Brien and Piggott had triumphed in the Derby.

The Minstrel was owned by Robert Sangster, the boss of Vernons Pools. Mr Sangster had been offered the enormous sum of £1 million for the colt the week before the Derby, but had turned away the bid as he wished for The Minstrel to stand as a stallion at his Coolmore Stud in Ireland.

The Minstrel went on to confirm his class and courage in the Irish Derby and then again when taking the King George VI and Queen Elizabeth Diamond Stakes at Ascot. The flashy, hard-as-nails chestnut then went on to a fine career at stud, sadly passing away in 1990 at the age of sixteen.

# SHIRLEY HEIGHTS

The favourite for the 1978 Derby was Inkerman. The horse had never raced as a two-year-old, but had taken both his races at three. True, the 1978 Derby was a very open race, but there seemed little reason for Inkerman to be installed as the clear favourite. After all, the inexperienced colt had not taken any of the major trials, but the fact that Inkerman was trained by Vincent O'Brien and ridden by Lester Piggott was good enough to propel him to the top of the betting market as punters sought a solution to a puzzling-looking contest. A win for Inkerman would have provided Ireland with their fourth Derby win of the decade.

Next in the betting came Whitstead and Shirley Heights. Whitstead, a chestnut sired by the 1973 Derby winner Morston, was trained by Ryan Price and had shown his liking for the Derby distance by winning the Lingfield Derby Trial. Even more impressive in his Derby warm-up had been the bay son of Mill Reef, Shirley Heights. Trained in Sussex by John Dunlop, Shirley Heights had first gained recognition when winning the Royal Lodge Stakes as a juvenile. After winning at Newmarket at three, Shirley Heights displayed his Derby potential with an attacking performance in the Dante Stakes at York, where he showed fine speed, a fluent action and plenty of battling spirit to see off the challenge of two very good horses in Julio Mariner and Sexton Blake. Also in his favour was that Shirley Heights was sired by the excellent 1971 Derby hero Mill Reef, a horse that was developing in to a super stallion.

The two horses Shirley Heights beat in the Dante, Julio Mariner and Sexton Blake, also had significant support at Epsom. Julio Mariner was a bay colt that stood out with his fine, athletic looks and was sired by the 1969 Derby winner

John Dunlop trained his first Derby winner in 1978.

Blakeney, making him a brother to the 1975 English and Irish Oaks heroine Juliette Marny. Julio Mariner was owned by Greek shipowner Captain Marcus Lemos, who had owned the 1973 Derby runner-up Cavo Doro, while the horse was trained by Clive Brittain, who was ultra-confident regarding the colt's chance. Sexton Blake had been the top juvenile in England the season before, winning three races, including the Champagne Stakes at Doncaster. The horse had been trained by Barry Hills with the Derby as his main objective ever since the end of his two-year-old campaign, and after finishing strongly behind Shirley Heights in

The Queen cheers on the runners in the 1978 race.

the Dante, the extra distance of the Derby was a test Sexton Blake was expected to relish. Hills had trained the 1972 runner-up Rheingold and he was also represented on this occasion by the Chester Vase second Hawaiian Sound, the mount of top American jockey Willie Shoemaker, who would be having his first Derby ride.

Others that held sound claims were Roland Gardens, Remainder Man and English Harbour. Roland Gardens had won the 2,000 Guineas, yet a combination of suspect stamina and poor homework had seen the Newmarket hero drift badly in the betting market, while Remainder Man had been runner-up in the Guineas and fourth in the Dante, but although his form was good, the firm going was expected to be detrimental to the soft-ground lover. There was also a Royal flavour to the 1978 Derby, with The Queen represented by the fast ground-specialist English Harbour – another son of Mill Reef – partnered by Joe Mercer.

On rock-hard ground, the field broke away, and as the twenty-five runners settled into their race rhythm, it was the American, Shoemaker, that rushed his mount Hawaiian Sound into the lead.

Shirley Heights (nearest rails) just holds off the brave Hawaiian Sound.

Jockey Greville Starkey.

No horse in recent times had made all of the running to win in the Derby, with Snow Knight in 1974 being the last to win having led a significant way out, yet the spirited ride Shoemaker was giving Hawaiian Sound suggested that was about to change, as the horse held command at the top of the hill and continued his confident march rounding Tattenham Corner, with Camacho, Julio Mariner, Hills Yankee, Remainder Man and the French challenger Pyjama Hunt closest to him.

The green Inkerman had not been running a bad race, but when the field straightened for home and the fight was on, he was found wanting and the horse eventually finished twenty-first, though no excuses were made by O'Brien or Piggott, both simply reasoning that the horse was neither experienced or good enough to win a Derby.

Sexton Blake was another that really seemed to struggle to cope with the rigours of the Derby, but while his chance was evaporating rapidly, Hawaiian Sound continued to cavalier towards the finishing line. Nearest to him were Remainder Man and Julio Mariner, but when the latter inexplicably weakened in the straight, he badly interfered with the close-tracking Whitstead, and jockey Brian Taylor was forced to snatch-up his mount, causing him to lose ground and momentum.

Making eye-catching progress as they passed the two-furlong marker was Shirley Heights. The horse had appeared to struggle adjusting to the downward spirals of Epsom, yet now he could extend his stride in the straight, the horse was able to show his true colours. Hawaiian Sound had now shaken off the majority of his pursuers, but Shirley Heights was charging at him relentlessly under Greville Starkey, and as they came out of the dip and met the rising ground for the final time, the fight to the line was as brutal as it was invigorating.

In the shadow of the post, Shirley Heights got up by a head to hand Hawaiian Sound the cruellest of defeats, but the winner had again – as at York – shown his toughness; his cause had looked lost at one point, so viciously had Hawaiian Sound struck for home under an inspirational ride from Shoemaker. Remainder Man, a son of the fine 1968 runner-up Connaught, had run a cracking race for trainer Reg Hollinshead and jockey Tony Ives, despite the fact that he would have much preferred easier conditions, and finishing a length-and-a-half third behind Hawaiian Sound was a noble effort. Pyjama Hunt came next, followed by the outsider Obraztsovy and then Julio Mariner. Despite appearing not to stay, Julio Mariner repaid his trainer's unwavering belief in him by winning the St Leger later in the season.

Shirley Heights' powerful late burst had presented John Dunlop with his first Derby win, and denied Barry Hills again. Indeed, it was the first English Classic for Dunlop, who had previously taken the Irish 1,000 Guineas back in 1970 with Black Satin. For Starkey, the win came fifteen years after he had guided Merchant Venturer into second place behind Relko on his first Derby ride. It was Starkey's first Derby win, though his first Classic had arrived courtesy of Homeward Bound in the 1964 Oaks.

It was the second Classic triumph for Shirley Heights' sire Mill Reef, with the Derby great also responsible for the recent French Derby winner Acamas. There would be plenty more Derby success for Mill Reef's offspring in the future. Hawaii, the sire of Hawaiian Sound, had now got two placed horses in the Derby, having also sired the 1975 third Hunza Dancer. In 1980, he would have the winner to his name, with Henbit destined to triumph.

Shirley Heights became the first Derby winner since St Paddy in 1960 to have previously won the Dante Stakes, while he was also the first winner since 1962 to be sired by a Derby winner (Larkspur by Never Say Die). Showing similar form next time out in the Irish Derby, Shirley Heights added a second Classic to his resume, while in his retirement at stud, the enthralling Derby winner of 1978 would pass on his ability to many good horses, including Slip Anchor, who followed his father's lead and won the Derby in 1985.

## 1978 DERBY RESULT

| FATE / HORSE | WEIGHT | JOCKEY | ODDS |
|---|---|---|---|
| **1st – Shirley Heights** | 9-0 | G. Starkey | 8/1 |
| **2nd – Hawaiian Sound** | 9-0 | W. Shoemaker | 25/1 |
| **3rd – Remainder Man** | 9-0 | T. Ives | 40/1 |
| 4th – Pyjama Hunt | 9-0 | A. Gibert | 22/1 |
| 5th – Obraztsovy | 9-0 | B. Rouse | 100/1 |
| 6th – Julio Mariner | 9-0 | E. Hide | 10/1 |
| 7th – Whitstead | 9-0 | B. Taylor | 8/1 |
| 8th – Roland Gardens | 9-0 | F. Durr | 25/1 |
| 9th – Formidable | 9-0 | P. Eddery | 18/1 |
| 10th – Goblin | 9-0 | M.L. Thomas | 200/1 |
| 11th – Orange Marmelade | 9-0 | P. Paquet | 66/1 |
| 12th – Admiral's Launch | 9-0 | W. Carson | 10/1 |
| 13th – Exdirectory | 9-0 | C. Roche | 15/1 |
| 14th – Majestic Maharaj | 9-0 | J. Bleasdale | 40/1 |
| 15th – Sexton Blake | 9-0 | E. Johnson | 9/1 |
| 16th – Gracias | 9-0 | J.C. Desaint | 66/1 |
| 17th – Camacho | 9-0 | A. Murray | 100/1 |
| 18th – English Harbour | 9-0 | J. Mercer | 12/1 |
| 19th – Hill's Yankee | 9-0 | P. Cook | 33/1 |
| 20th – Bilal | 9-0 | Y. Saint-Martin | 50/1 |
| 21st – Inkerman | 9-0 | L. Piggott | 4/1* |
| 22nd – Son Fils | 9-0 | G. Lewis | 50/1 |
| 23rd – Tom Strauss | 9-0 | R. Fox | 500/1 |
| 24th – Wareath | 9-0 | P. Waldron | 500/1 |
| Last – Cainan | 9-0 | A. Lequeux | 100/1 |

7 June 1978
Going – Firm
Winner – £98,410
Time – 2 mins 35.30 secs
Favourite – Inkerman
25 Ran

| Shirley Heights | Bay colt by Mill Reef – Hardiemma |
| Hawaiian Sound | Bay colt by Hawaii – Sound Of Success |
| Remainder Man | Chestnut colt by Connaught – Honerone |

Winner bred by Lord Halifax and Lord Irwin
Winner trained by J.L. Dunlop at Arundel, Sussex

# TROY

In 1979, the Derby celebrated its 200th running. The bicentennial edition always promised to be a special race, with a whole host of tantalising outcomes possible. Without a doubt, the most popular result would have been a win for Her Majesty The Queen – the Derby being the only English Classic she had failed to win as an owner. The Queen had won the 1957 Oaks with Carrozza, the 2,000 Guineas of 1958 with Pall Mall, the 1,000 Guineas of 1974 with Highclere and the 1977 Oaks and St Leger with Dunfermline. Her Aureole had chased home Pinza in the 1953 Derby, but her representative in 1979 came attached with perhaps the most hype and promise yet in her quest for that elusive Derby winner.

The horse in question was Milford, a son of the 1971 Derby winner Mill Reef and out of the Classic-winning dam Highclere, a pedigree that suggested an abundance of speed and stamina. Milford had won both his races at three: the White Rose Stakes at Ascot and then over the Derby distance in the Lingfield Derby Trial. Trained by Dick Hern, Milford was considered slightly immature and inexperienced for the Derby by some, including jockey Willie Carson, who opted to ride the stable's other candidate, Troy. The man who took Carson's place on Milford was none other than Lester Piggott. The jockey was given special permission to partner The Queen's horse by owner Robert Sangster, with whom Piggott had a written agreement to partner his horses. Piggott had ridden The Minstrel for Sangster in 1977, but the owner stated there was no animosity in the decision to let Piggott ride Milford, commenting that the great jockey would only have been released for The Queen. Sangster, on this occasion, ran the outsider Accomplice, trained by Vincent O'Brien.

On passing on the chance to ride Milford, Carson opted for a more experienced, stronger horse in the highly talented Troy. The bay colt had won two of his four races as a juvenile and had then progressed strongly at three, winning the Sandown Classic Trial on his reappearance before taking the Predominate Stakes at Goodwood in fine style, two weeks prior to the Derby. A powerful, slick mover, Troy had greatly impressed his trainer Hern in his preparatory work, and his chance was bolstered by a solid pedigree. His sire, Petingo – who had died shortly after Troy's birth – had got an Irish Derby winner in English Prince as well as a fine English and Irish Oaks winner in Fair Salinia, while all seven foals produced by Troy's late dam, La Milo, had won on the racecourse.

Guy Harwood trained the favourite Ela-Mana-Mou.

The 1979 Derby was one of the hottest editions of the race for many a year. The Irish were very confident one of their challengers could emerge victorious, as Accomplice, the Mick O'Toole-trained Dickens Hill and the dark-grey colt from Paddy Prendergast's yard, Noelino, took their places in the field. Prendergast rated Noelino as the best chance he had ever had of winning the Derby – his lifelong ambition – having had twenty-six previous runners. Noelino, however, was another horse with precious little experience, despite winning in eye-catching fashion in the Nijinsky Stakes at Leopardstown the month before Epsom. The horse had run just twice in his life, but Prendergast pointed to the fact he had sent out Dilettante II to be third to Santa Claus in the 1964 Derby having had just one lifetime race. Noelino gave his backers a big scare the day before the Derby when slipping in exercise on the Epsom track, however, Christy Roche's mount was none the worse for the mishap and went into battle carrying many Irish hopes and dreams with him.

Among the others in a magnificent line-up were the Dante winner Lyphard's Wish, Barry Hills' 2,000 Guineas winner Tap On Wood – who was a first Derby ride for the stylish American jockey Steve Cauthen – and the eventual race favourite, Ela-Mana-Mou. The lattermost was trainer Guy Harwood's first

Derby runner, and the horse had only been beaten once in six races, with his most recent victory coming in Newmarket's Heath Stakes.

The twenty-three runners were swiftly reduced to twenty-two when the 500/1 outsider Saracen Prince refused to take part, so it was the fancied Lyphard's Wish under Joe Mercer that set the early pace.

Perhaps taking a leaf out of Willie Shoemaker's book from the 1978 Derby, Mercer rode Lyphard's Wish vigorously, hoping to make all like Hawaiian Sound had so nearly done the year before. The leader certainly had many of the runners in trouble. Milford had been well in touch until seven furlongs out, but then faded away timidly to quash any hopes of a Royal victory. Noelino

too was prominent for a while, but in the straight the grey could find no more. The Guineas winner Tap On Wood had struggled throughout, apparently not taking well to Epsom.

Lyphard's Wish still held the lead turning in to the straight, and for a while it was puzzling as to where his challengers would emerge. Willie Carson on Troy had not enjoyed the smoothest or clearest of passages into the straight, and had been stacked against the rails towards the back coming round Tattenham Corner, but with two furlongs to run, he proved what a fine horse he was.

Picking up wonderfully for Carson, Troy unleashed a dazzling turn of speed to get to the leaders, and then with little more than a furlong to go, he shot clear like a rocket, exploding away from the pack. Dickens Hill, the French colt Northern Baby and the favourite Ela-Mana-Mou tried to go with him, but their cause was hopeless. Troy was simply too powerful to cope with, and he galloped further and further clear. As he passed the line, Troy had destroyed his opponents by seven lengths, which was the largest winning margin since Manna had won under six-time winner Steve Donoghue back in 1925. Next came Dickens Hill and Northern Baby, with the favourite – who, according to his jockey Greville Starkey, had encountered problems with handling the course – in fourth.

Troy's pulverising win gave a first Derby crown to the West Ilsley, Berkshire stable of Dick Hern and his colourful Scottish jockey Willie Carson. Hern described Troy as a horse that possessed a magnificent temperament while Carson backed up the praise by adding that Troy was the easiest Derby winner for a long time, and that he knew the horse would win from a long way out.

Troy was owned and bred by Sir Michael Sobell and his son-in-law, Sir Arnold Weinstock, while the horse, like all the Sobell-owned horses, was managed by Sir Gordon Richards, who unfortunately had been unwell on Derby day and had been unable to witness Troy crush his rivals.

Troy was one of the most convincing Derby winners of the modern era, a horse that seemed ideally made for Epsom – a calm, relaxed nature, coupled with physical attributes of both power and quickness – and his win looked very straightforward, despite early traffic problems in a strong field that saw the runner-up Dickens Hill later win the Eclipse Stakes at Sandown and Northern Baby the Champion Stakes at Newmarket. Like a number of the recent Derby winners, Troy went on to take the Irish Derby and then the King George VI and Queen Elizabeth Diamond Stakes later in the year before finishing a respectable third in the Prix de l'Arc de Triomphe. From a multiple Classic-winning family, Troy seemed sure to prove a hit at stud. Sadly, however, he was cut down in his prime, dying of a twisted gut in the mid-1980s. One would be hard pressed to call him the best Derby winner of the decade when the likes of Nijinsky, Mill Reef and The Minstrel had strutted their stuff at Epsom to such memorable effect, but Troy certainly ranks near the top of the pile of the finest winners of the modern era, and on Derby day in 1979, he was an unstoppable machine that flew into the history books.

**1979 DERBY RESULT**

| FATE / HORSE | WEIGHT | JOCKEY | ODDS |
|---|---|---|---|
| **1st – Troy** | 9-0 | W. Carson | 6/1 |
| **2nd – Dickens Hill** | 9-0 | A. Murray | 15/1 |
| **3rd – Northern Baby** | 9-0 | P. Paquet | 66/1 |
| 4th – Ela-Mana-Mou | 9-0 | G. Starkey | 9/2* |
| 5th – Lyphard's Wish | 9-0 | J. Mercer | 11/1 |
| 6th – Hardgreen | 9-0 | P. Cook | 25/1 |
| 7th – Man Of Vision | 9-0 | B. Raymond | 33/1 |
| 8th – Cracaval | 9-0 | W. Shoemaker | 22/1 |
| 9th – Niniski | 9-0 | J. Reid | 80/1 |
| 10th – Milford | 9-0 | L. Piggott | 15/2 |
| 11th – Noelino | 9-0 | C. Roche | 12/1 |
| 12th – Tap On Wood | 9-0 | S. Cauthen | 15/2 |
| 13th – Morvetta | 9-0 | G. Baxter | 500/1 |
| 14th – Two Of Diamonds | 9-0 | E. Johnson | 25/1 |
| 15th – Son Of Love | 9-0 | A. Lequeux | 200/1 |
| 16th – Accomplice | 9-0 | Y. Saint-Martin | 50/1 |
| 17th – New Berry | 9-0 | P. Eddery | 25/1 |
| 18th – Chetinkaya | 9-0 | B. Rouse | 500/1 |
| 19th – Lake City | 9-0 | B. Taylor | 50/1 |
| 20th – Leodegrance | 9-0 | P. Waldron | 500/1 |
| 21st – Halyudh | 9-0 | G. Lewis | 200/1 |
| Last – Laska Floko | 9-0 | E. Hide | 40/1 |
| Left – Saracen Prince | 9-0 | J. Lynch | 500/1 |

6 June 1979
Going – Good
Winner – £153,980
Time – 2 mins 36.59 secs
Favourite – Ela-Mana-Mou
23 Ran

| Troy | Bay colt by Petingo – La Milo |
|---|---|
| Dickens Hill | Chestnut colt by Mount Hagen – Priddy Maid |
| Northern Baby | Bay colt by Northern Dancer – Two Rings |

Winner bred by Ballymacoll Stud Farm Ltd
Winner trained by W.R. Hern at West Ilsley, Berkshire

# HENBIT

No trainer had won the Derby in consecutive years since the Second World War. The last trainer to achieve the feat was Frank Butters, who won in 1935 and 1936 with Bahram and Mahmoud. Troy's victory in 1979 had been a total destruction of his opposition, a beautiful exhibition of a Derby horse at his very best. Now the trainer of the previous year's hero, Dick Hern, went in search of more glory with another talented warrior.

Hern's charge on this occasion was the American-bred horse Henbit – a big, rangy bay colt whose sire, Hawaii, had got placed horses before in the Derby. Henbit had won both his three-year-old starts (the Sandown Classic Trial and the Chester Vase) to leap near the top of the Derby betting. As in Troy's year, jockey Willie Carson had a choice to make regarding which horse he would partner at Epsom. Unlike 1979, when Carson had readily passed over The Queen's horse Milford in favour of the more advanced Troy, the jockey deliberated and pondered before selecting Henbit over his talented stablemate Water Mill, who consequently became the mount of Tony Murray.

The favourite for the 1980 Derby was a horse trained by Paddy Prendergast in Ireland, the unbeaten Nikoli. A win for Nikoli would have been welcomed by everyone, as Prendergast was seriously ill at home and was unable to make the journey to Epsom, with handling responsibilities going to the trainer's son Kevin. Nikoli was a large and power-packed horse that tended to sweat profusely before his races. Prendergast had purchased the horse for 52,000 guineas on behalf of the owner, Lord Iveagh, and a win would have presented the trainer with the only English Classic missing from his résumé. Nikoli was sired by Great Nephew, who had got the 1975 winner Grundy, so Nikoli was expected to cope

with the mile-and-a-half trip of the Derby, despite the fact that he had shown great speed to win the Irish 2,000 Guineas on his latest start. If he could win the Derby, Nikoli would join a group including Hard Ridden, Santa Claus and Grundy, that had tasted glory at Epsom after triumphing at The Curragh.

Representing the powerful team of Vincent O'Brien, Robert Sangster and Lester Piggott on this occasion was the top two-year-old of the year before, Monteverdi. Unbeaten in four runs at two, including the Dewhurst Stakes, Monteverdi had inexplicably proved a total flop in the current campaign, being soundly outpointed on all three of his starts. The colt seemed to have developed a lazy, unenthusiastic attitude to his racing, and Piggott went as far as to describe him as useless after Monteverdi had finished a disappointing fifth in the Irish 2,000 Guineas. Given Piggott's excellent judgement of Derby horses, a win for Monteverdi would have come as a surprise, despite the horse's starting price of 8/1.

Among those that held solid claims in 1980 were Tyrnavos, Hello Gorgeous and Garrido. Tyrnavos was trained in Newmarket by Bruce Hobbs and had won the Craven Stakes at his local track earlier in the season, before finishing seventh to the subsequently disqualified Nureyev in the 2,000 Guineas. Being by the 1969 Derby winner Blakeney, Tyrnavos was expected to give jockey Edward Hide a distinct chance of riding his second Derby winner. Henry Cecil had prepared a number of fancied Derby contenders in recent years, and it appeared only a matter of time before the talented trainer captured the Blue Riband. He was represented on this occasion by the soft-ground-loving Hello Gorgeous. The horse, who had won the Dante Stakes at York, would not have conditions in his favour on Derby day, however, with the Epsom going good-to-firm. Garrido was one of the top outsiders. The horse, trained in France by Francois Boutin, had recently won the Italian Derby, and the tough colt was trying to compensate his trainer for seeing his brilliant Nureyev disqualified at Newmarket.

It was another French hope, in Blast Off, that did just as his name suggested as the field left the starting stalls, rocketing away to assume early control.

With twenty-three others biting at his heels behind, the 66/1 chance courageously led the field down the hill and round Tattenham Corner, and still had his head in front entering the straight, with his nearest pursuers from a hungry pack being Braughing, Rankin, Moomba Masquerade, Henbit and Hello Gorgeous. To nobody's great surprise, Monteverdi had not run a fluent race, and as the main players began to lay down their cards, his chance of winning was remote at best.

It was Greville Starkey – going for his second win in three years – who powered Rankin past the long-time leader at the two-furlong post and set sail for home, but there were still a host of challengers well in contention,

The courageous Henbit beats
Master Willie in 1980.

including Henbit, Hello Gorgeous, Garrido, Pelerin and the fast-improving chestnut, Master Willie. Nikoli had held a decent position in the straight, but as the pace increased devilishly with Rankin's charge, his battle was soon lost.

Carson drove Henbit up to duel with Rankin and, a furlong out, the battle looked to be between the two of them, as the likes of Hello Gorgeous, Garrido and Pelerin began to struggle. The fight was grim; as Henbit nosed in front, it appeared it would be he that would fly away to victory. But something had happened to Henbit. Jinking on the ground inside the final furlong, he wondered off a true line, allowing Rankin another chance. Even more dangerous to Henbit's bid was the burst being delivered by the Philip Waldron-ridden Master Willie, who was coming with such an emphatic late charge it appeared highly likely Henbit would succumb under the pressure. With bravery and heart like no Derby winner before him, Henbit somehow found the extra courage and drive to fend off the lightning-bolt run of Master Willie by three-quarters-of-a-length, with Rankin just a length away in third. What made the result truly remarkable was the fact that at the point in the closing stages where Henbit had jinked on the ground, the horse had fractured an off-fore cannon bone, and had relied on sheer guts to make it home.

It was a truly special effort by Henbit, and even though Hern and Carson had recorded back-to-back victories in the great race, it was the horse – described as being so brave by Hern – that was the undoubted hero of the day. The runner-up, Master Willie, had also run a fine race considering that trainer Henry Candy's charge had missed a lot of work prior to the Derby with an infected throat. Master Willie would go on to win the Eclipse Stakes at Sandown as a four-year-old.

Henbit gave Willie Carson a second consecutive Derby win.

## 1980 DERBY RESULT

| FATE / HORSE | WEIGHT | JOCKEY | ODDS |
|---|---|---|---|
| **1st – Henbit** | 9-0 | W. Carson | 7/1 |
| **2nd – Master Willie** | 9-0 | P. Waldron | 22/1 |
| **3rd – Rankin** | 9-0 | G. Starkey | 14/1 |
| 4th – Pelerin | 9-0 | P. Eddery | 18/1 |
| 5th – Garrido | 9-0 | P. Paquet | 28/1 |
| 6th – Hello Gorgeous | 9-0 | J. Mercer | 9/1 |
| 7th – Julius Caesar | 9-0 | P. Cook | 50/1 |
| 8th – Nikoli | 9-0 | C. Roche | 4/1* |
| 9th – Star Way | 9-0 | Y. Saint-Martin | 22/1 |
| 10th – Water Mill | 9-0 | A. Murray | 14/1 |
| 11th – Moomba Masquerade | 9-0 | G. Baxter | 40/1 |
| 12th – Tyrnavos | 9-0 | E. Hide | 9/1 |
| 13th – Saint Jonathon | 9-0 | S. Cauthen | 33/1 |
| 14th – Monteverdi | 9-0 | L. Piggott | 8/1 |
| 15th – Prince Spruce | 9-0 | J. Matthias | 200/1 |
| 16th – Bozovici | 9-0 | B. Taylor | 33/1 |
| 17th – Braughing | 9-0 | J. Lynch | 200/1 |
| 18th – Blast Off | 9-0 | M. Philipperon | 66/1 |
| 19th – Noble Shamus | 9-0 | G. McGrath | 100/1 |
| 20th – Ribot Charter | 9-0 | T. Carberry | 100/1 |
| 21st – Running Mill | 9-0 | A. Kinberley | 100/1 |
| 22nd – Pimpont | 9-0 | G. Doleuze | 40/1 |
| 23rd – Marcello | 9-0 | B. Rouse | 200/1 |
| Last – Majestic Star | 9-0 | J. Reid | 33/1 |

4 June 1980
Going – Good to Firm
Winner – £166,820
Time – 2 mins 34.77 secs
Favourite – Nikoli
24 Ran

| | |
|---|---|
| Henbit | Bay colt by Hawaii – Chateaucreek |
| Master Willie | Chestnut colt by High Line – Fair Winter |
| Rankin | Chestnut colt by Owen Dudley – Cup Cake |

Winner bred by Mrs Jack G. Jones in the USA
Winner trained by W.R. Hern at West Ilsley, Berkshire

Henbit was originally being aimed at the French Derby by Hern, but was rerouted to Epsom when the excellent French colt Nureyev was withdrawn from the Derby. Henbit was bred in Kentucky, USA by Mrs Jack Jones and was a first Derby winner for the fine stallion Hawaii. The horse's winning time of 2 minutes 34.77 seconds was the fastest time since Nijinsky in 1970, and was only a second outside of Mahmoud's all-time record set in 1936.

After the Derby, X-rays showed a five-inch crack in Henbit's cannon bone, and he was confined to three months of box rest. Sadly, the horse was never sound enough to race again, but he became a dual-purpose stallion, siring horses for both the flat and jumps. Without a doubt, Henbit was the bravest of modern Derby winners, richly deserving his place on Epsom's distinguished roll of honour.

# SHERGAR

There had been some brilliant performances in the modern era of the Derby. Sea Bird II showed total authority in 1965, Sir Ivor an electric turn of foot in 1968, Nijinsky the class that made him a legend in 1970 and Henbit the courage of a wounded soldier in the most recent running. However, the outcome of the 1981 race would prove astounding, such was the performance conjured up by the winner. It would also prove to be a result that had a far-reaching impact, not just on the racing community, and would cruelly turn from triumph to tragedy.

Shergar, a deeply attractive, dark-bay colt with a striking white face, had been made the overwhelming favourite for the Derby after two devastating victories as a three-year-old. After one win from two runs in his juvenile season, Shergar reappeared at three by handing a ten-length slaughtering to the highly respected bay horse Kirtling in the Sandown Classic Trial. What made this victory even more impressive, and subsequently elevated Shergar to a new level, was the fact that Kirtling – a son of Grundy – then came out and won Chester's Dee Stakes by six lengths and followed that by securing an all-the-way win in Milan's Gran Premio d'Italia. If his performance at Sandown was not enough, Shergar then thrashed his opponents by twelve lengths in the Chester Vase. The way Shergar adapted his blazing style to the bends of Chester boded well for his chances in the Derby. Shergar was trained by Michael Stoute at Newmarket, and no Newmarket-based horse had won the Derby since Royal Palace in 1967. Stoute had been training for ten years, but had not enjoyed any luck with his three previous Derby runners: Running Mill, Hardgreen or Hills Yankee – although he had won the 1978 Oaks at Epsom

with Fair Salinia. Shergar was owned by the Aga Khan, whose grandfather had won the race five times through Blenheim in 1930, Bahram in 1935, Mahmoud in 1936, My Love in 1948 and Tulyar in 1952. Stoute had enormous belief in the nineteen-year-old jockey of Shergar, Walter Swinburn, who the trainer believed had an extremely bright future. On the back of his destructive warm-up races, Shergar started a red-hot favourite at 10/11, as he tried to become the first favourite to win the race since Roberto in 1972.

Shergar at home in his box.

Trainer Clive Brittain saddled three horses among the relatively weak opposition to Shergar: the Lingfield Derby Trial second Sheer Grit, an outsider in Silver Season and an even bigger outsider in Golden Brigadier – a horse that was a first Derby ride for Paul Bradwell. However, the main threats to the favourite appeared likely to come from Shotgun, Riberetto, Al Nasr and Glint Of Gold. Shotgun was the mount of Lester Piggott and had been runner-up in the Dante Stakes, while Riberetto had displayed stamina and a liking for the soft ground present at Epsom when leading all the way to win the Lingfield Derby Trial. Another soft-ground lover was Al Nasr, trained at Chantilly in France by Andre Fabre. Al Nasr was a big, rangy, unbeaten colt, but was considered to be immature in nature and was turned down by Piggott in favour of Shotgun. Glint Of Gold was noted as a possible dark-horse. The bay colt was a son of Mill Reef and had won over the course and distance prior to the Derby and looked certain to give a bold account of himself.

At the start of the race, one of the French horses, the Criquette Head-trained Lydian, had to be withdrawn after proving utterly stubborn going in to the stalls. Once the field was on their way, it was Riberetto and Silver Season that made the early headway.

Coming down the hill, there was some bumping and barging involving King Of Hush, Kalaglow and Glint Of Gold, but these incidents had no bearing on the final result whatsoever.

This particular Derby would be as clear-cut as one could find and, quite frankly, the result was easy to predict from a long way out. Swinburn had Shergar positioned on the heels of the leaders early on, and as the field came

Shergar comes home unopposed in 1983.

Shergar and teenage jockey Walter Swinburn.

round Tattenham Corner, the favourite was absolutely cruising behind Riberetto and Silver Season, with Scintillating Air, Shotgun and The Queen's horse, Church Parade – trained by Dick Hern, who was going for an unprecedented third consecutive win – next in line.

No sooner had the contenders lined themselves up for a shot at glory in the straight when Swinburn elected to ignite Shergar's equine cylinders and, from three furlongs out, the favourite put in a burst never before witnessed in the Derby. The sight of Shergar pulling further and further clear on the most competitive final stretch in racing was a breathtaking sight to behold. Shergar was simply not stopping and the gap between himself and the stunned pack was as wide as an ocean. Inside the final furlong, with the race long since over, Swinburn gradually eased the horse down to a more sedate pace, otherwise the record-breaking winning distance of ten lengths that he actually achieved would have been significantly greater. Almost in another time zone came Glint Of Gold in second with 50/1 shot Scintillating Air third.

There had never been such a convincing winner of the Derby, and although the field assembled for the 1981 Derby was not the strongest and the time was on the slow side, Shergar had emphatically put his rivals in their place on

slower-than-normal ground. Swinburn's picture-perfect ride on the winner earned him high praise from both Stoute and his jockey-father Wally. The teenager had only ridden his first winner three years previously, and in his first Derby he had shown the coolness and tactical class that would ascend him to become one of the finest jockeys of his era and bring him further Derby success in future years.

The Shergar juggernaught kept on rolling with no signs of stopping. The horse next won the Irish Derby, becoming the fifth Epsom winner since 1975 to carry off the double, and then went on to win the King George VI and Queen Elizabeth Diamond Stakes, beating the previous year's Derby runner-up Master Willie in the process. In winning at Ascot, Shergar joined a group that consisted of Nijinsky, Grundy, The Minstrel and Troy that had won the Derby, Irish Derby and King George in the same season.

After such a fine season of unbelievable performances, few could begrudge Shergar a sub-par day, and it arrived in Doncaster's St Leger, a race where he bore the affects of a long but highly satisfying year, and the horse trained-off in the autumn and was retired to the Aga Khan's Ballymany Stud in Ireland.

A newspaper report regarding the missing Shergar.

## 1981 DERBY RESULT

| FATE / HORSE | WEIGHT | JOCKEY | ODDS |
|---|---|---|---|
| **1st – Shergar** | 9-0 | W.R. Swinburn | 10/11* |
| **2nd – Glint Of Gold** | 9-0 | J. Matthias | 13/1 |
| **3rd – Scintillating Air** | 9-0 | G. Baxter | 50/1 |
| 4th – Shotgun | 9-0 | L. Piggott | 7/1 |
| 5th – Church Parade | 9-0 | W. Carson | 25/1 |
| 6th – Sheer Grit | 9-0 | J. Mercer | 28/1 |
| 7th – Silver Season | 9-0 | E. Johnson | 100/1 |
| 8th – Riberetto | 9-0 | P. Eddery | 22/1 |
| 9th – Sunley Builds | 9-0 | P. Waldron | 200/1 |
| 10th – King's General | 9-0 | B. Taylor | 150/1 |
| 11th – Sass | 9-0 | J. Reid | 500/1 |
| 12th – Krug | 9-0 | B. Raymond | 66/1 |
| 13th – Kalaglow | 9-0 | G. Starkey | 11/1 |
| 14th – Robellino | 9-0 | P. Cook | 28/1 |
| 15th – Golden Brigadier | 9-0 | P. Bradwell | 150/1 |
| 16th – Kind Of Hush | 9-0 | S. Cauthen | 25/1 |
| 17th – Al Nasr | 9-0 | A. Gibert | 16/1 |
| Last – Waverley Hall | 9-0 | B. Crossley | 1000/1 |

3 June 1981
Going – Good to Soft
Winner – £149,900
Time – 2 mins 44.21 secs
Favourite – Shergar
18 Ran

| | |
|---|---|
| Shergar | Bay colt by Great Nephew – Sharmeen |
| Glint Of Gold | Bay colt by Mill Reef – Crown Treasure |
| Scintillating Air | Bay colt by Sparkler – Chantal |

Winner bred by Owner (H. H. Aga Khan)
Winner trained by M. Stoute at Newmarket

Being by Great Nephew, who had sired the 1975 Derby winner Grundy, Shergar seemed destined for greatness at stud. Sadly, the bitter hand of fate intervened in an episode that still wreaks of cruel, injustice to this day, not to mention a feeling of total sorrow. In February 1983, the great Shergar was kidnapped by the IRA, who demanded a £2 million ransom for the horse's return. Shortly after, it appeared his kidnappers panicked under the uncertainty and impracticality of possessing such an animal. Tragically, there is strong evidence to suggest that Shergar was killed shortly after. Despite several reported discoveries, Shergar's body was never recovered. It was a truly upsetting episode for all connected with the horse, and robbed racing of a genuine superstar along with countless potential gems that would have emerged from his offspring. However, what nobody could ever steal was the memory of Shergar powering home for a wonderful and everlasting victory in the Derby of 1981.

Golden Fleece cruises home a very comfortable winner in 1982.

# GOLDEN FLEECE

With two days to go before the 1982 Derby, the Champion Jockey and eight-time Derby winner Lester Piggott was without a ride in the big race. The horse he was due to partner, Simply Great, had injured a foot in exercise and had been scratched from the contest. Almost unbelievably given his record, time ran out on Piggott, and for the first time since 1962, the Derby would be missing the great man, who was instead signed by ITV Television to be part of their race coverage. Piggott was by no means done with his relationship with the Epsom Classic; however, slowly but surely, a new batch of riders were staking their claims to be labelled the next great jockey. Willie Carson had already proven himself a fine horseman with a spirited fight to his riding that had already earned him two Derby wins, young Walter Swinburn was as natural a rider as one could find and had shot to stardom aboard Shergar the year before, the excellent American Steve Cauthen was based in England now and had rapidly proved his worth, while the soft-spoken but immensely competitive Pat Eddery had won the 1975 Derby on Grundy and was establishing himself as the most likely long-term successor to Piggott.

It was Eddery who had the mount on the outstanding favourite for the 1982 Derby. Trained by Vincent O'Brien, Golden Fleece was a giant of a horse, known for having a nervous disposition. As well as his incredible size, the bay was a terrific athlete with a turn of foot so mean and potent that O'Brien believed was comparable, if not superior, to his previous Derby winners, and that was high praise indeed, considering that group included Sir Ivor and Nijinsky. Golden Fleece was an unbeaten colt sired by the Triple Crown winner Nijinsky, and the horse had shown considerable talent when easily

winning his two starts at three – the Ballymoss Stakes at The Curragh and the Nijinsky Stakes at Leopardstown – with both races being a mile-and-a-quarter in distance, though O'Brien expressed total confidence in Golden Fleece's ability to see out the Derby trip. Two weeks prior to the Derby, Golden Fleece had returned home lame from work and there was, for a while, some doubt surrounding his participation. However, the big horse soon recovered to take his place at the head of the betting market.

Among a deep group of challengers on this occasion were Persepolis, Jalmood and Peacetime. Persepolis was considered to be the top three-year-old colt in France, having won both his races, including the Prix Lupin, and had been sent to Epsom by his trainer Francois Boutin in preference to a crack at the French equivalent. Persepolis was partnered by the veteran jockey Yves Saint-Martin, successful aboard Relko nineteen years previously. Jalmood was an American-bred colt from John Dunlop's yard. The horse was a son of Blushing Groom – the favourite that had failed to stay in The Minstrel's Derby – and had taken the important Lingfield Derby Trial on his second run of the season (and consequently shared second place in the betting with Persepolis). Peacetime, yet another well-fancied son of Nijinsky, was trained by Jeremy

Golden Fleece is greeted by the owner's wife, Mrs Susan Sangster, having won the 1982 Derby.

Tree and was ridden by Joe Mercer, a jockey riding in his twenty-ninth Derby. Peacetime had captured Sandown's Classic Trial earlier in the season.

Cantering to the start, Golden Fleece looked in superb condition, equipped with a sheepskin noseband, with his long, raking stride carried him stylishly to the stalls, although some wondered if such a big horse would act successfully in the race itself.

Florida Son, one of three horses in the race priced at 250/1, was the runner that broke away in front, and for a substantial period of the race, it was he that held the lead. Ridden by the winning rider of the 1969 Derby, Ernie Johnson, Florida Son still had control bounding into the straight, tracked by Norwick, Lobkowicz, the maiden Touching Wood and the cruising Peacetime. As they straightened for home, the favourite Golden Fleece was well back, although he appeared to be travelling smoothly.

It was Mercer on Peacetime that really gripped the race by the throat, and for a moment, the charge he delivered looked likely to be decisive. However, Eddery was simply radiating confidence aboard Golden Fleece, and making rapid but extremely casual progress from the rear, the favourite came to stalk Peacetime like the Grim Reaper, casting his immense shadow over his opponent.

Florida Son had dropped back quickly and the subsequent leader Norwick was now in trouble too, while Peacetime had no answer as the big favourite loomed up beside him. Eddery asked Golden Fleece to show his acceleration and, with a quarter-of-a-mile to run, the horse did not disappoint, shooting clear in dominant style to put the matter to bed. Staying on behind Golden Fleece were Touching Wood, Silver Hawk – who had encountered traffic problems at the top of the hill under Tony Murray – and the French horse Persepolis. At the line, Golden Fleece had a distinctly comfortable three lengths to spare over Touching Wood, and it was a victory that screamed class and style. Among the beaten horses, Peacetime had flattered to deceive in the straight and eventually finished seventh, while the fancied Jalmood had always been under heavy pressure and came home a remote fourteenth. Golden Fleece had beaten a high-class field though: Touching Wood went on to prove his ability when winning both the English and Irish St Legers, while Silver Hawk proved to be a magnificent stallion, getting, among others, the 1997 Derby winner, Benny The Dip. The first three horses home in the 1982 Derby were sired by former Derby winners as, besides Nijinsky siring Golden Fleece, both Touching Wood and Silver Hawk were sired by Roberto.

Golden Fleece, in a contrasting style to Shergar the year before, had carved a perfect destruction of his opposition. Pat Eddery described the winner as an unreal horse and the best he had ever sat on, while O'Brien compared Golden Fleece in favourable terms to his other Derby winners, of which the newest hero was now the sixth. It was also the second time Eddery and owner Robert Sangster had tasted Derby success.

The winning time of 2 minutes 34.27 seconds ranked Golden Fleece as one of the fastest Derby winners of all time, and his win was only half a second outside the record set by Mahmoud in 1936. With size, speed, stamina and class, Golden Fleece's attributes made him one of the finest Derby winners of the modern era and his eye-catching cruising ability made him perhaps the best Derby winner of the 1980s. Sadly, from Epsom onwards, the career of Golden Fleece was severely stunted. Picking up a bad virus, the horse never raced again and went to the Coolmore Stud in County Tipperary in 1983 carrying a value of £15 million. Before he had established himself as a potentially great stallion, Golden Fleece sadly died, a mere two years removed from his memorable Epsom win.

## 1982 DERBY RESULT

| FATE / HORSE | WEIGHT | JOCKEY | ODDS |
|---|---|---|---|
| 1st – Golden Fleece | 9-0 | P. Eddery | 3/1* |
| 2nd – Touching Wood | 9-0 | P. Cook | 40/1 |
| 3rd – Silver Hawk | 9-0 | A. Murray | 14/1 |
| 4th – Persepolis | 9-0 | Y. Saint-Martin | 4/1 |
| 5th – Norwick | 9-0 | G. Starkey | 33/1 |
| 6th – Palace Gold | 9-0 | T. Ives | 25/1 |
| 7th – Peacetime | 9-0 | J. Mercer | 6/1 |
| 8th – Rocamadour | 9-0 | W.R. Swinburn | 20/1 |
| 9th – Count Fahlen | 9-0 | G. Baxter | 33/1 |
| 10th – Fitzwarren | 9-0 | R. Weaver | 250/1 |
| 11th – Tidworth Tattoo | 9-0 | B. Rouse | 300/1 |
| 12th – Super Sunrise | 9-0 | E. Hide | 20/1 |
| 13th – Father Rooney | 9-0 | S. Cauthen | 28/1 |
| 14th – Jalmood | 9-0 | W. Carson | 4/1 |
| 15th – Lobkowiez | 9-0 | B. Taylor | 200/1 |
| 16th – Reef Glade | 9-0 | P. Waldron | 250/1 |
| 17th – Wongchoi | 9-0 | D. Brosnan | 150/1 |
| Last – Florida Son | 9-0 | E. Johnson | 250/1 |

2 June 1982
Going – Good to Firm
Winner – £146,720
Time – 2 mins 34.27 secs
Favourite – Golden Fleece
18 Ran

| | |
|---|---|
| Golden Fleece | Bay colt by Nijinsky – Exotic Treat |
| Touching Wood | Bay colt by Roberto – Mandera |
| Silver Hawk | Bay colt by Roberto – Gris Vitesse |

Winner bred by Paul & Mrs Hexter in the USA
Winner trained by M.V. O'Brien at Cashel, Co. Tipperary, Ireland

Geoff Wragg (pictured 2000), trainer of Teenoso.

# TEENOSO

Even though it lacked true star quality for the first time in a number of years, the 1983 edition of the Derby certainly had a deep, competitive look to it. Eight of the runners were priced at 16/1 or less, so an exciting renewal of the race seemed assured. The extra ingredient in 1983 had arrived in terms of the weather. A treacherous period of rain had preceded the 1 June fixture and, when a spectacular thunderstorm hit Epsom on the eve of the race, the ground for Derby day was left extremely heavy. To win this particular running of the Derby, the winning horse would have to own considerable amounts of stamina for the war of attrition that lay ahead.

The horse with the best credentials for the race appeared to be the Geoff Wragg-trained Teenoso, a bay colt by a French Derby winner in Youth and out of a mare, Furioso, that was sired by the great Ballymoss. Wragg was in his first season as a license holder, but had gained a huge deal of experience as an assistant to his father Harry, who had retired the year before at the age of eighty, having trained a winner of every British Classic – including the 1961 Derby with Psidium – except the Oaks. Teenoso had been beaten on his seasonal debut at Haydock, but had then won at Newmarket before really staking his claim for Derby consideration with a win over a mile-and-a-half in the Lingfield Derby Trial in the middle of May. At Lingfield, Teenoso had proved he could handle coming down a hill, and that fact coupled with the booking of a certain Lester Piggott to ride (Steve Cauthen had ridden the horse at Lingfield) meant that Teenoso started as the 9/2 favourite.

If the favourite was to be overturned, the chances were that his conqueror would come from a strong quartet owned by Robert Sangster. Two of his team,

Lomond and Salmon Leap, were trained in Ireland by Vincent O'Brien. Lomond had shown great acceleration when winning the 2,000 Guineas and had a superb pedigree. He was a son of the great Northern Dancer and was a half brother to the special American Triple Crown winner Seattle Slew. A win for Lomond would make Bill Shoemaker, the horse's jockey, the first American to win the Derby since Frank O'Neill on Spion Kop in 1920. Salmon Leap, also a son of Northern Dancer, had been running very well in Ireland during the season – albeit over shorter trips – winning races at Leopardstown and The Curragh. He entered the Derby as an unbeaten colt, and was trying to emulate Golden Fleece the year before by winning Leopardstown's Nijinsky Stakes before triumphing at Epsom.

The other two Sangster-owned horses were Shearwalk and The Noble Player. Shearwalk was a grey colt trained by Michael Stoute and had recently finished runner-up to Teenoso at Lingfield. The Noble Player was the least fancied of the quartet but was a hardy, genuine horse that had been fourth in the Dante Stakes at York before winning at Kempton nine days before the Derby, where he beat a horse called Diesis that had won the much respected Middle Park Stakes and Dewhurst Stakes as a two-year-old.

Among the other interesting challengers in 1983 were Morcon, Pluralisme, Slewpy and Carlingford Castle. Morcon, like his sire – the 1973 Derby winner Morston – was inexperienced, having only run three times in his life. Even so, Willie Carson's mount had made a favourable impression in May when winning the Predominate Stakes at Goodwood over the Derby trip. Pluralisme was the main hope of France on this occasion, although his trainer Alec Head was very pessimistic over his Derby chance. In his favour was that Pluralisme was sired by one of the gamest Derby winners of modern times, The Minstrel. Despite being unconsidered in the betting market, the challenge of Slewpy garnered plenty of attention for the fact the horse was trained in America. The

Teenoso was Lester Piggott's ninth and last Derby winner.

horse had won four races from twelve in the States, including a recent third in the Louisiana Derby, but had only raced once before on grass with his other runs coming on dirt tracks. One horse that came in for support because of his proven ability in the mud was Carlingford Castle. A flashy-looking chestnut that was trained in Ireland by Liam Brown, the horse was one of the few contenders that seemed certain to benefit from the stamina-sapping conditions as he also had a reputation as a tough stayer.

With half an inch of rain having fallen on the course, the race began at a sedate gallop; the jockeys obviously realising their mounts were going to have to preserve every ounce of energy for the battle ahead.

With seven furlongs to run, it was the 500/1 shot Mitilini that had the edge, followed by Neorion, Teenoso, Tivian, Guns Of Navarone and Carlingford Castle, but the race was turning into a brutal, uncompromising affair. Matters came to a head at the five-furlong post, where some severe scrimmaging occurred. Gianfranco Dettori aboard Tolomeo veered sharply across the back-pedalling outsider Holmburg, with the latter's jockey, Mick Miller, having to snatch his horse up violently. The consequences of this incident were dangerous to say the least, as the hampered Holmburg was cannoned into at his quarters by Shearwalk, with Yawa then going into the back of Shearwalk. Yawa was lucky not to capsize, but his jockey, Philip Waldron, was thrown from the saddle and dumped alarmingly to the turf. Of the horses involved in the rough and tumble, Shearwalk was very hard done by as he had been travelling sweetly and consequently lost a good deal of ground.

Mitilini still led going in to the straight, but really imposing himself just behind and looking full of confidence and composure was Teenoso, and the favourite appeared desperate to unleash his challenge. Three furlongs out, and Piggott decided to grant the horse his wish and he plunged Teenoso into the lead.

Teenoso was quickly pursued by Guns Of Navarone and then Carlingford Castle, but the favourite continued his surge and powered clear and, rather surprisingly, he went on to win the race in very easy fashion. Having surged through the mud, Teenoso had three lengths to spare at the line with Carlingford Castle second and the unlucky grey Shearwalk storming home to take third, although his jockey Walter Swinburn stated Shearwalk would not have caught Teenoso, such was the purpose and strength of the favourite's finish. Salmon Leap had apparently failed to handle the Epsom hill with the desired effect yet had still run creditably to finish fourth for Pat Eddery, but Lomond had flopped dismally, having been last for a long way before returning home sixteenth. The American horse Slewpy had been prominent for half the race, but eventually faded to finish seventeenth. For his part in causing the mid-race havoc, the forty-two-year-old Dettori – a ten-time champion in Italy – was given a six-day suspension.

Piggott had now won an incredible nine Derbys, and Teenoso's win came twenty-nine years after he had ridden Never Say Die to victory in the 1954 race at the age of eighteen. Piggott vouched that Teenoso was indeed a very good horse and was amazed by the simplicity of the colt's win, but contrasted that the field had been a poor group on this occasion, with the winning time being the slowest for ninety-two years.

Teenoso was owned by Eric Moller and was bred by the same man at White Lodge Stud in America. Previously, Moller's colours had been carried by Freefoot into third place behind Morston in the 1973 Derby.

Teenoso was beaten in his next two races, but as a four-year-old, he captured the King George VI and Queen Elizabeth Diamond Stakes. When his racing career came to an end, Teenoso was sent to Highclere Stud with a value of £6 million and later developed in to a top National Hunt sire based at Shade Oak Stud in Shropshire.

**1983 DERBY RESULT**

| FATE / HORSE | WEIGHT | JOCKEY | ODDS |
| --- | --- | --- | --- |
| **1st – Teenoso** | 9-0 | L. Piggott | 9/2* |
| **2nd – Carlingford Castle** | 9-0 | M. Kinane | 14/1 |
| **3rd – Shearwalk** | 9-0 | W.R. Swinburn | 18/1 |
| 4th – Salmon Leap | 9-0 | Pat Eddery | 11/2 |
| 5th – Guns Of Navarone | 9-0 | P. Robinson | 20/1 |
| 6th – Naar | 9-0 | J. Mercer | 100/1 |
| 7th – Pluralisme | 9-0 | F. Head | 18/1 |
| 8th – Morcon | 9-0 | W. Carson | 17/2 |
| 9th – Tolomeo | 9-0 | G. Dettori | 14/1 |
| 10th – Gordian | 9-0 | C. Asmussen | 25/1 |
| 11th – The Noble Player | 9-0 | S. Cauthen | 16/1 |
| 12th – Mitilini | 9-0 | G. Baxter | 500/1 |
| 13th – Neorion | 9-0 | B. Rouse | 150/1 |
| 14th – Wassl | 9-0 | A. Murray | 10/1 |
| 15th – Tivian | 9-0 | A. Barclay | 500/1 |
| 16th – Lomond | 9-0 | W. Shoemaker | 9/1 |
| 17th – Slewpy | 9-0 | Y. Saint-Martin | 100/1 |
| 18th – Appeal To Me | 9-0 | J. Reid | 500/1 |
| 19th – Holmbury | 9-0 | M. Miller | 1000/1 |
| 20th – Zoffany | 9-0 | G. Starkey | 28/1 |
| Last – Yawa | 9-0 | P. Waldron | 50/1 |

1 June 1983
Going – Heavy
Winner – £165,080
Time – 2 mins 49.7 secs
Favourite – Teenoso
21 Ran

| | |
| --- | --- |
| Teenoso | Bay colt by Youth – Furioso |
| Carlingford Castle | Chestnut colt by Le Bavard – Rache Ruysch |
| Shearwalk | Grey colt by Godswalk – Sairshea |

Winner bred by Owner (Mr E.B. Moller) & White Lodge Stud, USA
Winner trained by G. Wragg at Newmarket

# SECRETO

Sometimes racehorses are put on a pedestal and proclaimed as invincible warriors. This particularly happens in Flat racing when a horse has enjoyed a successful and fruitful two-year-old campaign. The prospect of seeing the same horse progress again at three is often too much to resist, and the horse can find itself labelled the 'new' Nijinsky or Mill Reef. Sadly, more often than not, the bubble is burst and the search for a new equine wonder begins again. Sometimes a horse will capture a race early in their three-year-old season, perhaps the 2,000 Guineas at Newmarket, and then head to Epsom for the Derby with the result apparently done and dusted in their favour. What nobody can truly foresee is how that particular horse will handle the unique and uncompromising challenge of the Derby. In previous years, Blushing Groom, Wollow and Green Dancer all arrived at Epsom with reputations as high as the sky, only to leave with their egos battered and bruised. The 1984 Derby was graced by a horse ranked with the very best in recent memory, and his starting price of 8/11 made him one of the most respected colts to line-up at Epsom in years.

The horse in question was a beautifully balanced bay colt named El Gran Senor. Trained by Vincent O'Brien, El Gran Senor was unbeaten in six lifetime races, and had won both his races at three, including when obliterating a strong field in the 2,000 Guineas at Newmarket. Before the Guineas, El Gran Senor had won at The Curragh, beating his stablemate Sadler's Wells, a horse that would go on to win the Irish 2,000 Guineas and ultimately become a supreme stallion. El Gran Senor was indeed a brilliant son of Northern Dancer, with his main traits being splendid acceleration and a fine, relaxed attitude on the racecourse that allowed him to settle and cruise through his races. Owned

by Robert Sangster and ridden by Pat Eddery, the only worry surrounding the favourite was whether he would truly stay the full, taxing distance of the Derby. One interesting point emerged before the race when O'Brien did not gallop El Gran Senor round Tattenham Corner the day before to provide his horse with some experience of Epsom. O'Brien's six previous Derby winners had all worked on Epsom before their victories, but this time O'Brien reasoned that El Gran Senor had done more than enough strong work at home in Ireland.

In truth, it was difficult to look past the favourite on this occasion, such was his lofty status. There were so many outsiders in the field of seventeen that the realistic challengers could be counted comfortably on one hand. Among those expected to give El Gran Senor most to contend with were Alphabatim, Claude Monet and Kaytu. The American-bred Alphabatim was a solid stayer that Lester Piggott hoped would give him a tenth Derby win. Trained by Guy Harwood, Alphabatim had won the Lingfield Derby Trial, having previously triumphed at Sandown. Claude Monet was sired by the US Triple Crown winner Affirmed and was out of a dam, Madelia, that had won the French Oaks, although Claude Monet had been hampered by wind problems throughout his career. Despite this deterrent, Henry Cecil's charge had won both his starts at three, including the Dante Stakes. Willie Carson's mount Kaytu was similar to the jockey's 1980 winner Henbit in that he was ultra-tough and a true stayer. Trained by Dick Hern, Kaytu was considered to be a horse on the rise having won the Chester Vase in May.

One other talented – but far less heralded – challenger from Ireland was Secreto. Trained by Vincent O'Brien's son David, Secreto was a tough warrior who required a good deal of homework to get fit. Secreto, another bay colt by Northern Dancer, had won his first start at three before finishing, staying on, behind Sadler's Wells in the Irish 2,000 Guineas. Christy Roche took the ride on the 14/1 chance.

With Ever Ready sponsoring the race for the first time, the contest was by far the richest edition of the Derby yet, with the 1984 winner scheduled to earn £60,000 more than when Teenoso had won the year before.

On good ground, it was Cataldi that made the early running from Northern Fred, At Talaq, Claude Monet, Telios, Ilium and Secreto, although Telios soon took over until At Talaq stole the show at the halfway stage.

At Talaq was a 250/1 outsider ridden by Richard Hills, and rounding Tattenham Corner, the unconsidered colt swept in to a shocking five-length lead and, at the two-furlong marker, he still held command from Telios. In behind, El Gran Senor was absolutely cruising under an extremely patient ride from Eddery, while further back, Roche was beginning to drive the hardy Secreto into contention.

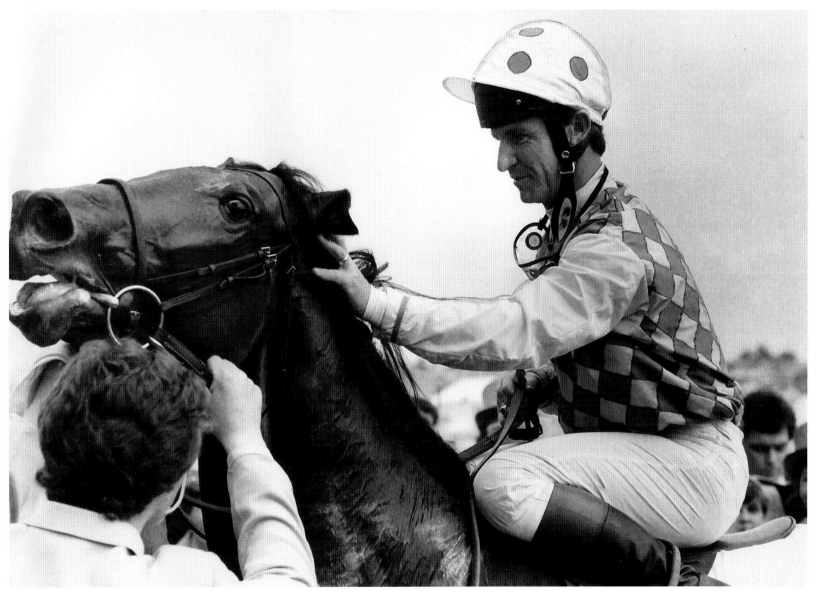

Secreto and jockey Christy Roche return having upset the favourite El Gran Senor.

It was not long before Eddery eased El Gran Senor in to the lead, sweeping past the plucky outsiders as he did so, and the one to go with him was Secreto, although it appeared the favourite had his number too. Roche was working furiously to get the underdog to stay with El Gran Senor, but Secreto was as wholehearted as he was brave, and the further the race progressed, the more anxious Eddery appeared to become. Those that had doubted El Gran Senor's true stamina now had cause to shout, and from a near certain-looking win for the favourite, the result was now up for grabs. As Secreto kept battling relentlessly while El Gran Senor tried desperately to repel him, the outcome was a breathtaking finish as both horses flashed together past the line. Mighty Flutter finished well back in third having run on well, with the game At Talaq fourth in front of the never-dangerous Alphabatim.

It had been a thrilling if perhaps unexpected finish, but as the crowd watched the replay of the duel, gasps of disbelief could be heard as it emerged it was Secreto and not El Gran Senor that had clinched the race by a nose. The finish had been desperate, and Eddery then added to the tension by objecting to the winner for leaning into his mount. It was the first objection in the Derby for thirty-two years, and none had been successful since 1913; not surprisingly, the atmosphere could be cut with a knife as the result was being decided. After ten seemingly endless minutes, it was announced that the places remained unaltered and that Secreto had won the Derby.

A true sportsman in an obviously disappointing moment, Vincent O'Brien was quick to proclaim his joy for his son David winning the race. Having only been in training for four seasons, David O'Brien became the youngest ever – at just twenty-seven – to have won the Derby, though he had previously won the Irish and French versions. It was also a first Derby success for Italian owner Luigi Miglitti, who lived in Venezuela and had purchased Secreto at the Kentucky Sales.

Pat Eddery came in for much criticism for not unleashing El Gran Senor at the two-furlong marker when he appeared in total control, but the truth was Eddery had been instructed to wait so as to preserve the favourite's stamina. In contrast, Roche received considerable credit for the strong, forceful ride he had given Secreto in the titanic battle.

For the great sire Northern Dancer, Secreto was now his third son to have won the Derby, following Nijinsky and The Minstrel, and he became the first sire to record a one-two in the Derby since Swynford in 1924.

While El Gran Senor gained some consolation by later winning the Irish Derby, it was the extremely brave Secreto that was the real hero of the day. Secreto did not train on as a four-year-old, instead being sent to stud in America and ultimately Japan.

## 1984 EVER READY DERBY RESULT

| FATE / HORSE | WEIGHT | JOCKEY | ODDS |
|---|---|---|---|
| **1st – Secreto** | 9-0 | C. Roche | 14/1 |
| **2nd – El Gran Senor** | 9-0 | Pat Eddery | 8/11* |
| **3rd – Mighty Flutter** | 9-0 | B. Rouse | 66/1 |
| 4th – At Talaq | 9-0 | R. Hills | 250/1 |
| 5th – Alphabatim | 9-0 | L. Piggott | 11/2 |
| 6th – Telios | 9-0 | G. Baxter | 100/1 |
| 7th – Long Pond | 9-0 | G. Duffield | 150/1 |
| 8th – Kaytu | 9-0 | W. Carson | 12/1 |
| 9th – Sheer Heights | 9-0 | P. Cook | 100/1 |
| 10th – Ilium | 9-0 | A. Murray | 16/1 |
| 11th – Pigwidgeon | 9-0 | G. Starkey | 150/1 |
| 12th – Elegant Air | 9-0 | B. Raymond | 50/1 |
| 13th – Claude Monet | 9-0 | S. Cauthen | 12/1 |
| 14th – My Volga Boatman | 9-0 | W.R. Swinburn | 33/1 |
| 15th – Sassanoco | 9-0 | T. Rogers | 500/1 |
| 16th – Cataldi | 9-0 | A. Clark | 250/1 |
| Last – Northern Fred | 9-0 | G. Moore | 150/1 |

6 June 1984
Going – Good
Winner – £227,680
Time – 2 mins 39.12 secs
Favourite – El Gran Senor
17 Ran

| | |
|---|---|
| Secreto | Bay colt by Northern Dancer – Betty's Secret |
| El Gran Senor | Bay colt by Northern Dancer – Sex Appeal |
| Mighty Flutter | Brown colt by Rolfe – Lettuce |

Winner bred by E.P. Taylor in the USA
Winner trained by D.V. O'Brien at Rahimaghmore, Co. Tipperary, Ireland

Henry Cecil trained his first Derby winner in 1985.

# SLIP ANCHOR

After Lester Piggott had won his ninth Derby aboard Teenoso in 1983, the jockey stated that he would love to have one more winner of the great race for trainer Henry Cecil. The Newmarket-based trainer had risen to a high status in the training ranks, but as of pre-Epsom in 1985, Cecil had yet to train the winner of the Blue Riband. Piggott would certainly have wished he was able to partner Cecil's principal hope for the 1985 Derby, as on this occasion, the trainer had in his yard the hottest property among the three-year-old generation.

The horse that had Cecil on the brink of breaking his Derby duck was a relentless-galloping bay colt called Slip Anchor, and the horse was to be ridden by American Steve Cauthen, who was the reigning Champion Jockey. Having won over ten furlongs at Newmarket earlier in the season, Slip Anchor then really shot to prominence with an effortless success in the Lingfield Derby Trial. What made Slip Anchor such an interesting and in some ways unusual candidate for Epsom was that, in both his three-year-old wins, the horse had made all from the front to simply crush his rivals. These were tactics that were rarely successful in the Derby, but perhaps the most significant pointer came from Cauthen, who firmly believed that Slip Anchor would gallop his opponents into submission come Derby day. Slip Anchor was by the 1978 winner Shirley Heights and was owned by Lord Howard de Walden, whose last Derby runner had been Oncidium, a disappointment behind Santa Claus in the 1964 race.

The field of fourteen was the smallest in number since 1970, but nevertheless, there were some worthy challengers to the 9/4 favourite Slip Anchor. One of these, trained by Michael Stoute, was the narrow winner of the 2,000 Guineas, Shadeed. A naturally explosive racehorse, Shadeed – like his father Nijinsky – was somewhat headstrong and got worked up in race preliminaries, leading some to believe the colt to be unbalanced mentally. All his faults considered, Shadeed remained a very talented horse and his form was strong, having beaten the improving stayer Damister in the Craven Stakes prior to his Guineas win. That form was significantly franked when Damister – also a Derby runner – won York's Dante Stakes.

Others with strong claims included Law Society, Theatrical and Lanfranco. Vincent O'Brien was represented by the talented but lazy Law Society, a brown colt sired by the dual Prix de l'Arc de Triomphe winner Alleged. A classy juvenile whose only ever defeat had come in the Dewhurst Stakes, Law Society had attracted some Derby interest when winning the Chester Vase earlier in the season. Law Society's jockey, Pat Eddery, was one man that was eager to make amends for finishing second in 1984, when he had suffered an agonising defeat aboard El Gran Senor. Theatrical was a first Derby runner for Irish trainer Dermot Weld. The horse was unbeaten, having won the Leopardstown Derby Trial on his latest outing, and had Lester Piggott in the saddle. Sired by the 1963 Derby winner Relko, Lanfranco was undoubtedly the second-string colt from Henry Cecil's yard. The horse, ridden by American Cash Asmussen, had won the mile-and-a-half Predominate Stakes at Goodwood most recently.

A relentless galloper, Slip Anchor destroyed the 1985 Derby field.

From the very early stages, the 1985 Derby was all about one horse. Just as he had done in his two victories prior to Epsom, Steve Cauthen pushed Slip Anchor into the lead a mere fifty yards after bolting out of the starting stalls, and very quickly the jockey had his horse settled into a smooth, steady gallop. Even at the infant stage of the race, none of the field seemed willing to take on the favourite, so Cauthen joyfully let Slip Anchor churn along happily.

Slip Anchor was adapting really well to Epsom's undulations, and coming down the hill he gave the impression of a horse that was relishing the Derby experience, so well was he travelling. The Guineas winner Shadeed had appeared to be going satisfactorily at the top of the hill, yet the longer the race went on, the more it became obvious he was in trouble, and soon he was out of contention, finishing miserably under Walter Swinburn.

It was at Tattenham Corner that the 1985 Derby result was well and truly decided. Kicking Slip Anchor on again, the favourite slipped ever more into a pounding gallop mode and forged clear of his pursuers. Entering the straight, he was a mammoth fifteen lengths clear from Petoski, Phardante, Supreme Leader, Law Society and Theatrical.

Three furlongs out and the Irish raider Law Society emerged from the pack to give chase to the runaway leader, but Slip Anchor was too powerful and too determined a galloper to be hauled back now, and careering on to the finish, Slip Anchor stormed in to become one of the most convincing and deserving Derby winners in history, romping home by seven lengths from Law Society and the plugging-on Damister. Shadeed's Epsom adventure had been a total flop, with the Newmarket hero beating only one horse home, the 200/1 outsider Main Reason.

Slip Anchor's victory was emphatic and perfectly scripted, with Cauthen correct in his pre-race prediction. The remainder of the jockeys admitted that the winner had annihilated them, while Slip Anchor's winning margin had only been bettered by Manna in 1925 and Shergar in 1981 since records had been kept.

For Henry Cecil, Slip Anchor was the first of what seemed likely to be many Derby winners and was undoubtedly the best horse he had trained to date, while Cauthen compared Slip Anchor favourably to his brilliant 1978 US Triple Crown winner Affirmed. The jockey had not had the greatest of starts to Derby day when the helicopter transporting himself, Piggott and Swinburn from Newmarket to Epsom was delayed by fog, meaning they had to miss the first race on the card.

Winning owner Lord Howard de Walden – who owned three studs in Yorkshire, Newmarket and Berkshire – had bred Slip Anchor by Shirley Heights out of a German mare called Sayonara. Sadly, Sayonara had died shortly after foaling Slip Anchor. The Derby win was a fulfilment of a longstanding dream of the owner, and he was a very proud man after the race.

While Law Society went on to win the Irish Derby, Slip Anchor suffered a bad injury after Epsom and was denied a tilt at Ascot's King George VI and Queen Elizabeth Diamond Stakes. When he finally returned to the racecourse, Slip Anchor was never quite the same, disappointing in defeats at Kempton and Newmarket at the end of his three-year-old season, while also losing his only race at four. Despite the anticlimactic end to his racing career, Slip Anchor had been a totally dominating force in the 1985 Derby, and was a fine winner of the race. When he was finally retired to stud in 1987, he took with him a value of £5 million.

**1985 EVER READY DERBY RESULT**

| FATE / HORSE | WEIGHT | JOCKEY | ODDS |
|---|---|---|---|
| **1st – Slip Anchor** | 9-0 | S. Cauthen | 9/4* |
| **2nd – Law Society** | 9-0 | Pat Eddery | 5/1 |
| **3rd – Damister** | 9-0 | Y. Saint-Martin | 16/1 |
| 4th – Supreme Leader | 9-0 | P. Robinson | 10/1 |
| 5th – Lanfranco | 9-0 | C. Asmussen | 14/1 |
| 6th – Reach | 9-0 | T. Quinn | 33/1 |
| 7th – Theatrical | 9-0 | L. Piggott | 10/1 |
| 8th – Phardante | 9-0 | G. Starkey | 40/1 |
| 9th – Royal Harmony | 9-0 | M. Hills | 40/1 |
| 10th – Snow Plant | 9-0 | G. Curran | 100/1 |
| 11th – Petoski | 9-0 | W. Carson | 33/1 |
| 12th – Seurat | 9-0 | E. Legrix | 33/1 |
| 13th – Shadeed | 9-0 | W.R. Swinburn | 7/2 |
| Last – Main Reason | 9-0 | P. Waldron | 200/1 |

5 June 1985
Going – Good
Winner – £204,160
Time – 2 mins 36.23 secs
Favourite – Slip Anchor
14 Ran

| | |
|---|---|
| Slip Anchor | Bay colt by Shirley Heights – Sayonara |
| Law Society | Bay or brown colt by Alleged – Bold Bikini |
| Damister | Bay colt by Mr Prospector – Batucada |

Winner bred by Owner (Lord Howard de Walden)
Winner trained by H. Cecil at Newmarket

# SHAHRASTANI

It is fairly infrequent that a horse that deserves to win a race fails to do so. But it can happen, albeit normally in races with bigger fields. For example, in National Hunt racing, the Grand National annually attracts a field of forty runners, and during the race, runners that may be going particularly well at the time can be brought down or knocked over by loose, rampaging horses that have already fallen. In Flat racing, it is possible for the Derby to fall into this same category. Normally having large fields, the added problems of the undulations and Tattenham Corner means that the race can get rough. The likes of Shantung in 1959 and Prince Regent in 1969 are horses that, in hindsight, may have won the Derby had they not received ill luck in running. Jockeyship too plays a big part in success or failure, and often it is the early part of the Derby, when jockeys are battling for position, that can be critical.

Without any shadow of a doubt, the class horse of the 1986 Derby field was the Guy Harwood-trained Dancing Brave. A beautifully smooth-actioned bay colt, Dancing Brave was unbeaten in four races – two as a juvenile and two in the current campaign. Dancing Brave looked a wonderfully relaxed horse during races before arriving with late bursts of speed and power, as he had done to devastating effect in the 2,000 Guineas – where he had beaten the good Green Desert – and this was how Harwood envisioned Dancing Brave running at Epsom. Dancing Brave was owned by Khalid Abdullah and was partnered in the race by the oldest jockey in Britain, Greville Starkey. Starkey had won the race aboard Shirley Heights in 1978, but rated Dancing Brave not only classier than that horse but the best he had ever ridden. Despite all the positives, Dancing Brave had never raced beyond a mile, so there were obvious stamina doubts attached to his bid. What remained to be seen was

whether Dancing Brave would follow the lead of Wollow, Blushing Groom and El Gran Senor as very well-fancied favourites that did not quite see out the entire Derby trip or else prove similar to Sir Ivor and Nijinsky, horses that had stamina questions before their Derbys but possessed the class and clinical acceleration to win the race.

Waiting to test the favourite's resolve were a variety of challengers with useful form. One ironic outcome would have been a win for Allez Milord, given that he was from the same stable as Dancing Brave. Blatantly not as fancied, Allez Milord did have fine form over the Derby distance, having proved his stamina in the mud at Goodwood when winning the Predominate Stakes. Allez Milord started as the 8/1 third favourite, and gave the Sussex-based Harwood realistic hopes of being the first to train the Derby one-two since Richard Carver in 1948 with My Love and Royal Drake.

Unbeaten in both his races at three, the chestnut colt Shahrastani was a horse that appeared to be on the rise. From the same Shergar team of 1981 – the Aga Khan, Michael Stoute and Walter Swinburn – Shahrastani was a horse who, by the trainer's own admission, took a while to get to the top of his game. However, having won at Sandown, the colt then won well in the Dante Stakes to confirm himself ready to run at Epsom, and he took second place in the betting at 11/2.

Among the others in the field were Wise Counsellor and Bold Arrangement. The former was a son of the two-time Arc winner Alleged and was a horse looking to give Vincent O'Brien a seventh Derby win and Pat Eddery a third. Bold Arrangement had been unfortunate not to have won the Kentucky Derby in May, finishing a brave second. The horse was partnered by top American rider Chris McCarron, who had flown over from California to ride the horse, despite having never ridden at Epsom before.

The start of the race was delayed by Willie Carson's mount Sharrood, who had to be reshod. When the race finally got underway, it was Nomrood and Nisnas that set a hot early pace, although the tempo calmed down considerably after a couple of furlongs.

The decline in pace had something of a ripple effect. Though the horses at the front, including the well-placed Shahrastani, stayed clear of any incident, those at the back got stacked up and had little room to manoeuvre. These included Dancing Brave who found himself with nowhere to go, and Starkey frustratingly had to bide his time before he could make a move forward.

As they came round Tattenham Corner, it was an outsider in Faraway Dancer – giving Willie Ryan a superb first Derby ride – that had the edge, although Swinburn had Shahrastani beautifully poised just in behind. In bleak contrast, Dancing Brave was virtually last having suffered a bad run, and Starkey later claimed that the horse had been unbalanced coming down the hill.

Despite the desperate late charge of the favourite, Dancing Brave, Shahrastani (nearest rails) held on to win the 1986 race.

Shahrastani and jockey Walter Swinburn are led in by owner the Aga Khan (top hat).

Having received a charmed run the entire race, Swinburn sent Shahrastani past Faraway Dancer with two-and-a-half furlongs to run, and the horse began to bound clear in willing style for his rider, and it appeared a surprisingly easy victory may be on the cards. But Dancing Brave had not given up. Passing horse after horse in the straight, he showed fantastic speed and power, and with Shahrastani visibly slowing in front, the favourite still had a glimmer of hope.

But Swinburn had stolen this race. With none of his rivals willing to attack in the straight, the jockey had urged his mount into an unassailable advantage, and try as Dancing Brave did to catch him, the favourite simply ran out of ground, showing that although he did stay, he was bereft of luck in running.

At the line, Shahrastani had courageously held on for victory by half-a-length from Dancing Brave, with the Henry Cecil-trained Mashkour running on for third. Of the others, Allez Milord had never been in a position to threaten, while Eddery was forced to pull-up his mount Wise Counsellor, who returned sore having failed to negotiate the hill.

Not surprisingly, Greville Starkey came in for a torrent of abuse from punters and racing fans alike that were horrified at the ride he had given Dancing Brave. The result left a disbelieving Starkey and Harwood totally glum, such was the magnitude of the defeat. For Starkey, it was not the end of the nightmare. Trouncing Shahrastani on a number of subsequent meetings, Dancing Brave went on to win the Eclipse Stakes, King George and Prix de l'Arc de Triomphe and was second in the Breeders Cup Turf at Santa Anita in America, proving himself to be one of the very best horses in the modern era not to have won the Derby. However, for the last three of those races, including his last ever at Santa Anita, Dancing Brave was partnered by Pat Eddery, who had displaced Starkey.

Lost somewhat in the Dancing Brave situation was the victory of Shahrastani, a horse that had responded admirably to a superb ride from Swinburn. The jockey understandably did not rate the winner in the class of Shergar, but Shahrastani had toughness and resilience. The horse went on to win the Irish Derby and when he was retired and sent to the Three Chimneys Stud in America, Shahrastani – a second Derby winner sired by Nijinsky – carried with him a value of £16 million.

**1986 EVER READY DERBY RESULT**

| FATE / HORSE | WEIGHT | JOCKEY | ODDS |
|---|---|---|---|
| **1st – Shahrastani** | 9-0 | W.R. Swinburn | 11/2 |
| **2nd – Dancing Brave** | 9-0 | G. Starkey | 2/1* |
| **3rd – Mashkour** | 9-0 | S. Cauthen | 12/1 |
| 4th – Faraway Dancer | 9-0 | W. Ryan | 33/1 |
| 5th – Nisnas | 9-0 | P. Waldron | 40/1 |
| 6th – Flash Of Steel | 9-0 | M.J. Kinane | 25/1 |
| 7th – Sirk | 9-0 | P. Robinson | 50/1 |
| 8th – Sharrood | 9-0 | W. Carson | 25/1 |
| 9th – Mr John | 9-0 | T. Ives | 50/1 |
| 10th – Allez Milord | 9-0 | C. Asmussen | 8/1 |
| 11th – Nomrood | 9-0 | T. Quinn | 20/1 |
| 12th – Jareer | 9-0 | B. Rouse | 16/1 |
| 13th – Then Again | 9-0 | R. Guest | 33/1 |
| 14th – Bold Arrangement | 9-0 | C. McCarron | 12/1 |
| 15th – Arokar | 9-0 | Y. Saint-Martin | 18/1 |
| 16th – Fioravanti | 9-0 | C. Roche | 33/1 |
| Last – Wise Counsellor | 9-0 | Pat Eddery | 16/1 |

4 June 1986
Going – Good
Winner – £239,260
Time – 2 mins 37.13 secs
Favourite – Dancing Brave
17 Ran

| | |
|---|---|
| Shahrastani | Chestnut colt by Nijinsky – Shademah |
| Dancing Brave | Bay colt by Lyphard – Navajo Princess |
| Mashkour | Chestnut colt by Irish River – Sancta Rose |

Winner bred by Owner (H.H. Aga Khan) in the USA
Winner trained by M. Stoute at Newmarket

American Steve Cauthen won his second Derby in 1987.

# REFERENCE POINT

Steve Cauthen had come to ride in England back in 1979 from Kentucky, USA. He had been Champion Jockey in America at the tender age of seventeen and had since become the only ever jockey to be Champion on both sides of the Atlantic, having taken the English title in 1984 and 1985. Cauthen had won all five of the English Classic races: the 1979 2,000 Guineas with Tap On Wood, the 1985 fillies Triple Crown (1,000 Guineas, Oaks and St Leger) with the brilliant Oh So Sharp and, of course, the 1985 Derby with Slip Anchor. Cauthen had only started watching the Derby in 1978 after he had been offered the ride on that year's runner-up, Hawaiian Sound, although he turned the mount down to avoid missing out on the final leg of the US Triple Crown, which he won on Affirmed. Now, two years after Slip Anchor had pulverised the 1985 Derby field, Cauthen again partnered the Derby favourite on a horse whose style was remarkably similar to the hero of 1985.

The horse was Reference Point, a big, lazy individual trained by Henry Cecil. Like Slip Anchor, Reference Point was a horse that appreciated front-running tactics where he could use his huge galloping stride to maximum effect. The colt had done this on his only start of the season, when winning the Dante Stakes at York after recovering from a serious sinus problem that required an operation. There were those that thought Reference Point's price of 6/4 was incredibly short, given that the horse had only run once in the season and that his wins to date had come at galloping tracks like Sandown, Doncaster and York. But the horse had the benefit of being sired by Mill Reef, while Slip Anchor had shown that a front-running, strong-galloping style could be used to win a Derby. Cecil also saddled Legal Bid, a horse that had shattered the record

time for winning the Lingfield Derby Trial on his previous start, despite getting his tongue stuck through the ring of the bit after it had slipped through his mouth during the race. Legal Bid was a half brother to the 1985 runner-up Law Society, and Cauthen knew that, having had the option to ride him, he was risking passing on a potential Derby winner. When Cauthen decided to ride Reference Point, it was Tony Ives that took the mount on Legal Bid.

Splitting the Cecil-trained pair in the betting was the exciting French challenger Sadjiyd. Trained by Alain de Royer-Dupre, Sadjiyd had taken two important French trials in the Prix Noailles and the Prix Hocquart, and the horse was partnered at Epsom by the veteran Yves Saint-Martin. Sadjiyd's good form in France had seen a major gamble take place on the horse, and eventually the colt started as the 11/2 second-favourite.

Trying to make up for the painful defeat of Dancing Brave the year before was owner Khalid Abdullah. He was represented on this occasion by the naturally relaxed, brown colt Bellotto. The American-bred horse had come with a late but fruitless rally behind the excellent Don't Forget Me in the 2,000 Guineas, sparking hopes the horse may appreciate the longer distance of the Derby. Trained by Jeremy Tree, Bellotto was attempting to emulate Mill Reef, Grundy and Roberto as 2,000 Guineas runner-ups that progressed to win the Derby.

The favourite, Reference Point, returns back the winner of the 1987 Derby.

It was a deeply talented field that contested the 1987 Derby, and among the other chief contenders were Entitled, Ajdal, Groom Dancer and Most Welcome. Having been a sick horse the year before, the Vincent O'Brien-trained Entitled had bounced back to finish second in the Irish 2,000 Guineas and, while he had natural speed, his pedigree suggested that stamina should also be in his locker, as he too was sired by Mill Reef, while his dam's sire was the 1968 Derby winner Sir Ivor. A son of Northern Dancer, Ajdal had been a fine two-year-old, and his wins had included the Dewhurst Stakes. However, the horse was beaten when favourite for both Guineas races in England and Ireland, and Ray Cochrane's mount was perceived to have a lack of stamina. Sired by the 1977 Derby favourite Blushing Groom, Groom Dancer was another with stamina doubts. However, the horse was unbeaten in three races during the season, including when winning Longchamp's valuable Prix Lupin. Trained in France by Tony Clout and ridden by confident eighteen-year-old jockey Dominic Boeuf, Groom Dancer's connections were little known in England – or perhaps the horse would have started shorter than 16/1. Most Welcome, a chestnut trained by Geoff Wragg, had run well in the 2,000 Guineas, although the horse had hung left and eventually been disqualified. Ridden by Champion Jockey Pat Eddery's younger brother Paul, Most Welcome carried the extreme confidence of his trainer into the battle.

In attendance for the 1987 Derby were The Queen, The Queen Mother, the Prince and Princess of Wales and the Duchess of York, and on an overcast afternoon, it was Cauthen aboard the favourite that soon took the lead, tracked by his stablemate Legal Bid, Ibn Bey, Ascot Knight, Water Boatman and Ajdal.

The first notable occurrence of the 1987 Derby had arrived when the French raider Sadjiyd had grown quarrelsome in the stalls, seriously threatening his chances in the race. As a result, the horse was reluctant to race when they eventually started, and was soon tailed off.

Coming down the hill, it was evident that Cauthen was working constantly to get Reference Point racing, as the lazy-minded colt appeared to be distracted by the large crowd around him. Even so, he was going strongly and looked to have every chance rounding Tattenham Corner.

One horse that was travelling well just in behind the favourite was the Michael Stoute-trained Ascot Knight, but he was soon to fade dramatically at the three-furlong marker, and it was the chestnut Most Welcome that emerged from the challenging pack to tackle Reference Point in the straight.

Inside the final two furlongs the race was at boiling point as Reference Point rattled along, hard-driven by Cauthen and harassed all the time by Most Welcome. The chestnut got right to the favourite's quarters at one point, but Reference Point was not only a supreme galloper, but he was also mightily resilient once he had his mind focused and he simply would not let Most Welcome past. Coming from a different galaxy, Pat Eddery was flashing home Bellotto in one last desperate thrust, but neither he nor Most Welcome could unship Reference Point from his lead, and as they hurtled past the post, the favourite had won the Derby by a length-and-a-half from Most Welcome with Bellotto third. Sadjiyd had picked off some weakening horses to finish a disappointing eighth, while Legal Bid had fared even worse, trailing home fourteenth.

Cecil and Cauthen were overjoyed at Reference Point's game, all-the-way win, describing the horse as a beautifully relaxed animal with an abundance of class and courage. It was Cauthen's belief that the horse was not ideally suited to Epsom, as the sheer size of the colt naturally made him unbalanced at the trickier moments, so it proved what a high-class individual the winner was to adapt to the challenge. When the dust had settled, the brutal, never-ending gallop Reference Point had set was enough to register the fastest ever electrically timed win in the race, with only Mahmoud's hand-timed effort in 1936 faster.

Reference Point was owned by Louis Freedman, who had also bred the horse at his Cliveden Stud near Maidenhead in Berkshire, with the result being a huge boost for British breeding – considering the phenomenal recent success for the American-based stallions, particularly Northern Dancer. It was a second Derby success for Mill Reef, having also sired the 1978 winner Shirley Heights.

Reference Point was an above-average winner of the Derby and he went on to confirm his superiority when winning the season's King George at Ascot and St Leger at Doncaster. The horse was then retired to stud the following year with a value of £11 million. Sadly, he died at a young age, passing away in 1991.

**1987 EVER READY DERBY RESULT**

| FATE / HORSE | WEIGHT | JOCKEY | ODDS |
|---|---|---|---|
| **1st – Reference Point** | 9-0 | S. Cauthen | 6/4* |
| **2nd – Most Welcome** | 9-0 | Paul Eddery | 33/1 |
| **3rd – Bellotto** | 9-0 | Pat Eddery | 11/1 |
| 4th – Sir Harry Lewis | 9-0 | J. Reid | 66/1 |
| 5th – Entitled | 9-0 | C. Asmussen | 11/1 |
| 6th – Mountain Kingdom | 9-0 | M. Roberts | 33/1 |
| 7th – Groom Dancer | 9-0 | D. Boeuf | 16/1 |
| 8th – Sadjiyd | 9-0 | Y. Saint-Martin | 11/2 |
| 9th – Ajdal | 9-0 | R. Cochrane | 25/1 |
| 10th – Persifleur | 9-0 | A. Cruz | 33/1 |
| 11th – Ascot Knight | 9-0 | W.R. Swinburn | 25/1 |
| 12th – Love The Groom | 9-0 | W. Carson | 33/1 |
| 13th – Ibn Bey | 9-0 | T. Quinn | 40/1 |
| 14th – Legal Bid | 9-0 | T. Ives | 8/1 |
| 15th – Gulf King | 9-0 | P. Cook | 100/1 |
| 16th – Water Boatman | 9-0 | B. Rouse | 150/1 |
| 17th – Angara Abyss | 9-0 | G. Starkey | 100/1 |
| 18th – Alwasmi | 9-0 | R. Hills | 150/1 |
| Last – Romantic Prince | 9-0 | W. Ryan | 150/1 |

3 June 1987
Going – Good
Winner – £267,600
Time – 2 mins 33.90 secs
Favourite – Reference Point
19 Ran

| | |
|---|---|
| Reference Point | Bay colt by Mill Reef – Home On The Range |
| Most Welcome | Chestnut colt by Be My Guest – Topsy |
| Bellotto | Brown colt by Mr Prospector – Shelf Talker |

Winner bred by Cliveden Stud
Winner trained by H. Cecil at Newmarket

# 1988

## KAHYASI

Since the first running of the Dante Stakes at York back in 1958, only four horses had won that race and progressed to win the Derby. Indeed, after St Paddy had won at York and Epsom in 1960, no horse achieved the double until Shirley Heights in 1978. However, after Shahrastani and Reference Point took both races in the previous two years before 1988, the Dante rapidly became a more important and recognised trial for the Derby.

The 1988 winner of the York race was a horse that was being compared to the excellent 1982 Derby winner Golden Fleece by the jockey of both horses, Pat Eddery. The big, talented horse in question was named Red Glow and was trained by Geoff Wragg. The trainer had sent out Teenoso to win the Derby in 1983, yet he believed Red Glow to be a colt with superior acceleration – a fact evident when the horse came from last to first, quickening admirably off a sluggish pace, to win at York. The Dante was only Red Glow's third lifetime race, but his fine performance, coupled with truly sensational workouts, saw the horse begin the Derby as the 5/2 favourite in an open-looking field.

It had looked for a while like being a firm-ground Derby, but in the days leading up to the race, the heavens opened, significantly softening the turf, meaning stamina would be a huge part of any potential winner's design. One horse that possessed such a quality was the Dick Hern-trained Unfuwain, one of four horses owned by Hamdan Al Maktoum. Hern also trained the 2,000 Guineas runner-up Charmer and the gritty Minster Son – a horse bred and ridden by Willie Carson – but it was Unfuwain that had captured the attention of punters. Unfuwain, a son of Northern Dancer, was unbeaten as a three-year-old and was similar in build to the previous year's winner, Reference

Kahyasi was a third Derby winner for the Aga Khan.

Point, and like that horse and the 1985 winner Slip Anchor, Unfuwain was a relentless, long-striding galloper. Twice a winner over a mile-and-a-half, Steve Cauthen's mount had really impressed when thrashing his opponents to win the Chester Vase earlier in the season.

Hoping to welcome in his third Derby winner was the Aga Khan, and he was represented on this occasion by Doyoun and Kahyasi. Doyoun, a bay son of Mill Reef, was considered an uncertain stayer by his trainer Michael Stoute, yet the horse was unbeaten in his three lifetime races. However, all three of his wins were at Newmarket at a distance of around a mile. The colt had won the season's 2,000 Guineas when favourite and if he could win the Derby, he would be the first to complete the double since the great Nijinsky in 1970. Though Doyoun attracted a lot more public interest, the dark-horse of the race, Kahyasi, was potentially a colt far better equipped for the Derby test. Like Doyoun, unbeaten in his only three lifetime races, the little bay Kahyasi had shown quickness and heart to win the Lingfield Derby Trial. Kahyasi was a second Derby ride for jockey Ray Cochrane, while the horse was trained at Newmarket by Luca Cumani.

Despite the grey horse Sheriff's Star making a big fuss on entry to the starting stalls, the fourteen-strong field broke away to a good start, and straightaway,

The Queen shows her enthusiasm for racing during the 1988 Derby.

the pace was red hot, as the four horses owned by Hamdan Al Maktoum – Unfuwain, Al Mufti (a son of Roberto), Maksud and Al Muhalhal – sparred aggressively for the lead. It was the pounding galloper Unfuwain that emerged as the winner of that particular battle, and Cauthen's mount proceeded to lead on in relentless fashion. Early on, the favourite, Red Glow, who had sparkled and stood out in the preliminaries, took up a position at the rear, while it was evident that Cochrane was finding some difficulty in getting Kahyasi to settle, such was the ferocity of the gallop.

Kahyasi and jubilant jockey
Ray Cochrane.

It appeared that Cauthen was trying to adopt the same tactics he had used so mercilessly when winning with Slip Anchor and Reference Point, as Unfuwain charged on. Reaching Tattenham Corner, the leader was still going strong, tracked by the improving Barry Hills-trained bay colt Glacial Storm. Red Glow too was moving forward fast, but Kahyasi drifted very wide coming round the famous corner.

The question entering the straight was whether any horse could force their way past Unfuwain. The answer fell in the positive, as the leader was about to be challenged by a whole host of colts hungry as wolves for Derby glory.

Red Glow was trying to creep into a threatening position, while Doyoun – well positioned on the inside – and the surprising Kefaah on the outside made their plays, yet the first to engulf the now tiring Unfuwain was Glacial Storm, who had quietly been running a big race.

Inside two furlongs and Michael Hills went for home on Glacial Storm, as the partnership looked to give Barry Hills a first Derby win, having been second twice before through Rheingold and Hawaiian Sound. In behind Glacial Storm, Red Glow simply could not find the necessary acceleration to get to the lead, much to the disappointment of favourite backers, but little Kahyasi was now starting to motor and was picking up majestically for Cochrane.

Kahyasi had really been struggling earlier but now the horse showed his courage and determination as he charged up the centre of the track and was level with Glacial Storm with just a half a furlong to run. Showing fine battling qualities and no shortage of finishing speed, Kahyasi overthrew Glacial Storm and drove home to a length-and-a-half win. Doyoun had run a gallant race for a supposed non-stayer, but had just failed to find extra reserves at the end, coming home third ahead of Red Glow. Having attempted to win from the front, Unfuwain eventually faded to finish seventh. The fancied pair of Minster Son and Charmer had never been factors in the race, although both returned home lame.

Kahyasi's win had given the Aga Khan his third Derby win following those of Shergar and Shahrastani. The Aga Khan's grandfather had won the race five times between 1930 and 1952, yet the current Aga Khan had only had his racing interest evoked when his father Aly Khan – who never won the Derby – was killed in a car crash. Now, forty years after his grandfather had been first and third in the 1948 race with My Love and Noor, the Aga Khan had done the same with Kahyasi and Doyoun. It was Doyoun that wore the owner's first colours of green with red armlets, while Kahyasi carried the green and chocolate hoops that had been worn by the Aga Khan's grandfather's horse Tulyar when he won the 1952 Derby.

It was the first Derby success for both Cumani and Cochrane. The thirty-year-old Cochrane had switched to a brief career in jump racing in 1977 when his weight had increased, but in 1988, he proudly trailed only Pat Eddery and Cauthen in the jockey's title race having been reborn in the Flat game, largely due to his association with the Newmarket-based Cumani, who incidentally had also saddled the fifth-placed Kefaah. Cochrane – who in later years would be involved in a horrific helicopter accident with the Italian jockey Frankie Dettori – had contacted the wife of the then-incarcerated jockey Lester Piggott before the race to get some advice from the great champion. Piggott had told Cochrane to be in a challenging position round Tattenham Corner so as to have a chance. Despite being wide on the course at that point, Cochrane had ridden a fine race in just his second Derby.

The tough Kahyasi was one of the smallest of all Derby winners at just 15.2 hands high, but the head-spinning early pace coupled with his strong finish had given the horse the fastest winning time since the race was recorded electronically. Kahyasi was sired by a decent middle-distance performer in Ile De Bourbon, while he was the first foal of Kadissya, who was in turn sired by the 1977 Derby third Blushing Groom. Kahyasi followed up his Epsom win by taking the Irish Derby, while in his retirement he was placed at the same Ballymany Stud that Shergar had been sent to.

## 1988 EVER READY DERBY RESULT

| FATE / HORSE | WEIGHT | JOCKEY | ODDS |
|---|---|---|---|
| **1st – Kahyasi** | 9-0 | R. Cochrane | 11/1 |
| **2nd – Glacial Storm** | 9-0 | M. Hills | 14/1 |
| **3rd – Doyoun** | 9-0 | W.R. Swinburn | 9/1 |
| 4th – Red Glow | 9-0 | Pat Eddery | 5/2* |
| 5th – Kefaah | 9-0 | J. Reid | 25/1 |
| 6th – Sheriff's Star | 9-0 | T. Ives | 18/1 |
| 7th – Unfuwain | 9-0 | S. Cauthen | 9/2 |
| 8th – Minster Son | 9-0 | W. Carson | 6/1 |
| 9th – Project Manager | 9-0 | K.J. Manning | 66/1 |
| 10th – Al Mufti | 9-0 | R. Hills | 14/1 |
| 11th – Charmer | 9-0 | Paul Eddery | 11/1 |
| 12th – Clifton Chapel | 9-0 | W. Newnes | 100/1 |
| 13th – Maksud | 9-0 | M. Roberts | 200/1 |
| Last – Al Muhalhal | 9-0 | P. D'Arcy | 500/1 |

1 June 1988
Going – Good
Winner – £296,500
Time – 2 mins 33.84 secs
Favourite – Red Glow
14 Ran

| Kahyasi | Bay colt by Ile De Bourbon – Kadissya |
|---|---|
| Glacial Storm | Bay colt by Arctic Tern – Hortensia |
| Doyoun | Bay colt by Mill Reef – Dumka |

Winner bred by Owner (H. H. Aga Khan)
Winner trained by L.M. Cumani at Newmarket

# NASHWAN

Every so often, a special horse comes along to take the racing world by storm. In Flat racing, these explosions usually last no more than a season or two – such are the bountiful riches these horses can command at stud. In the modern history of the Derby, the likes of Crepello, Sea Bird II, Sir Ivor, Nijinsky, Mill Reef and Shergar are the ones that certainly fit into the superstar category, and it was Nijinsky that was being used in comparison to the 1989 equine god that had surfaced to try and join the list of greats.

Back in 1970, Nijinsky had become the thirty-fifth and last horse to win both the 2,000 Guineas and the Derby en route to taking the Triple Crown. Now, nineteen years later, a tall, handsome, powerful chestnut called Nashwan attempted to become the thirty-sixth. Trained by Dick Hern and ridden by Willie Carson, Nashwan had won at Newbury and Ascot as a two-year-old and had been aimed at the Derby as a three-year-old. However, after sparkling immensely at home, connections decided to let Nashwan run in the Guineas, and they were rewarded with a performance of the highest class as Nashwan showed amazing speed and power to win in the fastest time for forty years. Nashwan had never run beyond a mile, and his sire Blushing Groom had failed to see out the trip in the 1977 Derby, but the rest of the colt's pedigree suggested an abundance of stamina, as his dam, Height Of Fashion, was a daughter of the St Leger winner Bustino, as she also produced the durable 1988 Derby runner Unfuwain, so Nashwan appeared to have all the ingredients to win the Derby. There was a feeling before the race that Nashwan may be extra special, and both Hern and Carson were in no doubts that the horse would stay and win.

Nashwan crosses the line a magnificent winner of the Derby.

Deemed as Nashwan's biggest rival was another giant of a horse with a glowing reputation – the Guy Harwood-trained Cacoethes. An American-bred horse (like Nashwan), Cacoethes had won at Brighton earlier in the season before really making his mark in the Lingfield Derby Trial. Three of the past six Derby winners – Teenoso, Slip Anchor and Kahyasi – had won at Lingfield before Epsom, and the huge bay Cacoethes had been equally, if not more, impressive than those horses as he won the trial in record time. Greville Starkey's mount, being a big horse, naturally had many wondering if his long galloping stride would be suited to Epsom, but his performance at Lingfield had been so impressive that a bold run seemed assured, and he started at 3/1 behind the 5/4 favourite Nashwan.

Understandably, most of the hype surrounding the 1989 Derby focused on the battle between Nashwan and Cacoethes, but other interesting contenders included Warrshan, Mill Pond and Prince Of Dance. Warrshan was a colt

Willie Carson shows his delight with Nashwan's win.

trying to give his great sire Northern Dancer a remarkable fourth Derby win, which would have tied a twentieth-century mark posted by both Cyllene – who got the 1905 winner Cicero, the 1909 winner Minoru, Lemberg in 1910 and Tagalie in 1912 – and Blandford, who got the winners of 1929, 1930, 1934 and 1935, Trigo, Blenheim, Windsor Lad and Bahram. A lazy type of horse, Warrshan had been beaten in the Chester Vase earlier in the season, before retaliating to win the Predominate Stakes at Goodwood. After some excellent Derby success in the 1950s and 1960s, the French had only registered one win since Sea Bird II in 1965, that being the Maurice Zilber-trained Empery in 1976, and their only challenger on this occasion was the lightly-raced outsider Mill Pond. Trained by Patrick Biancone, Mill Pond was a son of Mill Reef – who had developed into the most influential sire in recent years besides Northern Dancer – having got the Derby winners Shirley Heights and Reference Point. A stablemate of Nashwan, Prince Of Dance – a son of the 1983 Oaks and St Leger heroine Sun Princess – was the dark-horse of the race. An outstanding two-year-old, Prince of Dance had won his only race of his three-year-old season, the Newmarket Stakes, and was by a stallion in Sadler's Wells who in time would emerge as a sire of monumental status. One man who would be hoping that Prince Of Dance would not win was Carson, who had rejected him in favour of Nashwan. Carson had passed over Milford to win on Troy in 1979 and chose Henbit when he won a year later over stablemate Water Mill. The jockey hoped he had got it right for a third time.

The smallest field since 1970 broke away on ground that had been softened by recent rain, and it was Cacoethes' stablemate, the 250/1 outsider Polar Run, that took the early lead from Torjoun, Ile De Nisky and Cacoethes, while the favourite Nashwan was quickly settled nicely in behind.

Polar Run had been put in the race as a pacemaker for Cacoethes; and he ensured that the race was given a fast-beating pulse, and he continued to lead approaching Tattenham Corner, where he unsurprisingly began to drift away.

Coming round Tattenham Corner, it was Ray Cochrane on the Aga Khan's horse Torjoun that narrowly had the advantage from Cacoethes and Ile De Nisky – a son of the previous year's winning sire Ile De Bourbon. There had been a slight worry that the long-striding, tall-structured Nashwan may have some trouble acting on the course, but never far from the leaders, those worries were cast aside as Carson had the easiest of times. Nashwan glided down the hill like a swan, and the favourite melted away any lingering doubts as he cruised smoothly into contention once in the straight.

Cacoethes was the first to play his hand in the straight as Starkey urged the big horse on three furlongs out, yet Nashwan always had him on his radar, and it was not long before the favourite had gobbled up his rival a furlong later. As soon as Carson asked his horse to show his acceleration, the matter was laid

Dick Hern celebrates Nashwan's victory.

to rest, as Nashwan exhibited his total class to pull away from the pack. Flashing home from the rear of the field was the 500/1 shot Terimon – a totally unconsidered grey horse – with Michael Roberts on board, but no horse in the field could live with Nashwan, and the favourite cruised home a five-length winner. The Clive Brittain-trained Terimon, who had won a Leicester maiden the week before, astounded many by taking second with a somewhat demoralised Cacoethes third, having hung awkwardly in the straight. Warrshan and Prince Of Dance both failed to run to their potential and never got into the race. Sadly, Prince Of Dance had lost the action in his back legs during the race, and a post-race examination led to the discovery of spinal cancer, and the talented horse had to be put down.

Carson and Hern were jubilant in the success of Nashwan, and both stated the horse was the best they had ridden and trained respectively. Nashwan was owned by Sheikh Hamdan Al Maktoum, for whom it was a lifetime ambition to win the Derby. Nashwan, meaning 'joyful' in Arabic, was the eighteenth Derby runner for the Maktoum family, with Touching Wood's second place in 1982 being the closest to victory prior to 1989.

For Major Dick Hern, Nashwan was a third Derby success – as it was for Carson – and nobody present at Epsom could have begrudged the trainer that fact, as he had been confined to a wheelchair since a hunting accident four years previously. In a wonderful career, Hern finished Champion Trainer four times and won sixteen British Classics.

Nashwan (blue colours) again defeated Cacoethes in the King George VI and Queen Elizabeth Diamond Stakes after the Derby.

## 1989 EVER READY DERBY RESULT

| FATE / HORSE | WEIGHT | JOCKEY | ODDS |
|---|---|---|---|
| **1st – Nashwan** | 9-0 | W. Carson | 5/4* |
| **2nd – Terimon** | 9-0 | M. Roberts | 500/1 |
| **3rd – Cacoethes** | 9-0 | G. Starkey | 3/1 |
| 4th – Ile De Nisky | 9-0 | G. Duffield | 20/1 |
| 5th – Mill Pond | 9-0 | Pat Eddery | 16/1 |
| 6th – Gran Alba | 9-0 | B. Rouse | 80/1 |
| 7th – Classic Fame | 9-0 | J. Reid | 33/1 |
| 8th – Torjoun | 9-0 | R. Cochrane | 11/1 |
| 9th – Flockton's Own | 9-0 | R. Hills | 500/1 |
| 10th – Prince Of Dance | 9-0 | S. Cauthen | 11/2 |
| 11th – Warrshan | 9-0 | W.R. Swinburn | 13/1 |
| Last – Polar Run | 9-0 | A. Clark | 250/1 |

7 June 1989
Going – Good
Winner – £296,000
Time – 2 mins 34.90 secs
Favourite – Nashwan
12 Ran

| | |
|---|---|
| Nashwan | Chestnut colt by Blushing Groom – Height Of Fashion |
| Terimon | Grey colt by Bustino – Nicholas Grey |
| Cacoethes | Bay colt by Alydar – Careless Notion |

Winner bred by Owner (Hamdan Al Maktoum) in Kentucky, USA
Winner trained by W.R. Hern at West Ilsley, Berkshire

Nashwan was a truly excellent Derby winner. He was a horse that had everything: speed, toughness, courage, immense power and balance. He compared very favourably to Nijinsky in the fact that he had the raw speed to win the Guineas, but also the class and staying power for the Derby. Later he became the first horse to win the Guineas, Derby, Eclipse and King George in the same season, but many were disappointed when he was targeted at the Arc instead of a tilt at the St Leger and the chance to become the sixteenth ever Triple Crown winner. However, in his warm-up race for the Arc, the Prix Niel in France, Nashwan was surprisingly beaten. He then picked up a virus that ruled him out of the Arc and was retired to stud in Norfolk, having been syndicated for £18 million. Hern knew Nashwan was a great horse – the fact that he rated him higher than the great Brigadier Gerard spoke volumes. At stud, the two-time King George winner of the 1990s, Swain, was probably the best of Nashwan's offspring. Sadly, at the age of sixteen, Nashwan passed away due to complications from an operation.

Khalid Abdullah, narrowly beaten with his Dancing Brave in 1986, saw his Quest For Fame win in 1990.

# QUEST FOR FAME

To say that the 1990 Derby was an open race is an understatement. On paper, well over half the field had a realistic chance of winning, and very few could be written off completely. Some labelled it a weak renewal before the race had even taken place, with big names such as the 2,000 Guineas winner Tirol and the hugely impressive but now injured Lingfield Derby Trial winner Rock Hopper absent, yet much of the uncertainty stemmed from the inexperience of many of the contenders. Of the eighteen runners in the field, only five had run in as many as three races in the current campaign.

Henry Cecil trained two of the fancied horses in River God and the race favourite, Razeen. A physically imposing colt, Razeen had not run as a juvenile because of a wind problem, but had made up for lost time by winning all three of his races at three years old, including an easy victory in Goodwood's Predominate Stakes on his latest start. Sired by Northern Dancer, Razeen was a brother to the 1989 Derby failure Warrshan, and Cecil harboured strong doubts that the colt owned enough experience for a race like the Derby. River God, like his stablemate, was owned by Sheikh Mohammed, and entered the race as something of a dark-horse, having won his only race of the season very easily at Doncaster not long before Epsom.

Behind Razeen in the betting came Linamix and Zoman. The grey horse Linamix was an interesting raider from France. The colt had beaten Zoman when winning the Poule d'Essai des Poulains (the French 2,000 Guineas) in course-record time earlier in the season, although no horse had won that race and gone on to win the Derby since Relko in 1963. Linamix was trained by François Boutin and ridden by twenty-three-year-old Gerald Mosse, who was having his first Derby ride. Talented a horse as Linamix was, he was bred to be a miler and there was a strong feeling he would lack the necessary stamina for the Derby. Perhaps the 'buzz' horse in the 1990 Derby field was Zoman, trained at Whatcombe by a super-confident Paul Cole. Zoman's only run of the season had come behind Linamix at Longchamp, and therefore experience was a major worry for Cole's challenger. However, the Whatcombe gallops had produced Derby winners in Blakeney and Morston with similar experience, and the normally reserved Cole seemed extremely bullish over Zoman's chance of winning. Ridden by Richard Quinn, Zoman was a son of the American Triple Crown winner Affirmed.

With uncertainty surrounding a number of the fancied horses, two colts with definite stamina on their sides were Blue Stag and Quest For Fame. After trainer Barry Hills had seen three of his charges finish runner-up in the race, there were few that would have begrudged him a first Derby success. In Blue Stag, Hills had a tough little horse in the Kahyasi mould, and the bay son of Sadler's Wells had performed with credit to win the Dee Stakes at Chester earlier in the season. A runner-up at Chester, this time in the Vase, was Pat Eddery's mount Quest For Fame. Trained by first-year trainer Roger Charlton at Beckhampton in Wiltshire, Quest For Fame had won a Newbury maiden earlier in the season, and was by a sire in Rainbow Quest that had won an Arc, while Quest For Fame's dam, Aryenne, had won the 1,000 Guineas of 1980. The horse's stable had won the French Derby at Chantilly three days before Epsom with Sanglamore, and Quest For Fame was a horse rated higher by Eddery.

The pacemaker for Walter Swinburn's mount Digression – Aromatic – fluffed his lines as he missed the break when the field shot away, and it was Treble Eight – fighting for his head – that steamed into an early lead from River God, Elmaamul, Duke Of Paducah and Quest For Fame.

Quest For Fame and jockey Pat Eddery are led in having won the 1990 Derby.

Roger Charlton, trainer of Quest For Fame.

It was not long before it became obvious that the French challenger Linamix was struggling to act on the course, while Cash Asmussen was well towards the rear on Blue Stag as the runners swooped down the hill, where Zoman and Razeen made progress to get within touching distance of the leaders.

At Tattenham Corner, Treble Eight still held the lead, with Quest For Fame, Zoman, Elmaamul and Razeen all well positioned, while Blue Stag encountered traffic problems, making it difficult for Asmussen to mount a challenge on the little stayer.

Once in the straight, the action began to hot up considerably. First, the long-time leader Treble Eight was swallowed up by Zoman and Elmaamul, while Razeen suddenly went out like a light and began to drop away timidly. However, it was Eddery on Quest For Fame that had been travelling the smoothest from a long way out and just when Cole's faith in Zoman seemed ready to be justified, Quest For Fame rocketed past him and was away.

Though Blue Stag finally emerged from his uncomfortable passage to chase the leader, Eddery drove Quest For Fame all the way home and, in the end, he fully deserved his three-length victory. Blue Stag became Hills' fourth Derby runner-up, while Elmaamul came third after a solid performance. The fancied horses disappointed on this occasion. Zoman had looked a serious proposition early in the straight, but once passed, he could find no more and finished seventh. Linamix had not enjoyed his run, ending up ninth, with the favourite Razeen failing miserably in fourteenth, two places ahead of his stablemate River God.

Quest For Fame's victory gave the Charlton stable a second Derby victory in four days, and it was Eddery who had advised Charlton to send Sanglamore to Chantilly and keep Quest For Fame for Epsom. Eddery then turned down a chance to ride Digression and opted for the eventual winner. Having previously won the Derby on Grundy and Golden Fleece, Eddery stated that

Quest For Fame's win was the easiest of the three. Charlton became the first trainer to win the English and French Derbys in the same year since Charles Semblat in 1950 with Scratch II and Galcador. The forty-year-old Charlton had spent twelve years as an assistant to Jeremy Tree before taking over from his ill mentor at the start of the season.

Quest For Fame was owned by Khalid Abdullah and the win made up for the misery the owner had endured with Dancing Brave's defeat to Shahrastani in 1986. The winner was bred at the owner's Juddmonte Farm.

Quest For Fame had not beaten the strongest-ever Derby field assembled, but he had performed and won with a minimum of fuss. He was then injured when finishing fifth in the Irish Derby, and soon after, he was sent to America where he twice finished runner-up in the Breeder's Cup Turf. The Derby hero of 1990 was then retired to stud in the same country.

**1990 EVER READY DERBY RESULT**

| FATE / HORSE | WEIGHT | JOCKEY | ODDS |
| --- | --- | --- | --- |
| **1st – Quest For Fame** | 9-0 | Pat Eddery | 7/1 |
| **2nd – Blue Stag** | 9-0 | C. Asmussen | 8/1 |
| **3rd – Elmaamul** | 9-0 | W. Carson | 10/1 |
| 4th – Kaheel | 9-0 | M. Roberts | 33/1 |
| 5th – Karinga Bay | 9-0 | B. Rouse | 14/1 |
| 6th – Duke Of Paducah | 9-0 | R. Cochrane | 14/1 |
| 7th – Zoman | 9-0 | T. Quinn | 6/1 |
| 8th – Treble Eight | 9-0 | B. Raymond | 66/1 |
| 9th – Linamix | 9-0 | G. Mosse | 11/2 |
| 10th – Missionary Ridge | 9-0 | M. Hills | 50/1 |
| 11th – Digression | 9-0 | W.R. Swinburn | 14/1 |
| 12th – Sober Mind | 9-0 | A. Munro | 150/1 |
| 13th – Bookcase | 9-0 | J. Williams | 150/1 |
| 14th – Razeen | 9-0 | S. Cauthen | 9/2* |
| 15th – Bastille Day | 9-0 | S. Craine | 100/1 |
| 16th – River God | 9-0 | M.J. Kinane | 28/1 |
| 17th – Aromatic | 9-0 | A. Clark | 100/1 |
| Last – Mr Brooks | 9-0 | P. Shanahan | 66/1 |

6 June 1990
Going – Good
Winner – £355,000
Time – 2 mins 37.26 secs
Favourite – Razeen
18 Ran

Quest For Fame    Bay colt by Rainbow Quest – Aryenne
Blue Stag    Bay colt by Sadler's Wells – Snow Day
Elmaamul    Chestnut colt by Diesis – Modena

Winner bred by Juddmonte Farms
Winner trained by R. Charlton at Beckhampton, Wiltshire

Clive Brittain, trainer of the 2,000 Guineas winner Mystiko.

# GENEROUS

One of the really interesting aspects of the 1991 Derby was that the eleven-time Champion Jockey, Lester Piggott, was back for a thirty-third Derby ride at the age of fifty-five. Piggott had been absent from the Derby scene since partnering Theatrical in 1985, and in the interim, had spent time in prison. Now he was back, and his mount in 1991 was the Henry Cecil-trained outsider Hokusai, owned by the jockey's good friend Charles St George. Piggott, despite his long absence, was still regarded as the font of all Derby knowledge by his contemporaries, and similarly to when Ray Cochrane had asked for advice as to how to best ride the race before he won on Kahyasi in 1988, this time it was twenty-four-year-old Alan Munro – the rider of the fancied Generous – that spent some time at Piggott's Newmarket home days before the race, watching videos of the great champion's nine Derby wins.

Joint favourites for a second consecutive open-looking Derby were Corrupt and Toulon. Corrupt, a colt that possessed both speed and stamina, was the first Derby runner of trainer Neville Callaghan's twenty-year career. Corrupt had shown his ability to travel strongly and efficiently down a hill when destroying his opposition to win the Lingfield Derby Trial in May, a race that recent Derby victors Teenoso, Slip Anchor and Kahyasi had taken before triumphing at Epsom. Corrupt's jockey was Cash Asmussen, who was fresh from winning the French Derby on the exciting but disappointingly Epsom-absent Suave Dancer. The previous year's winning owner, Khalid Abdullah, was represented on this occasion by Toulon, a horse that had won over the Derby distance earlier in the season when winning the Chester Vase, showing

fine acceleration in the process. Toulon was trained in France by Andre Fabre, and both horses started at 4/1 in the betting. Encouraging for the two market leaders was the fact that six of the previous ten Derby favourites – Nashwan, Reference Point, Slip Anchor, Teenoso, Golden Fleece and Shergar – had won, while two others, Dancing Brave and El Gran Senor, were second, while another in Red Glow had run well to be fourth. Only Razeen the year before had flopped badly.

Trained by Clive Brittain, Mystiko was the winner of the 2,000 Guineas. A free-running sort of horse that had stamina doubts, Mystiko had survived a late scare when having a corn removed a week before the Derby. Brittain, who used to work for the late Sir Noel Murless, was enjoying a super season and was extremely bullish over the chances of the grey Mystiko – a son of the 1984 Derby winner Secreto.

As well as Toulon, France had a serious challenger in the high-class Hector Protector. The horse, despite some niggling stamina reservations, was unbeaten in eight career races, and had won four Group One races, including the French 2,000 Guineas. Hector Protector was trained by Francois Boutin and ridden by the much-maligned Freddie Head, whose Epsom record was dismal, with a sixth aboard the favourite Green Dancer in 1975 his best effort.

Trained by Paul Cole, the flaxen-maned chestnut Generous had been a fine two-year-old. As a juvenile, he had won three times, including the Dewhurst Stakes, a race won by – among others – Derby winners Mill Reef, Grundy and The Minstrel. A powerful galloper, Generous was making his seasonal debut when finishing fourth to Mystiko in the 2,000 Guineas, a result which prompted owner Fahd Salman to replace Cole's stable jockey Richard Quinn with Munro, who would be having his second Derby ride.

Hector Protector was a high-class raider from France.

The chestnut Generous was a splendid winner of the 1991 Derby.

The field also contained some more-than-useful outsiders in Environment Friend, Star Of Gdansk and Hailsham. Trained by James Fanshawe and ridden by George Duffield, the grey-coloured Environment Friend showed his wealth of stamina when romping home in the Dante Stakes at York, while Ireland was represented by Star Of Gdansk, the Irish 2,000 Guineas runner-up trained by Jim Bolger. Despite being beaten by Environment Friend at York, Hailsham had performed well during the season. Sporting the red and white colours of Sheikh Mohammed, the colt had taken the Sandown Classic Trial and the Italian Derby.

The afternoon did not start particularly well for the Guineas winner Mystiko as the horse got very worked up in the parade, and the eleven-time South African Champion Jockey Michael Roberts was forced to lead him down to the start. One horse that was taking the preliminaries far better was Generous, a colt with a history of boiling over in hot weather. However, Derby day in 1991 was cold and blustery, aiding Generous' cause tremendously.

Right from the start, the pace was electric as the outsider Arokat and the grey Mystiko blazed a trail. The tactics employed principally by Roberts on the grey ensured that the race would be truly run, and if Mystiko was to win, he would positively have to stay – or else play in to the hands of those that did.

Coming down the hill, the two in front continued their blistering gallop, with Piggott nicely tucked in behind aboard Hokusai with Generous for company. One horse that appeared uncomfortable though was Toulon, as the colt frequently changed his legs. Hector Protector was another that would be going into unchartered territory distance-wise, and the first signs that the classy horse may struggle came when Head was forced to niggle at him as the field made their descent.

It was Mystiko that boasted the lead round Tattenham Corner and heading into the straight, but in behind him, Munro was poised beautifully on the chestnut Generous.

Like lightning, Munro changed the pattern of the race as he charged Generous forward, picking off Mystiko with delightful ease and quickly flew into a five-length lead. The move appeared to stun the rest of the field. The long-time leader had no answer and he dropped away with no fuel left in his tank, while the remainder were soon searching for oxygen.

With a furlong to run, Generous' lead was insurmountable, and though Marju, with Willie Carson on board, emerged to give chase, the power and aggression of Generous' run had proved too much and had been clinical. Motoring home, Generous showed the rest no mercy and as he crossed the line five lengths clear of Marju, Munro punched his fist in to the air to celebrate his magnificent triumph. The Irish runner Star Of Gdansk and the game but stamina-lacking Hector Protector were a long way back in third and

Paul Cole saddled Generous to win in 1991.

fourth, while Corrupt and Toulon had never once threatened. Mystiko was made to pay for his dynamic gallop and wilted into tenth.

Cole, who was having his best season in terms of prize-money, and Yorkshireman Munro had always believed in Generous and knew he had the ideal traits of a Derby winner, of which his performance at Epsom made him a fine one. Even in his finest hour, Munro admitted to feeling sorry for the displaced Quinn, who ended up listening to the race on his way to an evening meeting at Beverley.

The fast gallop had suited Generous perfectly and he had simply roared home. The rest of the colt's season was spent battling the fine French Derby winner Suave Dancer. Generous confirmed himself a high-class Derby winner by beating his rival in winning both the Irish Derby and the King George, before Suave Dancer gained some revenge by toasting the Epsom hero in the Prix de l'Arc de Triomphe. Generous was retired to stud in 1992 with a value of £18 million and his first crop as a stallion produced forty-six foals.

**1991 EVER READY DERBY RESULT**

| FATE / HORSE | WEIGHT | JOCKEY | ODDS |
| --- | --- | --- | --- |
| **1st – Generous** | 9-0 | A. Munro | 9/1 |
| **2nd – Marju** | 9-0 | W. Carson | 14/1 |
| **3rd – Star Of Gdansk** | 9-0 | C. Roche | 14/1 |
| 4th – Hector Protector | 9-0 | F. Head | 6/1 |
| 5th – Hundra | 9-0 | B. Raymond | 66/1 |
| 6th – Corrupt | 9-0 | C. Asmussen | 4/1* |
| 7th – Hokusai | 9-0 | L. Piggott | 25/1 |
| 8th – Hailsham | 9-0 | S. Cauthen | 28/1 |
| 9th – Toulon | 9-0 | Pat Eddery | 4/1* |
| 10th – Mystiko | 9-0 | M. Roberts | 5/1 |
| 11th – Environment Friend | 9-0 | G. Duffield | 11/1 |
| 12th – Arokat | 9-0 | Paul Eddery | 250/1 |
| Last – Mujaazif | 9-0 | W.R. Swinburn | 33/1 |

5 June 1991
Going – Good to Firm
Winner – £355,000
Time – 2 mins 34 secs
Joint Favourites – Corrupt & Toulon
13 Ran

| | |
| --- | --- |
| Generous | Chestnut colt by Caerleon – Doff The Derby |
| Marju | Brown colt by Last Tycoon – Flame Of Tara |
| Star Of Gdansk | Chestnut colt by Danzig Connection – Star Empress |

Winner bred by Barronstown Stud
Winner trained by P.F.I. Cole at Whatcombe, Oxon

Peter Chapple-Hyam saw his 'second-string' Dr Devious land the 1992 Derby.

# DR DEVIOUS

Before the 1992 Derby, some critics were labelling the race a weak renewal. Whether this was close to the mark or not, the competitive nature at the top of the Derby betting market was as strong as it had been for many a year. So much so, that on Derby morning, bookmakers William Hill had six horses – Alnasr Alwasheek, Assessor, Dr Devious, Muhtarram, Rodrigo de Triano and Rainbow Corner – grouped together as co-favourites, with a seventh, Great Palm, among the favourites with various other bookies.

The man that appeared to possess the strongest hand was the second-year trainer from Manton in Wiltshire, Peter Chapple-Hyam, as he trained two of the most fancied horses in the field – the English and Irish 2,000 Guineas winner Rodrigo de Triano and the tough, combative chestnut Dr Devious. The lightning-bolt Rodrigo de Triano was a son of the 1984 Derby runner-up El Gran Senor, and like his father, the biggest question surrounding Rodrigo de Triano was whether he would stay the full Derby distance. Rodrigo de Triano had been, undisputedly, the top juvenile of the year before, yet had disappointed on his three-year-old debut. However, once Lester Piggott was appointed to partner the colt, the horse then showed his brilliance to win his two Guineas races and consequently started the Derby as the 13/2 favourite, although the cast of challengers for that honour was fierce. Piggott had mentioned before the race that he planned to ride Rodrigo de Triano like he had Sir Ivor in the 1968 race, where that horse had been patiently ridden before pouncing late to beat Connaught. In total contrast to the fleet-footed Rodrigo de Triano, Chapple-Hyam's 'second-string' Dr Devious liked to pound out a relentless gallop from a long way

out, and was a horse with grit and stamina, while the colt was trying to emulate Generous the year before, as Dr Devious too had won the important Dewhurst Stakes as a juvenile. Dr Devious was owned by American Sidney Craig and the horse was originally going to stay in the States. However, Dr Devious was not at his best on the dirt tracks in America and had only finished seventh in the recent Kentucky Derby, so he was sent back to Chapple-Hyam's stables. The journey Dr Devious endured, however, was not without discomfort and wound up lasting a bewildering five days. This arduous trip, coupled with a grazed throat picked up while running on the dirt tracks, had taken a lot out of the horse, and it remained to be seen if his toughness would stretch to the heat of the Derby battle. Having been partnered by American Chris McCarron in Kentucky, John Reid came in for the ride at Epsom.

Four horses began the race grouped together at 9/1 – Assessor, Muhtarram, Alnasr Alwasheek and Rainbow Corner. The Lingfield Derby Trial winner Assessor, trained by Richard Hannon, was a soft-ground lover and had come in for much support as heavy rain hit the course in the days leading up to the race. Although Epsom saw some sun soon afterwards, the jockeys confirmed that the ground on the day was on the slow side, giving Assessor an excellent chance of becoming Walter Swinburn's third Derby winner. Muhtarram, who had finished fifth in the 2,000 Guineas behind fellow Derby runners Rodrigo de Triano and Silver Wisp, carried the same Nashwan colours of Hamdan Al Maktoum. Muhtarram was bred to stay, being by the dual Arc winner Alleged, but had not experienced the ideal preparation, with injury preventing him from running in York's Dante Stakes. The horse that had won the York race was the Michael Stoute-trained Alnasr Alwasheek – a horse that seemed sure to stay. He had previously won Newmarket's Craven Stakes and finished with momentous power in the Dante. Partnered by Steve Cauthen, a win for Alnasr

Dr Devious storms home to win from St Jovite and Silver Wisp (white face).

Alwasheek would have provided jockey and trainer with their third Derby wins respectively. Rounding out the quartet was Rainbow Corner, a horse by the same sire, Rainbow Quest, that had got the hero of 1990, Quest For Fame. Trained by Andre Fabre, Rainbow Corner was trying to become the first winner from France since Empery in 1976, and his most recent outing had seen him finish a narrow second in the French 2,000 Guineas.

The dark-horse in the eighteen-strong field was the Paul Cole-trained Great Palm. Trying to become the first grey horse to win the Derby since Airborne in 1946, Great Palm was a mountainous individual, though he lacked vital experience. He had only run in three lifetime races, and in the current campaign, had suffered injury problems before finishing runner-up in the Dante Stakes. He was definitely a horse with a large amount of talent, although Cole was by no means as confident with Great Palm as he had been with Generous the year before.

The early pace was only average, and it was the Henry Cecil-trained Twist And Turn that led from Great Palm, St Jovite and Pollen Count. The lattermost, trained by John Gosden, was ridden by Italian-born Frankie Dettori, having his first Derby ride. Dettori was the son of former jockey Gianfranco Dettori, and the twenty-one-year-old would develop into one of the most charismatic personalities in the racing game.

The favourite, Rodrigo de Triano, was settled quietly at the rear of the pack by Piggott, together with Assessor, although the latter seemed in trouble early on and was not making life easy for Swinburn.

Twist And Turn, ridden by Mick Kinane, was thoroughly enjoying the Derby experience, and going round Tattenham Corner, he bounded on from the giant grey Great Palm, the always well-positioned Dr Devious and the aggressively ridden St Jovite.

As they headed in to the straight, Twist And Turn was hanging on gamely, but Great Palm's stamina was soon to give out, and he began to hit a retreat. St Jovite was starting to respond to Christy Roche's urgings and Muhtarram too was putting in a challenge from some way back, but it was Dr Devious that really had his motor churning and as he steadily cut back Twist And Turn's advantage, he found himself in front with one-and-a-half furlongs to run.

Now Dr Devious could be seen at his best, and with stablemate Rodrigo de Triano well out of contention, Reid sent the chestnut into overdrive. St Jovite was trying hard and Silver Wisp under Paul Eddery was finishing fast, but Dr Devious was grinding on gamely, and with 200 yards to go, he put the matter beyond doubt with a strong finishing kick. Crossing the line as powerfully as at any point in the race, Dr Devious won the Derby from St Jovite and Silver Wisp, with Muhtarram fourth and the long time leader Twist And Turn fifth. Rodrigo de Triano had never looked like being a serious factor, and eventually coasted home in ninth, blatantly not staying.

The combination of Peter Chapple-Hyam and John Reid had each captured the Derby for the first time. The trainer had only recorded his first ever winner in April of 1991, yet now, in only his second season, he had collected three Classics. Reid had once ridden for the Vincent O'Brien stable, but was now a freelance rider in Britain having spent some time in Hong Kong when he was failing to find rides on quality horses back home. Reid's previous big race successes had come aboard Ile de Bourbon in the King George and Tony Bin in the Arc.

Dr Devious had been owned by three different people in the previous ten months. Robert Sangster had owned him originally before selling the horse to Italian Luciano Gaucci in the summer of 1991. Gaucci had then sold the colt to the wife of Sidney Craig, who gave the horse as a sixtieth birthday present to her husband. Sangster owned Dr Devious' stablemate Rodrigo de Triano, and still owned the winner's dam, Rose Of Jericho.

The form of the 1992 Derby, where fancied horses like Rodrigo de Triano, Rainbow Corner and Great Palm did not stay, was given a major boost when the runner-up St Jovite progressed to win the Irish Derby and the King George. As for the ultra-tough winner Dr Devious, he was sold to Japanese interests soon after the race for a fee of around £6 million.

## 1992 EVER READY DERBY RESULT

| FATE / HORSE | WEIGHT | JOCKEY | ODDS |
|---|---|---|---|
| **1st – Dr Devious** | 9-0 | J. Reid | 8/1 |
| **2nd – St Jovite** | 9-0 | C. Roche | 14/1 |
| **3rd – Silver Wisp** | 9-0 | Paul Eddery | 11/1 |
| 4th – Muhtarram | 9-0 | W. Carson | 9/1 |
| 5th – Twist And Turn | 9-0 | M.J. Kinane | 12/1 |
| 6th – Alflora | 9-0 | T. Quinn | 200/1 |
| 7th – Alnasr Alwasheek | 9-0 | S. Cauthen | 9/1 |
| 8th – Great Palm | 9-0 | A. Munro | 10/1 |
| 9th – Rodrigo de Triano | 9-0 | L. Piggott | 13/2* |
| 10th – Thourios | 9-0 | M. Roberts | 50/1 |
| 11th – Rainbow Corner | 9-0 | Pat Eddery | 9/1 |
| 12th – Well Saddled | 9-0 | J. Williams | 150/1 |
| 13th – Assessor | 9-0 | W.R. Swinburn | 9/1 |
| 14th – Paradise Navy | 9-0 | G. Duffield | 250/1 |
| 15th – Lobilio | 9-0 | R. Hills | 250/1 |
| 16th – Pollen Count | 9-0 | L. Dettori | 14/1 |
| 17th – Ninja Dancer | 9-0 | M. Hills | 100/1 |
| Last – Young Freeman | 9-0 | B. Raymond | 66/1 |

3 June 1992
Going – Good (Last 4 furlongs, Good to Soft)
Winner – £355,000
Time – 2 mins 36.19 secs
Favourite – Rodrigo de Triano
18 Ran

| | |
|---|---|
| Dr Devious | Chestnut colt by Ahonoora – Rose Of Jericho |
| St Jovite | Bay colt by Pleasant Colony – Northern Sunset |
| Silver Wisp | Bay colt by Silver Hawk – La Ninouchka |

Winner bred by Lyonstown Stud
Winner trained by P.W. Chapple-Hyam at Manton, Wiltshire

Darryl Holland enjoyed a fine first Derby ride aboard the outsider Blues Traveller.

# COMMANDER IN CHIEF

Trainer Peter Chapple-Hyam had possessed the top two in the betting market for the 1992 Derby, but it was his second-string in Dr Devious that won the race, not the favourite, Rodrigo de Triano. For the 1993 renewal, it was Newmarket-based trainer Henry Cecil that held the hot hand. Cecil was one of the top – if not the top – trainer to emerge from the twentieth century; a supremely gifted handler with a masterful habit of preparing his horses for precisely the right moment. At the time of the 1993 Derby, Cecil had been Champion Trainer nine times, although his last Classic success had come back in 1989 with Michelozzo in the St Leger. Cecil had once been married to the daughter of the late Sir Noel Murless, Julie, and his stepfather was Captain Cecil Boyd-Rochfort, who had trained Parthia to win the 1959 Derby. Cecil had already trained the Derby winner twice – Slip Anchor in 1985 and Reference Point two years later – and the odds of him adding to those victories in 1993 were extremely good, courtesy of a pair of Khalid Abdullah-owned horses, Tenby and Commander In Chief.

Tenby, named after a seaside resort in Wales, was the odds-on favourite for the race having slaughtered his rivals in magnificent style to win the Dante Stakes at York. Tenby was unbeaten in five lifetime races, having won all three as a two-year-old, including the Grand Criterium. It was difficult to oppose Tenby, who was a very small colt at just 15.1 hands high, but he was tough and well balanced and was a relentless galloper with grit and an injection of speed. Also on his side was an outstanding pedigree, with his sire being Caerleon – the same as the 1991 hero Generous – and his grandsire was

Nijinsky, while on his dam's side, there was a line through Mill Reef. There were those that remained convinced that Tenby would be prone to a fast-finishing horse, so the plan was for jockey Pat Eddery to make the race a true and thorough test of stamina. Second in the betting market, and like Tenby unbeaten, Commander In Chief was the baby of the race and was almost overlooked given the lofty status of his stablemate. A dark-coloured horse, Commander In Chief had been a late foal (18 May) and was expected to hit his peak later in the season if following the usual pattern of horses born around his birth date. The horse had not run as a two-year-old and had only graced the racecourse for the first time six weeks before the Derby, winning at Newmarket before beating the subsequent Italian Derby runner-up Needle Gun at York. Commander In Chief, like Tenby, was expected to have the necessary stamina for the Derby, with his sire being the bitterly unlucky 1986 Derby second Dancing Brave, while his dam was Slightly Dangerous, a runner-up to Time Charter (who also won a King George) in the 1982 Oaks. In addition, his maternal grandsire was the 1972 Derby hero Roberto. Taking the ride on Commander In Chief was the gifted Irishman Mick Kinane, whose previous best Derby performance had come aboard Carlingford Castle, runner-up to Teenoso in 1983.

In contrast to the perceived staying horses like Tenby, Commander In Chief and the respected Mark Tompkins-trained winner of the Lingfield Derby Trial, Bob's Return, a pair of colts relying on a speed finish to counter their suspect stamina were Barathea and Fatherland. The speedy Barathea had been runner-up in the 2,000 Guineas at Newmarket before winning the Irish 2,000. Barathea, trained by Luca Cumani, was trying a distance of more than a mile for the first time and was not really expected to stay, though his sire, Sadler's Wells, had produced winners of the Irish and French Derbys as well as the Epsom Oaks, also siring Blue Stag who finished runner-up to Quest For Fame in the 1990 Derby. Also by Sadler's Wells was the hardy Fatherland, representing the illustrious combination of trainer Vincent O'Brien and jockey Lester Piggott. Fatherland had finished fast to be denied by only Barathea in the Irish 2,000 Guineas and a victory for him would give Ireland its eleventh Derby winner. Fatherland's connections assured him of a lofty place in the betting market, making him the chief challenger from the Emerald Isle. For Piggott, his ride on Fatherland was his thirty-fifth in the Derby.

As the sixteen-strong field – including the first American challenger since Slewpy in 1983 in the shape of Wolf Prince, handled by former Yorkshire-based jumps trainer Michael Dickinson – broke away, it was clear the 1993 Derby was going to be a brutal battle.

Tenby, who often liked to race from the front, was being taken on for the lead by the headstrong Bob's Return, with Planetary Aspect also well to the fore. Perhaps understanding the greenness of his mount, Kinane wisely avoided placing Commander In Chief in the heart of the scrimmage for supremacy, instead settling the colt towards the rear.

The first signs that Tenby may be in trouble emerged at halfway. The horse appeared to be struggling to maintain his position, as those around him constantly snapped at his heels, and as they came to Tattenham Corner, Bob's Return and the outsider Blues Traveller were sweeping the favourite off his feet, while Commander In Chief was creeping steadily closer from midfield as the cauldron began to simmer to boiling point.

At odds of 150/1 and ridden by Darryl Holland, Blues Traveller was the first to go for home in the straight having discarded Bob's Return, while Barathea too – in the red and white colours of Sheikh Mohammed – began to make a charge. However, having been patiently and carefully ridden by Kinane in the early stages, it was Commander In Chief that emerged as the major player, screaming down the inside to take control at the two-furlong marker.

Running in his first Group One race, Commander In Chief belied his inexperience, and the youngest horse in the contrast stormed home to thump his rivals by a convincing three-and-a-half lengths. Blues Traveller had run a fine race but was just pipped for second by another 150/1 shot in Blue Judge, with Cairo Prince coming from a different galaxy to take fourth ahead of the game but non-staying Barathea. Blue Judge was trained in Ireland by Jim Bolger, who had sent out St Jovite and Star Of Gdansk to be placed in the previous two Derbys. Fatherland had never been in the hunt and finished ninth, but the huge disappointment was Tenby, who left connections absolutely perplexed by his failure. Eddery reported that Tenby finished distressed, yet shortly after the race, the horse appeared fine, and a routine dope test showed nothing. Whether Tenby was good enough to win a Derby was not altogether clear, but the horse had suffered from a bout of colic two weeks before the race and it was possible he may not have recovered sufficiently.

Whatever the reason for Tenby's display, Commander In Chief had proved himself a rapidly improving horse, shining wonderfully at Epsom and winning the race in a truly emphatic manner. His previous race, in the Glasgow Stakes at York, had proved something of a battle, and many believed that it had hardened the horse up for the Derby.

Kinane, eight times Champion Jockey in Ireland, had ridden a special race aboard the winner to claim his first Derby success. Kinane's father and brothers had been jump jockeys, and his father had won the 1978 Champion Hurdle on Monksfield. Earlier in the year, Kinane had turned down an offer to replace the departed American Steve Cauthen as number one jockey to Sheikh Mohammed.

The baby of the 1993 field, Commander In Chief ran out a most convincing Derby winner.

Commander In Chief was the second Derby winner for Khalid Abdullah following Quest For Fame's victory in 1990. The owner boasted a truly envious collection of three-year-olds in 1993. As well as Commander In Chief and Tenby, he also owned the brilliant 2,000 Guineas winner Zafonic and the classy Armiger, a horse hotly fancied for the Derby before being withdrawn from Epsom because of unsuitable ground.

Khalid Abdullah was one of many that believed that Commander In Chief would play second fiddle to Tenby. Indeed, Commander In Chief became the first Derby winner not to have raced as a two-year-old since Morston twenty years previously. He went on to win the Irish Derby after Epsom before, like the 1992 Dr Devious, being sold to Japan for £4 million to stand at stud.

**1993 EVER READY DERBY RESULT**

| FATE / HORSE | WEIGHT | JOCKEY | ODDS |
| --- | --- | --- | --- |
| **1st – Commander In Chief** | 9-0 | M.J. Kinane | 15/2 |
| **2nd – Blue Judge** | 9-0 | B. Raymond | 150/1 |
| **3rd – Blues Traveller** | 9-0 | D. Holland | 150/1 |
| 4th – Cairo Prince | 9-0 | W. Carson | 50/1 |
| 5th – Barathea | 9-0 | M. Roberts | 11/1 |
| 6th – Bob's Return | 9-0 | P. Robinson | 15/1 |
| 7th – Redenham | 9-0 | T. Quinn | 150/1 |
| 8th – Wolf Prince | 9-0 | L. Dettori | 40/1 |
| 9th – Fatherland | 9-0 | L. Piggott | 8/1 |
| 10th – Tenby | 9-0 | Pat Eddery | 4/5* |
| 11th – Desert Team | 9-0 | C. Roche | 25/1 |
| 12th – Planetary Aspect | 9-0 | J. Reid | 16/1 |
| 13th – Geisway | 9-0 | C. Asmussen | 25/1 |
| 14th – Canaska Star | 9-0 | A. Munro | 200/1 |
| 15th – Shareek | 9-0 | W.R. Swinburn | 40/1 |
| Last – Zind | 9-0 | R. Cochrane | 150/1 |

2 June 1993
Going – Good
Winner – £447,580
Time – 2 mins 34.51 secs
Favourite – Tenby
16 Ran

Commander In Chief   Bay or brown colt by Dancing Brave – Slightly Dangerous
Blue Judge           Bay colt by Rainbow Quest – Water Splash
Blues Traveller      Bay colt by Bluebird – Natuschka

Winner bred by Juddmonte Farms
Winner trained by H. Cecil at Newmarket

1994

Sheikh Mohammed, agonisingly close to owning the Derby winner with King's Theatre.

# ERHAAB

The field of twenty-five that lined up for the 1994 Derby was the biggest since the same number started in 1978 and 1973, while the number of starters had only been bettered in relatively recent times by the twenty-six that contested Blakeney's Derby of 1969. Eight of the field were listed at 100/1 or greater, and even before what would turn in to the roughest Derby since Larkspur won in 1962, there were serious concerns over the high number of perceived 'no hopers'.

Strikingly similar in size and ability to the previous year's favourite Tenby, the little brown colt Erhaab was the clear market leader having won what was generally considered the strongest Derby Trial to take place during the season. By beating fellow Derby contenders Weigh Anchor, Mister Baileys and King's Theatre in record time in York's Dante Stakes, the John Dunlop-trained Erhaab shot to the head of the betting market, having been beaten on his seasonal debut at Newmarket. Despite his somewhat diminutive stature, Erhaab was a little rock of a horse, tough-pulling and fully expected to have the necessary Derby stamina, although the Epsom race would be his first over the distance of a mile-and-a-half. Erhaab was also a late foal, but as Commander In Chief had proved the year before, that was not necessarily a detriment to winning the Derby, and Erhaab actually had more race experience than many in the 1994 field. Erhaab was partnered by the fiery Scot Willie Carson, while Dunlop also fielded Khamaseen, ridden by Lester Piggott in his thirty-sixth and final Derby.

The strength of Erhaab's victory at York was made clear by the fact that the horses he beat in the Dante also figured prominently in the Derby market.

Second at York, the Ian Balding-trained Weigh Anchor was trying to keep an incredible family run alive. Weigh Anchor's sire, Slip Anchor, grandsire Shirley Heights and great-grandsire Mill Reef had all won the Derby, though Weigh Anchor was a horse that certainly would have preferred softer going than was present at Epsom in 1994. A surprise winner of the 2,000 Guineas, the Mark Johnston-trained Mister Baileys was a horse that appeared not to stay at York, but his traits were gameness and toughness, and the Newmarket hero was a fine first ride for young Jason Weaver. Perhaps the 'sleeping giant' of the field was the talented but frustrating King's Theatre, a horse trained by Henry Cecil. Owned by Sheikh Mohammed, King's Theatre – an attractive bay son of the prolific sire Sadler's Wells – had been a multiple winner as a juvenile and had thus been installed as a solid winter favourite for the Derby. When King's Theatre beat fellow Derby contender Colonel Collins in Newmarket's Craven Stakes on his first run at three, a fine season appeared to lie in wait, but the classy horse flopped to finish thirteenth in the Guineas and then came fourth in the Dante. King's Theatre was, however, a Group One winner, and there were those that strongly believed Mick Kinane's mount required the Derby distance for his class to tell.

Having been beaten by King's Theatre in the Craven, the Peter Chapple-Hyam-trained chestnut Colonel Collins had gone on to be third in the Guineas, sparking a big Derby gamble on the consistent colt. Owned by Robert Sangster, Colonel Collins – a strong, good-looking animal – was sired by El Gran Senor, so stamina worries were present, yet Chapple-Hyam was

Erhaab gets up to defeat King's Theatre in 1994.

extremely confident that Colonel Collins could emulate his 1992 hero Dr Devious and win the Derby. One disadvantage for Colonel Collins was that, since starting stalls had been introduced to the Derby, no horse had won from stall one since Roberto in 1972; Colonel Collins was drawn in stall one.

Other leading fancies in a deep, talented Derby field included Linney Head, Broadway Flyer and Sunshack. Unbeaten in three runs, including both as a three-year-old, the John Gosden-trained Linney Head had many supporters on Derby day, having won the Sandown Classic Trial in impressive style, and had demonstrated a toughness that belied his relative inexperience. A lazy horse at home, Broadway Flyer had slammed his opposition to win at Newbury and Chester during the season and consequently had earned second place in the market at 6/1. Broadway Flyer was trained by Barry Hills' son, John, and was ridden by John's brother, Michael, while the horse was part-bred by the legendary South African golfer Gary Player. Trying to improve France's poor recent Derby record was the dark-horse of the race, Sunshack, a colt trained by Andre Fabre and owned by Khalid Abdullah. Sunshack appeared to have all the right credentials for the Derby. His sire, Rainbow Quest, had got the 1990 hero Quest For Fame and his brother, Raintrap, had won the 1993 French St Leger. Sunshack himself was a Group One winner, having taken the Criterium de St Cloud over a mile-and-a-quarter as a juvenile. As a bonus, Sunshack had three-time winning jockey Pat Eddery in the saddle.

With great excitement among the large crowd, the twenty-five runners charged away for what was to prove a real roughhouse Derby, and after some early jostling for places, it was the Guineas winner Mister Baileys that took control at the head of affairs.

The favourite Erhaab did not look entirely comfortable early on. Indeed, at the top of the hill, Erhaab only had the rank outsiders Jabaroot, Colonel Colt and Plato's Republic behind him. His position had his followers and trainer John Dunlop worried, but there had been a reason for him being marooned out the back. In front of the favourite, there had been much jostling as horses bumped and barged for room. Carson had been forced to refrain from letting Erhaab progress in order to avoid the carnage that was taking place. Matters came to a head at the halfway point when Foyer parted company with his jockey Willie Ryan. King's Theatre had been on Foyer's outside, and when Foyer was squeezed for room on the inside rails, he ditched Ryan, whose painful fall left the jockey with three broken ribs. Foyer was out of the race, while several other horses were almost down on their knees, prompting many jockeys after the event to call for a ban on horses that had little to no chance of winning a Derby and were seen as clogging up valuable space.

Meanwhile, Mister Baileys was making a bold effort to win from the front, and as the hungry army of challengers swooped round Tattenham Corner

Erhaab comes back in having given Willie Carson a fourth Derby victory.

– where Carson and Erhaab were pinned against the inside rails – Weaver sent his mount on in a bullish manner from Chickawicka, Khamaseen, Colonel Collins and King's Theatre, and with three furlongs to run, the horse had stolen a six-length chunk out of the field.

The lead Mister Baileys had gained surprised some, but as had been feared before the race, his stamina began to dither in the closing stages. Having progressed steadily, old adversaries Colonel Collins and King's Theatre emerged to swallow up the brave Guineas hero, and halfway up the straight, the race appeared between the two of them as they commenced the battle to the line.

Erhaab though had been guided through a minefield of hazards in masterful style by Carson, and charging like a rocket up the inside, he all of a sudden had the leading duo in his sights. A few hundred yards previously, it seemed impossible that the winner would not be either Colonel Collins or King's Theatre, but Erhaab was flying as the leaders met the rising ground with the winning line in view. King's Theatre had managed to shake off Colonel Collins and looked set to give Mick Kinane a second consecutive Derby win, but he could only watch in disbelief as Erhaab finished the strongest of all, snatching the lead in the last hundred yards before coming back on the bridle just before the line, winning in blazing style by a length-and-a-quarter from King's Theatre, with Colonel Collins a further length-and-a-half away in third. Mister Baileys had run a fine race but lacked the necessary stamina to win, while Piggott steered the unfancied Khamaseen in to a highly respectable fifth position in his Derby swansong. The York form had worked out beautifully, with only Weigh Anchor failing to shine from the Dante runners. Frankie Dettori's mount Linney Head had failed to handle the course while the French hope Sunshack had never been sighted. Broadway Flyer had endured an utterly miserable time, having been knocked around badly in the gunfight, losing his action and rhythm.

Erhaab's triumph was the second Derby success for both trainer John Dunlop and owner Hamdan Al Maktoum, while it was the fourth (and most hard earned) win for Carson. The Scottish jockey had truly deserved this victory, as he was forced to come from a long way back, weaving through traffic before letting Erhaab display his fine finishing speed.

It had been, at times, a brutal Derby, but Erhaab's decisive acceleration at the end had won him the day, forcing him past King's Theatre and Colonel Collins at the death. While King's Theatre won the King George at Ascot later in the season, the Derby was where Erhaab peaked. His next race would be his last and would see him finish third in the Eclipse Stakes at Sandown before the game little dark-brown colt was retired.

## 1994 EVER READY DERBY RESULT

| FATE / HORSE | WEIGHT | JOCKEY | ODDS |
|---|---|---|---|
| 1st – Erhaab | 9-0 | W. Carson | 7/2* |
| 2nd – King's Theatre | 9-0 | M.J. Kinane | 14/1 |
| 3rd – Colonel Collins | 9-0 | J. Reid | 10/1 |
| 4th – Mister Baileys | 9-0 | J. Weaver | 14/1 |
| 5th – Khamaseen | 9-0 | L. Piggott | 33/1 |
| 6th – Pencader | 9-0 | B. Thomson | 66/1 |
| 7th – Golden Ball | 9-0 | K. Darley | 50/1 |
| 8th – Just Happy | 9-0 | W.R. Swinburn | 50/1 |
| 9th – Star Selection | 9-0 | A. Munro | 100/1 |
| 10th – Linney Head | 9-0 | L. Dettori | 8/1 |
| 11th – Ionio | 9-0 | M. Roberts | 50/1 |
| 12th – Chocolat De Meguro | 9-0 | R. Cochrane | 40/1 |
| 13th – Weigh Anchor | 9-0 | C. Asmussen | 10/1 |
| 14th – Wishing | 9-0 | W. Newnes | 100/1 |
| 15th – Party Season | 9-0 | K. Fallon | 50/1 |
| 16th – Jabaroot | 9-0 | B. Raymond | 200/1 |
| 17th – Waiting | 9-0 | T. Quinn | 16/1 |
| 18th – Chikawicka | 9-0 | J. Carroll | 200/1 |
| 19th – Sunshack | 9-0 | Pat Eddery | 12/1 |
| 20th – The Flying Phantom | 9-0 | P. Robinson | 250/1 |
| 21st – Broadway Flyer | 9-0 | M. Hills | 6/1 |
| 22nd – Darkwood Bay | 9-0 | D. Holland | 100/1 |
| 23rd – Colonel Colt | 9-0 | B. Rouse | 500/1 |
| Last – Plato's Republic | 9-0 | D. Biggs | 500/1 |
| Unseated Rider – Foyer | 9-0 | W. Ryan | 20/1 |

1 June 1994
Going – Good
Winner – £473,080
Time – 2 mins 34.16 secs
Favourite – Erhaab
25 Ran

| | |
|---|---|
| Erhaab | Brown colt by Chief's Crown – Histoire |
| King's Theatre | Bay colt by Sadler's Wells – Regal Beauty |
| Colonel Collins | Chestnut colt by El Gran Senor – Kanmary |

Winner bred by Shadwell Farm Inc. & Shadwell Estate Co. Ltd in the USA
Winner trained by J.L. Dunlop at Arundel, Sussex

1995

Saeed Bin Suroor, trainer for the
Godolphin team.

# LAMMTARRA

The 1995 Derby was the first edition of the race to feature horses from the new Godolphin operation. The Maktoum family ran the set-up, with the real driving force being Sheikh Mohammed. The idea of Godolphin was to winter their horses in the fine weather of Dubai before sending them back to Britain and Europe to compete in all the top races. The man responsible for holding the training licence was the articulate Saeed Bin Suroor, and his two charges for the 1995 Derby were the French 2,000 Guineas winner Vettori and the talented but woefully inexperienced chestnut Lammtarra, the dark-horse of the race.

Sheikh Mohammed, the true power behind Godolphin, had never seen his famous red-and-white colours carried to success in the Derby (King's Theatre's second place the year before being his closest yet), but on this occasion, the two horses that were to represent him on an individual basis (independent from Godolphin), seemed sure to give him a golden chance of finally winning the race. The horses he sent forward were the excellent 2,000 Guineas hero Pennekamp and the tough, versatile Tamure, who like Pennekamp was unbeaten. Pennekamp, a beautiful bay horse with a white streak on his face, had not been conquered in six previous starts and had been made favourite for the Derby on the back of a highly impressive win in the 2,000 Guineas. Trained in France by Andre Fabre, Pennekamp had stalked and then accelerated devastatingly past one of the most talked-up horses of all time, Celtic Swing, to win at Newmarket. Celtic Swing had long been the Derby favourite before the Guineas, yet Pennekamp put him firmly and emphatically in his place at Newmarket, so much so that Celtic Swing – who never really

lived up to his sky-high reputation – eventually ran in (and won) the French Derby rather than at Epsom. Pennekamp's credentials were strong – he was a powerful colt with a fine turn of foot, while he also possessed a calm, laid-back temperament. Against the French challenger were the facts that he was unproven over the Derby distance and that the statistics showed that no horse had won the Derby with a French trainer and jockey since Relko in 1963. Derby debutant Thierry Jarnet was in the saddle, but Fabre was extremely confident his horse could deliver the goods. John Gosden, who also trained the durable Presenting – third in the Dante Stakes – was the handler of Tamure. Ridden by Frankie Dettori, Tamure was a tough stayer that finished his races well and came from a sire in Sadler's Wells that had provided recent Derby runner-ups in Blue Stag and King's Theatre, while Tamure's dam, Three Tails, was sired by Blakeney, so the colt's pedigree for the race seemed strong.

The horses expected to give the Sheikh Mohammed duo the most to do were Spectrum and Munwar. As confident as he had been before Dr Devious had triumphed in 1992, trainer Peter Chapple-Hyam's belief in his Irish 2,000 Guineas winner Spectrum was rock-solid. Having won both his races at three, Spectrum matched Pennekamp, Tamure, Lammtarra and the Irish raider Humbel in the fact that he was unbeaten throughout his racing life to date. Sired by Rainbow Quest, Spectrum's bid had gathered increased momentum after putting in a series of brilliant workouts at home to earn him the tag of second favourite at 5/1. Munwar became trainer Peter Walwyn's first Derby

Tamure (red & white colours) and Spectrum were two of the leading fancies for the 1995 Derby.

Bride, the Oaks winner – albeit through disqualification – of 1989, were factors well in his favour. The truth was that the racing and betting public knew little of what to expect from Lammtarra, and as such, he started adrift of the perceived favourites in the market.

As had happened the year before when Erhaab had survived a brutal passage to win, the 1995 edition of the Derby was not to be without its

runner since Naar in 1983, and the horse had been very impressive earlier in the season, winning the highly touted Lingfield Derby Trial on his latest start.

The horse that least was known about was the attractive chestnut Lammtarra. The horse had won the Washington Singer Stakes at Newbury as a juvenile, a race that remained the horse's only ever start before Epsom. Having been seriously ill with a near-fatal lung infection during his winter in Dubai, Lammtarra had not been seen on the racecourse prior to the Derby and his inexperience seemed a huge detriment to his chances. However, the horse had left an intriguing impression after his only race at two and the fact that he was sired by a great Derby winner in Nijinsky and that his dam was Snow

share of carnage. Although the fifteen-strong field was fewer by ten than the year before, it was the electric pace right from the start that was the main feature of the 1995 race.

The rank outsider Daffaq was the early pacesetter, blazing a kamikaze trail from Presenting, Court Of Honour and Maralinga. Lammtarra too was well forward initially, until some bumping and barging forced him right back on the run to Tattenham Corner.

It was the descent to Tattenham Corner where Pennekamp's Derby turned into a nightmare. Moving awkwardly, it became apparent that the classy horse had injured himself and, from there, he was never a factor in the race, being

Lammtarra (green colours) came from nowhere to snatch victory from Tamure (red & white) and Presenting (white).

eased home sympathetically by Jarnet. The horse returned back sore and lame, but the injury would prove to be very serious. It emerged later that Pennekamp had sustained a hairline fracture of a fetlock, and sadly he never raced again.

Meanwhile, it was Fahal, a 50/1 shot ridden by Richard Hills, that had led in to the straight and had command at the three-furlong marker from Court Of Honour. However, Tamure was being coaxed along sweetly by Dettori with the game Presenting there as well. Walter Swinburn had not enjoyed the smoothest of rides aboard Lammtarra and had been some eight lengths behind the leaders, tucked tightly on the inside, entering the straight. However, Swinburn began to stoke the fire in his colt's belly, and despite some scrimmaging with Munwar as he moved to the centre of the track, Lammtarra began to motor in the closing stages.

The finish was developing in to one of the best in recent years. Tamure still seemed likely to win as Dettori pushed him out from Presenting, Fahal and Court Of Honour, but with a style that his father Nijinsky would have been proud of, it was Lammtarra that came from the heavens to thunder home and take the race at the death. Lammtarra had been only sixth with a few hundred yards left to run, and his finish was so explosive and unlikely that it had to be seen again in slow motion to be believed. Flashing beautifully across the line, Lammtarra won by a length from Tamure to give Swinburn his third Derby victory, following those aboard Shergar and Shahrastani. Presenting finished third. As well as the dismay Pennekamp had endured, Spectrum had returned home jarred and lame in thirteenth, having not got into the race, although he was to recover to win the Dubai Champion Stakes later in the season. Sadly, the early leader Daffaq was tragically lost, having fractured a knee during the battle.

Lammtarra (nearest rails) proved himself a fine horse after the Derby by taking the Prix de l'Arc de Triomphe, beating Freedom Cry.

**1995 VODAFONE DERBY RESULT**

| FATE / HORSE | WEIGHT | JOCKEY | ODDS |
|---|---|---|---|
| **1st – Lammtarra** | 9-0 | W.R. Swinburn | 14/1 |
| **2nd – Tamure** | 9-0 | L. Dettori | 9/1 |
| **3rd – Presenting** | 9-0 | C. Asmussen | 12/1 |
| 4th – Fahal | 9-0 | R. Hills | 50/1 |
| 5th – Court Of Honour | 9-0 | B. Thomson | 66/1 |
| 6th – Vettori | 9-0 | R. Cochrane | 20/1 |
| 7th – Riyadian | 9-0 | T. Quinn | 16/1 |
| 8th – Humbel | 9-0 | M.J. Kinane | 25/1 |
| 9th – Munwar | 9-0 | W. Carson | 8/1 |
| 10th – Salmon Ladder | 9-0 | K. Darley | 50/1 |
| 11th – Pennekamp | 9-0 | T. Jarnet | 11/8* |
| 12th – Korambi | 9-0 | M. Roberts | 150/1 |
| 13th – Spectrum | 9-0 | J. Reid | 5/1 |
| 14th – Daffaq | 9-0 | B. Rouse | 500/1 |
| Last – Maralinga | 9-0 | M. Fenton | 200/1 |

10 June 1995
Going – Good to Firm
Winner – £504,500
Time – 2 mins 32.31 secs (New record)
Favourite – Pennekamp
15 Ran

| | |
|---|---|
| Lammtarra | Chestnut colt by Nijinsky – Snow Bride |
| Tamure | Bay colt by Sadler's Wells – Three Tails |
| Presenting | Brown colt by Mtoto – D'Azy |

Winner bred by Gainsborough Farm Inc.
Winner trained by Saeed Bin Suroor at Newmarket

Godolphin had won the Derby at their first attempt and had also won the Oaks the day before courtesy of Moonshell, and the gracious Sheikh Mohammed stated he was equally as pleased for his operation to triumph as he would have been if Tamure had held on to win. However, thoughts after the race soon focused on Lammtarra's late, former trainer Alex Scott. In a tragic episode, Scott had been shot dead the previous September, yet it was he who had proclaimed Lammtarra to be a Classic horse in the making, having won at Newbury as a two-year-old.

Lammtarra had stunned many with his truly devastating finish and became the first horse not to have run at three and won the Derby since Grand Parade in 1919. When the great Derby winners are discussed Lammtarra's name is not frequently mentioned, yet it is worth considering that he smashed the time record in winning – even though he encountered problems during the race (which ultimately led to a steward's enquiry). He also remained unbeaten in his career, as in his next two races, he won the King George and the Arc in battling style under Dettori. He was so inexperienced at the time he won the Derby that many thought it to be a flash in the pan, but his subsequent wins showed character, toughness and his trademark finishing speed. With his racing career brought to a stop after just four lifetime races, Lammtarra took in to his retirement one of the most polished and convincing records of all modern Derby winners.

Trainer Mark Tompkins and his well-fancied Derby runner Even Top.

Alex Greaves became the first ever female to ride in the Derby, partnering Portuguese Lil in 1996.

# SHAAMIT

The win of Lammtarra in the 1995 Derby had been an unusual one. True, the colt developed after Epsom into a horse of awesome powers, but his win in the Blue Riband remained a surprise due to his distinct lack of experience. Lammtarra had only ever raced once before the Derby and never as a three-year-old, prior to stunning the racing world with his explosive success. A similar victory for one of the class of 1996 seemed improbable, but not impossible.

The horse that most closely resembled the mould of Lammtarra was Shaamit, a twice-raced bay son of the excellent middle-distance horse Mtoto. Like Lammtarra, Shaamit had never raced at three, losing his maiden tag as a juvenile in a twenty-three-runner race at Doncaster. He had been scheduled to run in the Dante Stakes at York before an overreach put paid to that plan for Newmarket-based trainer William Haggas. A horse with such inexperience and an interrupted build-up hardly seemed likely to win the Derby and Shaamit may well have been totally unconsidered and a big outsider if it was not for the fact that he was supplemented for the race at a cost of £8,000 on the advice of Haggas' father-in-law, none other than the great Lester Piggott. In physique, Shaamit was a powerful, rangy individual with a mean turn of foot, and as when Ray Cochrane and Alan Munro had sought advice from Piggott prior to their respective Derby wins aboard Kahyasi and Generous, the nine-time Epsom winner passed on his words of wisdom to Shaamit's jockey Michael Hills.

Favourite for the race was the Khalid Abdullah-owned and Henry Cecil-trained Dushyantor, a tough, sure-staying bay colt. Dushyantor had a most impressive pedigree: he was sired by Sadler's Wells and his dam was Slightly Dangerous, making him a half-brother to the 1993 winner Commander In Chief. Whereas Commander In Chief was a tall, athletic sort of horse, Dushyantor was more a power-packed, stocky colt that idled in front but was wonderfully consistent, with enormous stamina and drive. Although he had only been runner-up in the Dante (a curse that had prevented any of that ilk from previously winning the Derby), Dushyantor had been trained to the minute by Cecil, who was looking to follow-up Lady Carla's win in the Oaks the day before where Pat Eddery had been aboard, as he would be on Dushyantor in the Derby.

The winner of that Dante Stakes had been the fleet-footed Glory Of Dancer. The horse was trained by the former top National Hunt jockey Paul Kelleway, a man who had won the Cheltenham Gold Cup and Champion Hurdle in his time. Glory Of Dancer was not a certain stayer, though he had an abundance of speed and had won a Group One race in Italy, from where he had been transferred over the winter. Glory Of Dancer was partnered at Epsom by the talented French debutant Olivier Peslier.

Shaamit beats the favourite Dushyantor in 1996.

Others to attract attention for the 217th Derby were Even Top, Alhaarth and the filly Portuguese Lil. With the bold 2,000 Guineas winner Mark Of Esteem absent because of injury, the Newmarket form was represented by the Mark Tompkins-trained Even Top. The horse had finished second in the Guineas and was well fancied for Epsom, although a minor setback suffered at home the week before the race had diluted his chance somewhat. Alhaarth had been made winter favourite for the race, following a fine juvenile campaign where he had won the Dewhurst Stakes and been crowned Champion European two-year-old. However, his reputation suffered a major hammering when he was beaten at odds-on in the Craven Stakes at three before finishing only fourth in the Guineas. Alhaarth was trained by Dick Hern and ridden by Willie Carson – a pair that had teamed-up for sixteen European Classics – and the race would be the jockey's last in the Derby. With virtually no chance of winning,

Portuguese Lil, trained by David Nicholls, was an interesting runner for the fact that the horse was partnered by Alex Greaves, who became the first ever female rider to compete in the Derby. Despite odds of 500/1, Greaves' presence attracted a lot of attention in the media.

With Epsom having recently unveiled the 'Piggott Gates' in honour of the great jockey's achievements at the course, the twenty-strong field were soon on their way amid the usual cauldron of excitement, with the ground on the firm side of good.

The Derby is never the most straightforward of passages for its contestants, but for the third consecutive year, the race proved to be particularly rough. One of the horses to suffer enormously from traffic problems was the favourite Dushyantor. Pat Eddery's mount was shuffled back at the top of the hill by Even Top and the horse was forced dramatically down on his knees, which

Trainer Willie Haggas shows his joy at Shaamit's Derby success.

Jockey Michael Hills collects his trophy after Shaamit's win.

obviously caused him to lose ground. By the same token, Even Top was struck into, and from there, Mark Tompkins' contender never managed to get back into the race. In contrast, Dushyantor demonstrated his toughness and determination by eventually clawing his way back into contention.

On the descent to Tattenham Corner, the leading pack was headed by Jack Jennings, with the Lingfield Derby Trial winner Mystic Knight, Chief Contender and Glory Of Dancer next in line. Just in behind, Michael Hills was heeding the advice of Piggott and had Shaamit beautifully poised and ready to pounce.

Turning into the straight, it was Glory Of Dancer that was the first to attack, Peslier lunging his mount in to a threatening lead that, for a brief moment, looked as though it may be decisive. But Shaamit had the Dante winner covered, and with one-and-a-half furlongs to run, Haggas' first ever Derby runner took command with a lethal injection of speed. The manner in which Shaamit swept past Glory Of Dancer was most impressive, and it appeared he would go on and win rather easily. However, having suffered through a succession of mid-race misfortunes, Dushyantor was finally in position for a clear and sustained run.

Screaming home at the finish, Dushyantor and Eddery tried desperately to peg back Shaamit, but despite their efforts, Shaamit had just too much pace and, in a thrilling finish, held off Dushyantor by a length-and-a-quarter to give jockey Hills his first Derby success. Sheikh Mohammed's horse Shantou – who would later win the St Leger – was also badly hampered courtesy of some scrimmaging during the race, but ran on stoutly to take third ahead of Glory Of Dancer, who simply had not lasted the distance. Alex Greaves and Portuguese Lil finished last.

The worry before the race for Dushyantor was that he may be susceptible to a horse with a real finishing kick and – race traffic aside – that is exactly how events transpired, ultimately succumbing to Shaamit's superior finishing speed. Second place for Dushyantor meant his sire, Sadler's Wells, had now provided four Derby runner-ups.

Shaamit had become the second consecutive horse to win the Derby having not run at three and great credit went to Haggas for the training performance. Haggas trained forty-two horses at Newmarket, and trained Shaamit for Dubai businessman Khalifa Abdulla Dasmal, an owner with just three horses in training.

Shaamit, whose name meant 'gloating' in Arabic, had impressed many with the style of his win, and it was hoped the horse would reach the heights Lammtarra had scaled the year before. Sadly, it was not to be as he never won again and was officially rated one of the more inferior Derby winners of modern times. In 2001, while standing at a small stud in Northern Ireland, he died, having suffered a haemorrhage in his intestine.

**1996 VODAFONE DERBY RESULT**

| FATE / HORSE | WEIGHT | JOCKEY | ODDS |
| --- | --- | --- | --- |
| **1st – Shaamit** | 9-0 | M. Hills | 12/1 |
| **2nd – Dushyantor** | 9-0 | Pat Eddery | 9/2* |
| **3rd – Shantou** | 9-0 | L. Dettori | 25/1 |
| 4th – Glory Of Dancer | 9-0 | O. Peslier | 6/1 |
| 5th – Alhaarth | 9-0 | W. Carson | 15/2 |
| 6th – Mystic Knight | 9-0 | K. Darley | 14/1 |
| 7th – Jack Jennings | 9-0 | J. Reid | 25/1 |
| 8th – Acharne | 9-0 | W.J. O'Connor | 200/1 |
| 9th – Chief Contender | 9-0 | D. Harrison | 15/1 |
| 10th – Double Leaf | 9-0 | J. Murtagh | 16/1 |
| 11th – Classic Eagle | 9-0 | A. Mackay | 200/1 |
| 12th – Tasdid | 9-0 | W.J. Supple | 200/1 |
| 13th – Even Top | 9-0 | P. Robinson | 11/2 |
| 14th – Spartan Heartbeat | 9-0 | M. Birch | 200/1 |
| 15th – Storm Trooper | 9-0 | M.J. Kinane | 15/2 |
| 16th – Zaforum | 9-0 | Dane O'Neill | 150/1 |
| 17th – St Mawes | 9-0 | T. Quinn | 20/1 |
| 18th – Busy Flight | 9-0 | C. Asmussen | 25/1 |
| 19th – Prince Of My Heart | 9-0 | B. Thomson | 100/1 |
| Last – Portuguese Lil | 8-9 | Alex Greaves | 500/1 |

8 June 1996
Going – Good (Good to Firm in places)
Winner – £523,100
Time – 2 mins 35.05 secs
Favourite – Dushyantor
20 Ran

| Shaamit | Bay colt by Mtoto – Shomoose |
| --- | --- |
| Dushyantor | Bay colt by Sadler's Wells – Slightly Dangerous |
| Shantou | Bay colt by Alleged – Shaima |

Winner bred by Owner (Khalifa Abdulla Dasmal)
Winner trained by W.J. Haggas at Newmarket

Entrepreneur started a hot favourite for the Derby, having previously won the 2,000 Guineas at Newmarket.

# BENNY THE DIP

When El Gran Senor and Dancing Brave lined up for the 1982 and 1986 Derbys respectively, the feeling was that both those horses were genuine superstars. Both were hyped considerably and were seen as virtual 'sure things' to land their Derbys. Both were beaten. However, over the course of their careers, El Gran Senor and Dancing Brave proved they were indeed special horses. The same kind of pre-race feeling was attached to the red-hot favourite for the 1997 Derby and, similarly, the horse was deemed to be unbeatable before the big race.

It was generally expected that the horse in question, Entrepreneur, would become the first son of Sadler's Wells to win the Derby after the perennial Champion Sire had gotten four previous seconds in the race. Entrepreneur was a deeply attractive bay colt that had rocketed to Derby favouritism after winning the 2,000 Guineas in exquisite, speed-rich fashion, beating the top juvenile of the year before, Revoque. Entrepreneur was a horse with a commendable attitude and temperament and his trainer, Michael Stoute, believed the horse had more pure, natural speed than the dynamic 1981 Derby king, Shergar. Entrepreneur was jointly owned by Michael Tabor and John Magnier, and had been purchased for 600,000 guineas. Tabor was a foreign currency dealer and Magnier was the joint-owner and managing director of the famous Coolmore Stud and was also the son-in-law of the legendary Vincent O'Brien. Together, Tabor and Magnier shared 100 horses and, as well as Entrepreneur's success in the Guineas, in the current season, they had seen their Desert King win the Irish equivalent at The Curragh (the same horse would later win the season's Irish Derby) as well as having runner-ups in both the English and Irish 1,000 Guineas races, courtesy of Oh Nellie and Strawberry Roan. Entrepreneur started the Derby as a rock-solid 4/6 favourite, yet like El Gran Senor and Dancing Brave, there was the question of stamina – or lack of it – although Stoute was convinced the colt possessed enough to win. Having partnered Shergar and Shahrastani for Stoute in previous Derby glories, Walter Swinburn was absent this time, as he was taking time off to deal with weight problems. In his place was the winning jockey of 1993, Mick Kinane.

The next horse in the betting was the likeable grey Silver Patriarch, trained by John Dunlop. Silver Patriarch was a tough, consistent sort of horse, similar in mould to the 1996 runner-up Dushyantor, and like that horse, there was a sneaking suspicion that Sliver Patriarch may get 'done' by a faster finisher. The grey, who possessed an outstanding temperament, had won the Lingfield Derby Trial on his latest start and appeared to relish the distance of that race. Silver Patriarch was partnered by Pat Eddery, a jockey looking for his fourth Derby win following those aboard Grundy, Golden Fleece and Quest For Fame.

Trained by John Gosden, who had seen his charges Tamure, Presenting and Shantou pick up places in recent Derbys, the good-looking brown colt Benny The Dip was an intriguing candidate for Epsom. The horse had been a marvellous two-year-old, winning the Royal Lodge Stakes before beginning his three-year-old campaign with defeat in the Sandown Classic Trial. His attributes were deceptive speed and gameness, and these qualities came in to play when he ran superbly to win the Dante Stakes at York, ousting the highly touted (but Epsom absent) Craven Stakes winner Desert Story. Gosden had expressed doubts that his charge would stay the full Derby distance, but knew he was an exceptional talent capable of winning if the tactics were orchestrated to the colt's benefit. One mild problem for Gosden was finding a jockey for Benny The Dip. Frenchman Olivier Peslier had ridden the horse before, but he elected to partner the French raider Cloudings, while Frankie Dettori was claimed for the Godolphin candidate Bold Demand. Ultimately, the job fell to Willie Ryan, formerly attached to the Henry Cecil stable and a jockey that had contested three previous Derbys, the most recent ending in agony when he took a crunching fall from Foyer in the 1994 race.

Other interesting challengers in 1997 were Cloudings, Romanov and Single Empire. Cloudings, a horse that had won on all types of going, was trained in France by Andre Fabre and was the latest to try and end the curse that had haunted Sheikh Mohammed in the Derby. Cloudings had won the Prix Lupin recently but came in for even more positive attention following a fine workout with the outstanding French Derby and subsequent Arc winner, Peintre Celebre, of whom he was a stablemate. Romanov had been unraced at two but had developed into a more-than-useful three-year-old, registering two

Trainer John Gosden tasted Derby glory in 1997.

wins as well as a third in the Irish 2,000 Guineas. Romanov was trained by Peter Chapple-Hyam, and the bay colt was sired by the brilliant Nureyev, responsible for recent big-race winner Peintre Celebre, and just the day before, responsible for the Oaks winner Reams Of Verse. Despite never having run over the Derby trip, Romanov seemed likely to stay and was closely related to the Irish Derby and Epsom Oaks winner of 1994, the excellent Balanchine. Possibly the most intriguing outsider was Romanov's stablemate Single Empire. The horse had recently won the Italian Derby and was a half-brother to the 1995 Derby fifth, Court Of Honour.

With the prize money for the 218th Derby reaching £1 million for the first time, the thirteen-runner field shot away on good ground, and were quickly headed by an outsider in Crystal Hearted. The same horse was to lead for much of the way, with Fahris – a chestnut son of Generous – and Single Empire his closest company.

Benny The Dip too was nicely positioned just in behind the lead, but one that had been caught out by the sharp early pace of the race was Silver Patriarch, and the grey was seen struggling out at the back for much of the contest.

Benny The Dip just had enough to defeat the grey Silver Patriarch in 1997.

Jockey Willie Ryan greets his Derby-winning partner Benny The Dip at John Gosden's stables.

For much of the race, the overwhelming favourite Entrepreneur appeared in contention, but all was not well. After the race, Kinane reported that the horse had received a bump from Cloudings at the mile marker and was never travelling encouragingly thereafter. The huge crowd began to realise the seemingly invincible Entrepreneur would not be winning as the field came round Tattenham Corner.

It was here that Benny The Dip began a charge for glory, accelerating swiftly round Tattenham Corner and shooting sublimely into the straight. Like dynamite, Benny The Dip had left Entrepreneur and the rest for dead, carving open a huge five-length lead.

Pat Eddery had been working tirelessly aboard Silver Patriarch, struggling to get his mount competitive early on. Indeed, he was still in a different galaxy to the leader coming round Tattenham Corner, and it seemed highly unlikely he would be involved in the final argument. However, Silver Patriarch was spirited and tough, and as he finally began to gather momentum entering the straight, the grey suddenly exploded into a silver bullet. His progress was thunderous entering the final furlong, as he passed horse after horse, finally closing in on Benny The Dip.

The final encounter was thrilling. Silver Patriarch was devouring the ground, yet Benny The Dip simply refused to yield what was, by now, the narrowest of advantages. Just as it seemed inevitable that the grey would overturn the leader, Benny The Dip gave one final burst, and it was enough to win by a short head. Silver Patriarch had thrown all that he had to give at the winner and surely would have won in a few more strides, indeed, he went on to prove his tenacity by recording a victory later that season in the St Leger. However, Ryan had stolen this Derby with his charge round Tattenham Corner where he took valuable lengths and Benny The Dip had done the rest by showing utter gameness and courage. Romanov had stayed on to take third while Entrepreneur, bitterly disappointing despite his problems, came fourth. The favourite would race one more time after the Derby before retirement beckoned, never achieving the superstar status he had promised to aspire to.

The final outcome was not announced until some minutes after the finish, such was the closeness of the matter, but when Benny The Dip's success was confirmed, it provided John Gosden with his first Derby win, and ensured Newmarket a fourth winner in five years. Gosden's father, Towser, had trained Charlottown as a two-year-old before ill-health led to Gordon Smyth taking over for the horse's 1966 Derby win. It was Gosden's third Classic success after winning the 1992 Irish St Leger with Mashaallah and the 1996 St Leger with Shantou.

Benny The Dip, whose sire was the 1982 Derby third Silver Hawk and whose grandsire was the 1972 hero Roberto, had three more races before his retirement at the end of the season. He split a pair of brilliant older horses in the eventual dual King George winner Pilsudski and Bosra Sham in the Eclipse Stakes and then ran third behind the highly regarded Singspiel in the Juddmonte International at York. The two performances suggested Benny The Dip was a decent Derby winner; after all, Silver Patriarch went on to win a Classic of his own as well as taking the Coronation Cup as a four-year-old, yet Benny The Dip's final race clouded his reputation somewhat, as he was soundly trounced by Pilsudski in the Champion Stakes at Newmarket.

**1997 VODAFONE DERBY RESULT**

| FATE / HORSE | WEIGHT | JOCKEY | ODDS |
| --- | --- | --- | --- |
| **1st – Benny The Dip** | 9-0 | W. Ryan | 11/1 |
| **2nd – Silver Patriarch** | 9-0 | Pat Eddery | 6/1 |
| **3rd – Romanov** | 9-0 | J. Reid | 25/1 |
| 4th – Entrepreneur | 9-0 | M.J. Kinane | 4/6* |
| 5th – The Fly | 9-0 | R. Cochrane | 12/1 |
| 6th – Fahris | 9-0 | R. Hills | 12/1 |
| 7th – Symonds Inn | 9-0 | K. Fallon | 33/1 |
| 8th – Mulsalsal | 9-0 | M. Hills | 40/1 |
| 9th – Bold Demand | 9-0 | L. Dettori | 20/1 |
| 10th – Cloudings | 9-0 | O. Peslier | 12/1 |
| 11th – Single Empire | 9-0 | D. Harrison | 33/1 |
| 12th – Crystal Hearted | 9-0 | A. McGlone | 66/1 |
| Last – Papua | 9-0 | G. Carter | 150/1 |

7 June 1997
Going – Good
Winner – £595,250
Time – 2 mins 35.77 secs
Favourite – Entrepreneur
13 Ran

| | |
| --- | --- |
| Benny The Dip | Bay or brown colt by Silver Hawk – Rascal Rascal |
| Silver Patriarch | Grey colt by Saddler's Hall – Early Rising |
| Romanov | Bay colt by Nureyev – Morning Devotion |

Winner bred by Owner (Landon Knight) in the USA
Winner trained by J.H.M. Gosden at Newmarket

# HIGH-RISE

The last time a filly had won the Derby was back in 1916, and even then, Fifinella's victory had come at Newmarket in a wartime replacement Derby. The last filly to really run with any credit had been Nobiliary, who had finished runner-up to Grundy in 1975. Since then, no filly had made an impact on the race. In 1998, however, a filly emerged that seemed ready to challenge the colts for the Blue Riband title, even though the field for the race was extremely strong and deep.

The scintillating 1,000 Guineas winner, Cape Verdi, was supplemented for the Derby as a cost of £75,000 by Godolphin. The filly was a bay by Caerleon, the sire of the 1991 hero Generous, and although there were doubts surrounding Cape Verdi's stamina, she was a very relaxed horse with some serious speed. Partnering Cape Verdi was Frankie Dettori, and the ride presented the jockey with his best chance of landing the Derby after six fruitless efforts. In a hot betting contest, Cape Verdi eventually started the 11/4 favourite.

One trainer rapidly starting to progress into the spotlight was the young handler based at Ballydoyle Stables in Ireland, Aiden O'Brien. Earlier in the year, O'Brien had trained the great Istabraq to the first of his three Champion Hurdle wins at the Cheltenham Festival, but it was with Flat horses that he would become a supreme power. For the 1998 Derby, O'Brien sent forward a trio of contenders – Group One winners all of them. First, there was Second Empire, a big, strong horse by the outstanding sire Fairy King, a stallion that had got the 1996 Arc winner Helissio and was a brother to Sadler's Wells. The big bay Second Empire had won all three of his races as a two-year-old, including the Grand Criterium, and thus was a hot winter fancy for the Derby. However,

The magnificent 2,000 Guineas winner King Of Kings.

muscle problems had interrupted his three-year-old campaign and he could finish only third in the Irish 2,000 Guineas. Second Empire was a horse with brute power and cheetah-like speed and was always to be aimed at the Derby by his trainer, yet he was another with stamina worries and had never raced beyond a mile. Saratoga Springs had won the Dante Stakes but then finished a puzzling fourth in the French Derby and was a surprise runner at Epsom having been ruled out early in Derby week – it was only when the ground changed from soft to good that he was allowed to take his chance. As well as Second Empire and Saratoga Springs, O'Brien also had in his army perhaps the most naturally talented horse in the entire field – the handsome and wonderfully athletic King Of Kings. A son of Sadler's Wells and a horse with a high head carriage, King Of Kings had illustrated his class by winning a talent-rich edition of the 2,000 Guineas in fine style, outclassing the favourite Xaar with an enchanting display of poise and finishing speed. Like Second Empire and Cape Verdi, King Of Kings had shown his best form at distances of around a mile and there were concerns that he too may not stay in the Derby, yet he was a horse with class in abundance and seemed destined to give a bold account of himself. One serious and unplanned negative factor surrounding the O'Brien horses was the nightmare journey the trio endured in getting to Epsom. Leaving Ireland on the morning of the race, their plane was delayed by fog at Shannon Airport, leaving the horses anxious and restless, a far-from-ideal beginning to Derby day.

Having owned the commanding winner of the 1979 Derby in Troy, Lord Weinstock's candidate on this occasion was the fast-improving and increasingly well-fancied Greek Dance. Yet another high-quality son of Sadler's Wells, Greek Dance had won a pair of lesser races – including the Glasgow Stakes at York – to book his place in the big-race field. Trained by Michael Stoute and ridden by Walter Swinburn, Greek Dance was a horse that gained considerable support in the run-up to the Derby following reports of some magnificent workouts.

There were countless horses that held realistic hopes of winning the 1998 Derby, among them the grinding-stayer The Glow-Worm, the Generous-sired Courteous and the attractive bay City Honours, runner-up in the Dante. One other very talented horse, but one that was strangely unconsidered before the race, was the unbeaten, Luca Cumani-trained High-Rise. A bay colt with resolute staying powers and a decisive turn of speed, High-Rise had won the Lingfield Derby Trial most recently, the same race that Cumani had used to prepare Kahyasi for his Derby triumph of 1988. Unlike his higher-profile rivals Cape Verdi, Second Empire and King Of Kings, High-Rise had proved at Lingfield that he stayed the mile-and-a-half of the Derby, yet started the race at very generous odds of 20/1.

With a record attendance of almost 100,000 people at Epsom, the fifteen runners set off in search of a place in history – and a near-£600,000 first prize.

It was Sunshine Street – a maiden and the race's big outsider trained by Noel Meade – that jumped off in front and began setting a decent gallop from the Henry Cecil-trained stayer Sadian, the Chester Vase winner Gulland, Greek Dance, Cape Verdi and City Honours. King Of Kings – who began the race as third favourite – was settled out the back early on by Pat Eddery, just behind High-Rise and Border Arrow.

After a number of recent rough-and-tumble Derbys, the 1998 edition was, for the most part, chaos-free, and as they came to the top of the hill, it was still Sunshine Street – giving Johnny Murtagh a superb ride – that continued to bowl along in front.

Greek Dance came through his trial races well to earn a lofty position in the Derby betting market.

As Tattenham Corner came into view, a number of horses were beginning to struggle. King Of Kings was still rooted to the back and something appeared to be amiss with the Guineas winner, while unlike his Derby-winning father, Courteous seemed not to handle the descent well, slightly falling into Cape Verdi as they plunged down the course.

Turning into the straight, the order remained similar to what it had been throughout, with Sunshine Street bounding on from Sadian, Gulland, Greek Dance and City Honours. Second Empire had been chugging along like a tank in mid-division, yet when the serious business began, he was unable to quicken sufficiently to attack the lead. Cape Verdi drew wide of the preceding Gulland to mount her challenge, yet she quickly and rather tamely found herself outpaced, and flying past her on her outside, having been eight lengths down at the beginning of the straight, was High-Rise.

High-Rise (yellow colours) beats City Honours (blue) in a fierce finish to the 1998 race.

High-Rise training in Dubai as an older horse, having been switched to Godolphin.

Peslier had been very patient aboard High-Rise, but at Tattenham Corner he had begun a serious drive that had caught out the likes of Second Empire and Cape Verdi. Really charging up the straight, High-Rise picked-off the leaders one by one – Gulland, Greek Dance and then Sunshine Street – until only City Honours, who in turn had been sent on vigorously by John Reid, lay ahead.

City Honours – certainly the most handsome horse in the race – was powering home in relentless fashion under Reid, but High-Rise's momentum had been ascending with every stride from Tattenham Corner and the horse was now in full flight. The battle raged all the way to the line, with neither warrior prepared to back down, but ultimately, it was High-Rise that got his head in front, and that was enough to deny the brave City Honours. Border Arrow had been last turning into the straight, but had made up considerable late ground to displace the gallant and surprising Sunshine Street from third position. Of the fancied runners, Second Empire and Cape Verdi had not stayed – the latter, apparently not acting sufficiently on the course, while Greek Dance had run well for a long way but had suffered a mid-race injury that had blunted his effectiveness. King Of Kings – who had never surfaced from the back of the field – finished dead last, but it was later revealed, after X-rays, that the horse had sadly aggravated an old knee injury. King Of Kings had undergone surgery to remove a bone-chip from the joint at the end of his two-year-old season and the decision was soon taken by O'Brien – who held the horse in the highest regard – to retire the 2,000 Guineas winner.

The jubilant Olivier Peslier became the first French jockey to win the Derby since Yves Saint-Martin on Relko in 1963, while the Italian Luca Cumani had now trained his second Epsom hero. Cumani had suffered badly in the early 1990s when the quality and quantity of horses in his yard was depleted. At the time, the trainer had lost approximately forty horses owned by the Aga Khan after that owner had withdrawn his horses from Britain following the disqualification of his Aliysa in the 1989 Oaks. (Aliysa had won the Oaks but had been disqualified for testing positive for a banned substance). Cumani also lost horses from rapidly departing American owners and many horses owned by the Maktoum family were sent to John Gosden's yard. However, following the Aga Khan's return to Britain, the quality of Cumani's yard had slowly begun to rise again, although High-Rise was owned by Sheikh Mohammed Obaid Al Maktoum – a cousin of Sheikh Mohammed.

High-Rise had come from further back to win than any Derby winner since Golden Fleece in 1982, and in doing so, had maintained his unbeaten record. High-Rise was a very relaxed horse and had shown speed and unflinching nerve to get the better of City Honours. High-Rise ran two more times in the season after Epsom, finishing a creditable second to the very good Swain in the King George before disappointing behind Sagamix in the Prix de l'Arc de

High-Rise was trainer Luca Cumani's second Derby winner after Kahyasi in 1988.

**1998 VODAFONE DERBY RESULT**

| FATE / HORSE | WEIGHT | JOCKEY | ODDS |
|---|---|---|---|
| **1st – High-Rise** | 9-0 | O. Peslier | 20/1 |
| **2nd – City Honours** | 9-0 | J. Reid | 12/1 |
| **3rd – Border Arrow** | 9-0 | R. Cochrane | 25/1 |
| 4th – Sunshine Street | 9-0 | J. Murtagh | 150/1 |
| 5th – Greek Dance | 9-0 | W.R. Swinburn | 5/1 |
| 6th – The Glow-Worm | 9-0 | D. Holland | 20/1 |
| 7th – Sadian | 9-0 | K. Fallon | 25/1 |
| 8th – Second Empire | 9-0 | M.J. Kinane | 9/2 |
| 9th – Cape Verdi | 8-9 | L. Dettori | 11/4* |
| 10th – Saratoga Springs | 9-0 | W. Ryan | 20/1 |
| 11th – Gulland | 9-0 | M. Hills | 12/1 |
| 12th – Courteous | 9-0 | T. Quinn | 14/1 |
| 13th – Mutamam | 9-0 | M. Roberts | 50/1 |
| 14th – Haami | 9-0 | R. Hills | 20/1 |
| Last – King Of Kings | 9-0 | Pat Eddery | 11/2 |

6 June 1998
Going – Good
Winner – £598,690
Time – 2 mins 33.88 secs
Favourite – Cape Verdi
15 Ran

| | |
|---|---|
| High-Rise | Bay colt by High Estate – High Tern |
| City Honours | Bay colt by Darshaan – Ikebana |
| Border Arrow | Chestnut colt by Selkirk – Nibbs Point |

Winner bred by Owner (Sheikh Mohammed Obaid Al-Maktoum)
Winner trained by L.M. Cumani at Newmarket

Triomphe. Unlike many Derby winners, High-Rise trained on for a lengthy career and became something of a globetrotter. As a four-year-old, having been switched to the guidance of Godolphin, he ran four times, including a third place in the rich Japan Cup in Tokyo, although he then finished dead last in the prestigious Dubai World Cup behind the Godolphin outsider Almutawakel. He even ran three times as a five-year-old, winning a race in Dubai before ending his career by coming last in a race at Belmont Park in America. He was then retired to stud in Japan.

At Epsom though in June 1998, High-Rise's win went down as the third-fastest electronically of any Derby and his success continued the fine recent run of Newmarket-based stables in the greatest Classic of them all.

# OATH

'Open' was very much the way to describe the 1999 Derby, the 220th. Of the sixteen runners, no fewer than eleven began the race at a price of 16/1 or less. The competitiveness in the market did not stem from a lack of class, as even though the 2,000 Guineas winner Island Sands was an absentee, many of the winners of the major Derby trials were present. Indeed, after the 1999 Derby, a number of the runners would progress to have outstanding careers.

As one of two horses representing the powerful Godolphin team, Dubai Millenium began the race as favourite. The bay, partnered by Frankie Dettori, had won twice before the Derby, including a very easy victory in the Predominate Stakes at Goodwood. Formerly trained by David Loder, the horse had been described as a 'machine' and Dettori had personally selected Dubai Millenium over Godolphin's other runner, Adair, a horse that had run just once before when winning at Belmont Park in the States as a two-year-old. Since arriving in Britain for the current campaign, Adair had been slow to adjust and many considered him – though not without talent – to be too inexperienced and backward for a race like the Derby.

Following Dubai Millenium in the betting were a pair of good stayers in Lucido and Oath. Lucido was a big horse, unbeaten at three, and was trained by John Dunlop. After winning the Lingfield Derby Trial in good style from another Derby contender, Daliapour, connections took the bold step of supplementing Lucido for the Derby at a cost of £75,000, believing that the trip would be ideal for their charge. Having been beaten by Lucido at Newbury in April, the Henry Cecil-trained Oath entered the Derby picture with form to reverse with Dunlop's horse. Oath, whose sire Fairy King had been responsible for the much-fancied 1998 Derby flop Second Empire, had progressed to win

Lucido, one of the leading contenders in 1999.

the Dee Stakes at Chester after Newbury, displaying a relentless-galloping style to accompany a compact, neat action. Oath was small but tough and the dark bay horse was a fourth Derby mount for Kieran Fallon.

Trained by Sir Michael Stoute and a grandson of the 1972 Derby winner Roberto, Beat All was another with high Derby aspirations. The brown colt had recently recovered from a bruised foot, but was a talented stayer that had won the Newmarket Stakes on his only start of the season, beating the subsequent Italian Derby winner Mukhalif in the process. Beat All was partnered at Epsom by the top American jockey Gary Stevens, who was having his first Derby ride.

Also among the chief contenders for the 1999 Derby were Saffron Walden, Salford Express and Daliapour. Having suffered bitter disappointment when none of his three fancied challengers for the 1998 Derby were able to impact on the race, trainer Aiden O'Brien was represented on this occasion by the laid-back but fleet-footed Irish 2,000 Guineas winner Saffron Walden. The big worry, however, for the Irish raider was the ground, as Saffron Walden – a doubtful stayer – distinctly preferred faster conditions than were present at Epsom in 1999. Salford Express, a front-running chestnut trained by David Elsworth, had won the Dante Stakes at York, a feat that two of the previous five Derby winners had also managed. Salford Express was ridden by Pat Eddery, a man searching for his fourth Derby win. Eddery had also finished runner-up on no fewer than four occasions. Ground on the soft side of good was certainly of no detriment to the combative front-runner representing trainer Luca Cumani and owner the Aga Khan, Daliapour. A small but solid bay colt, Daliapour was a son of Sadler's Wells and had already proved himself at Epsom, winning the Blue Riband Trial in April before finishing second to Lucido at Lingfield. In contrast to some of the other contenders, Daliapour was a sure stayer and, with his previous Epsom run a success, seemed sure to relish the heated battle of the Derby.

During the pre-race parade, Oath began to sweat profusely, leaving Fallon with no choice but to break away and head to the start before the remainder. Although this act carried a fine of £1,000, it was both sensible and necessary if Oath's chance was not to be destroyed before the race had even begun.

Breaking away cleanly from the starting stalls, it was an outsider in All The Way that made the early running with Salford Express for company. Having suffered somewhat before the race, Oath was planted in a wonderful position by Fallon once the race was underway, poised in true 'Piggott' style behind the leaders.

As the race progressed, it was clear that one horse that was struggling with the unique occasion was the favourite Dubai Millenium. Like many fancied horses before him, Dubai Millenium simply did not act on the unusual track,

pulling extremely hard and becoming unbalanced as they came down the hill. It had not helped that the horse had been somewhat quarrelsome beforehand, as well as getting barged around once the action had intensified. This was not to be the favourite's day, but golden times awaited him later in his career. In ten lifetime races, the Derby would be the only time he tasted defeat. He developed into a truly magnificent horse and emerged as a modern-day superstar. He won four Group One races, including his long-term target as a four-year-old, the Dubai World Cup at Nad al Sheba, simply slamming his rivals in the process in one of the most ruthless and convincing big-race destructions in many a year. He won almost £3 million in prize money before injury ended his career. Most tragically, he died of grass sickness at five before having a chance to have an impact at stud. He goes down as one of the finest racehorse of recent years.

Dubai Millenium aside, the Derby was beginning to heat up immensely as the field rounded Tattenham Corner and then straightened for home. It was to be the famous green and red colours of the Aga Khan that emerged to take control in the straight as Daliapour set sail for home, having swept past All The Way and the back-pedalling Salford Express.

Daliapour, with Gerald Mosse aboard, quickly opened up a useful advantage as the tough little horse surged forward, but one horse that had tracked his movement was Oath, and he was the one to chase him.

Thundering up the straight, Daliapour and Oath had the race to themselves. They had shaken off the remainder of the field and now settled down for their own private battle. Daliapour was a most difficult horse to overturn but, little by little, Oath was getting the better of him. Brilliantly coaxed home by Fallon, Oath finally overthrew Daliapour inside the last furlong and, having cut him down, powered home to a length-and-three-quarters victory. Daliapour was a genuine horse and was very consistent. He went on to prove himself time and again as a globetrotting older horse, winning four times, including the Hong Kong Vase and Epsom's Coronation Cup. Also second in the Irish Derby shortly after the Derby, Daliapour was now the fifth horse sired by Sadler's Wells to finish runner-up in the Derby. Beat All came from a long way back to rally into third, but Lucido left connections perplexed; having been well positioned in the straight, he faded most tamely to finished next to last.

A fourth Derby win for Cecil brought with it glowing praise for the trainer from Fallon, who expressed gratitude that Cecil had given him so many opportunities in his career. Cecil and Fallon became the first trainer/jockey combination to win the Derby and Oaks in the same year since Cecil had achieved the same honour with Steve Cauthen in 1985. Cecil and Fallon had taken the Oaks courtesy of Ramruma. Oath's win had also given Cecil a twentieth-century record of twenty-two British Classics.

Daliapour ran his heart out in the Derby but had to settle for second place.

Jockey Kieran Fallon secured his first Derby win in 1999 aboard Oath.

**1999 VODAFONE DERBY RESULT**

| FATE / HORSE | WEIGHT | JOCKEY | ODDS |
|---|---|---|---|
| **1st – Oath** | 9-0 | K. Fallon | 13/2 |
| **2nd – Daliapour** | 9-0 | G. Mosse | 10/1 |
| **3rd – Beat All** | 9-0 | Gary Stevens | 7/1 |
| 4th – Housemaster | 9-0 | W. Ryan | 12/1 |
| 5th – All The Way | 9-0 | J.P. Murtagh | 33/1 |
| 6th – Glamis | 9-0 | R. Cochrane | 40/1 |
| 7th – Saffron Walden | 9-0 | M.J. Kinane | 8/1 |
| 8th – Compton Admiral | 9-0 | T. Jarnet | 25/1 |
| 9th – Dubai Millennium | 9-0 | L. Dettori | 5/1* |
| 10th – Brancaster | 9-0 | J. Fortune | 20/1 |
| 11th – Val Royal | 9-0 | O. Peslier | 14/1 |
| 12th – Zaajer | 9-0 | R. Hills | 16/1 |
| 13th – Adair | 9-0 | D. O'Donohoe | 16/1 |
| 14th – Salford Express | 9-0 | Pat Eddery | 12/1 |
| 15th – Lucido | 9-0 | T. Quinn | 13/2 |
| Last – Through The Rye | 9-0 | M. Hills | 100/1 |

5 June 1999
Going – Good (Good to Soft in places)
Winner – £611,450
Time – 2 mins 37.43 secs
Favourite – Dubai Millennium
16 Ran

| | |
|---|---|
| Oath | Bay colt by Fairy King – Sheer Audacity |
| Daliapour | Bay colt by Sadler's Wells – Dalara |
| Beat All | Bay or brown colt by Dynaformer – Spirited Missus |

Winner bred by Mrs Max Morris
Winner trained by H. Cecil at Newmarket

Oath, who had worn a white bridle to win, had gained the widest margin of victory since Commander In Chief had won in 1993. The horse then bypassed a tilt at the Irish Derby because of poor workouts and ran next in the King George VI and Queen Elizabeth Diamond Stakes at Ascot. However, in finishing seventh behind the fantastic grey Daylami, Oath cracked a bone in his near foreleg and was subsequently retired. Soon after, owner Ahmed Salman sold the Derby hero of 1999 to Yushun Farm in Japan for £8 million, where he was placed at stud.

# SINNDAR

The huge disappointment surrounding the 2000 Derby was the fact that King's Best, the splendid winner of the 2,000 Guineas at Newmarket, was absent. King's Best, trained by Sir Michael Stoute, had been the strong ante-post favourite for the Derby until a recurrence of an old muscle problem struck forty-eight hours before the race to cruelly rob him of a place in the field.

The absence of King's Best understandably took some of the gloss off the 2000 Derby, yet a strong field remained, together with the possibility that Henry Cecil could become the first trainer to win the Derby and the Oaks in the same year for consecutive years since Alec Taylor in 1918. Taylor had achieved the 1917 double with Gay Crusader and Sunny Jane and repeated the trick a year later courtesy of Gainsborough and My Dear. The day before the Derby, Cecil had recorded a remarkable seventh Oaks win after his Love Divine had scorched home, and not surprisingly, the attention then turned largely to his two runners to see if either could follow-up in the Derby. Cecil was represented by the useful stayer Wellbeing – ridden by Willie Ryan – and, more notably, by Beat Hollow, the mount of Cecil's first-year retainer Richard Quinn. The 7/2 favourite, Beat Hollow was a striking bay colt with a standout white face, yet he was not without problems. The colt had suffered an interrupted preparation, much to the concern of Cecil, and had only ever run twice in his life and only once at three. Having won his only race as a juvenile at Yarmouth, Beat Hollow was hampered by mucus in his lungs that forced him to miss the start of his three-year-old campaign. When he did see the racecourse, he behaved poorly, acting up in the preliminaries, but he ultimately displayed a keen turn of foot and a great deal of potential to win the

Henry Cecil's Derby hopeful Beat Hollow.

Newmarket Stakes. If Beat Hollow was going to win the Derby, he would have to buck the trend that had cursed favourites since Nashwan had triumphed in 1989. In the years following Nashwan, no favourite had won the Derby apart from Erhaab in 1994, and only Dushyantor in 1996 had run with much credit otherwise.

Meaning 'generous' in Arabic, Sakhee was a seriously good challenger from the John Dunlop yard. A big, high-class individual, Sakhee had won on all ground types and had taken two key trials during the season: the Sandown Classic Trial and the Dante Stakes. The Dante was a race that Dunlop's previous Derby winners, Shirley Heights and Erhaab, had taken before Epsom.

Despite having not won the Derby since Secreto saw off El Gran Senor in 1984, Irish hopes were high courtesy of two very realistic challengers, Aristotle and Sinndar. Despite seeing his four previous Derby winners crumble miserably on the big day, Aiden O'Brien had supreme confidence in the well-balanced Aristotle. A useful juvenile, Aristotle had won the Prix Greffulhe at Longchamp on his reappearance at three – the same race that French legend Sea Bird II had won before the Derby – only to be demoted to third, and together with the likes of Beat Hollow and Wellbeing, attempted to give a much-deserved first Derby win to his sire Sadler's Wells. Sinndar was a first ever runner in the Derby for trainer John Oxx. A highly talented bay colt by the excellent miler Grand Lodge and out of a mare, Sinntara, that was a listed winner over two miles, Sinndar was unbeaten at two and had beaten the useful Bach at Leopardstown as a three-year-old. Having gone close to another Derby winner with Daliapour the year before, the Aga Khan hoped Sinndar would prevail on this occasion. Johnny Murtagh, who had experienced fine rides aboard outsiders All The Way and Sunshine Street in recent Derbys, took the ride on Sinndar.

Fifteen horses entered the starting stalls, including the classy chestnut Best Of The Bests, one of four runners representing Godolphin. One element of the Godolphin team missing from this particular Derby, however, was Frankie Dettori. The popular jockey had been involved in a terrible helicopter accident together with former Derby winner Ray Cochrane, and the crash had claimed the life of the pilot. Dettori would have most likely partnered Best Of The Bests at Epsom, his place going to the fine American rider Chris McCarron.

Kingsclere, a son of the 1999 Derby-winning sire Fairy King, was the early leader in the race, yet bizarrely, after five furlongs, the Ian Balding-trained horse charged ridiculously wide on the course, totally lost his place, and then tailed off and eventually finished last.

With the unusual antics of Kingsclere behind them, the horses that would prove to be the major players in the race came to the fore. It was Best Of The Bests that swooped round Tattenham Corner in the lead, but Sakhee was waiting to pounce as soon as they straightened for home. Just in behind came Sinndar, who was calmly poised and hovering like a hawk under Murtagh, with Beat Hollow next, although that horse had suffered a degree of interference during the race. Aristotle had not been far away either, but as the leaders began their charge for home, the Irish horse could find nothing.

Irish hope Aristotle (leading string) works on the Ballydoyle gallops of Aiden O'Brien prior to his challenge for the Derby.

It was Sakhee that was sent for home first by Richard Hills – the colt's long, heavy stride leaving Best Of The Bests for dead. The Godolphin horse was beaten, while Beat Hollow simply could not reach the leader. All his challengers were beaten off, with the vital exception of Sinndar. Sakhee and Sinndar pulled five lengths clear of the favourite, and reaching the final furlong, their duel proved to be titanic.

Whereas the year before when it was apparent that Oath was gradually wearing down Daliapour, Sakhee and Sinndar could not be separated. Either horse – as the future would prove – would have been a brilliant and richly deserving winner, yet close to home, it was Sinndar that emerged the stronger, overpowering the gallant Sakhee right at the death. Sakhee had run his heart out, having gone for home a long way out, but Sinndar had shown both class and courage, relentlessly thrusting at Sakhee and refusing to be beaten, similar to The Minstrel's defeat of Hot Grove in the 1977 Derby. Beat Hollow had run a respectable race given his circumstances, coming home third ahead of Best Of The Bests.

Sinndar beats Sakhee in an epic finish in 2000.

Johnny Murtagh salutes Sinndar's fine Derby victory.

Oxx, who trained at County Kildare in Ireland, had won the Derby with his first ever runner in the race, and in the process, had presented the Aga Khan with his fourth Epsom victor. The spiritual leader of the Ismaili Muslims, the present Aga Khan (IV) had now achieved a post-war record of four Derby wins, with Sinndar's victory following those of Shergar, Shahrastani and Kahyasi. The Aga Khan was now only one Derby win behind his grandfather, Aga Khan (III) who had five.

Murtagh had been sacked as Oxx's jockey in 1992 because of weight problems and allegations he had cheated the scales. Eventually though, Murtagh was able to win back the trust of his boss and went on to become Champion Jockey in Ireland three times.

Sinndar was an excellent Derby winner, certainly the best since Lammtarra, and both he and Sakhee gave the 2000 renewal great credit by progressing into superb racehorses **after** Epsom. The runner-up really blossomed as a four-

Johnny Murtagh, trainer John Oxx and the Aga Khan (top hat) recount Sinndar's success.

**2000 VODAFONE DERBY RESULT**

| FATE / HORSE | WEIGHT | JOCKEY | ODDS |
|---|---|---|---|
| **1st – Sinndar** | 9-0 | J.P. Murtagh | 7/1 |
| **2nd – Sakhee** | 9-0 | R. Hills | 4/1 |
| **3rd – Beat Hollow** | 9-0 | T. Quinn | 7/2* |
| 4th – Best Of The Bests | 9-0 | C. McCarron | 12/1 |
| 5th – Wellbeing | 9-0 | W. Ryan | 7/1 |
| 6th – Hatha Anna | 9-0 | K. Darley | 66/1 |
| 7th – St Expedit | 9-0 | R. Hughes | 28/1 |
| 8th – Barathea Guest | 9-0 | P. Robinson | 12/1 |
| 9th – Zyz | 9-0 | J. Fortune | 100/1 |
| 10th – Aristotle | 9-0 | M.J. Kinane | 5/1 |
| 11th – Inchlonaig | 9-0 | Pat Eddery | 16/1 |
| 12th – Broche | 9-0 | C. Soumillon | 40/1 |
| 13th – Going Global | 9-0 | J. Reid | 25/1 |
| 14th – Cracow | 9-0 | M. Hills | 66/1 |
| Last – Kingsclere | 9-0 | O. Peslier | 16/1 |

10 June 2000

Going – Good

Winner – £609,000

Time – 2 mins 36.75 secs

Favourite – Beat Hollow

15 Ran

| | |
|---|---|
| Sinndar | Bay colt by Grand Lodge – Sinntara |
| Sakhee | Bay colt by Bahri – Thawakib |
| Beat Hollow | Bay colt by Saddler's Wells – Wemyss Bight |

Winner bred by Owner (H.H. Aga Khan)

Winner trained by John M. Oxx at Currabeg, Co. Kildare, Ireland

year-old, having being switched to Godolphin, winning the Group One Juddmonte International Stakes at York in great style before his finest hour when he equalled the record winning distance of the great Italian colt Ribot and the legendary Sea Bird II when winning the Prix de l'Arc de Triomphe by six lengths. Sakhee trained on as a five-year-old and his last ever race came in the Prix Gontaut-Biron at Deauville in France over one mile two furlongs, where he was narrowly beaten into second place by another member of the Derby Class of 2000, Wellbeing. As for the Derby hero Sinndar, he went on to win the Irish Derby and Longchamp's Prix Niel before crowning his glorious season by preceding Sakhee in winning the Arc. Sinndar was then retired at the end of his three-year-old season.

# GALILEO

Without a doubt, the leading big race trainer of the 2001 Flat racing season had been Aiden O'Brien. The young Irishman had begun his training career in 1993 at the age of twenty-four and had accumulated five Jumps Trainers titles in Ireland. In 1998, O'Brien began training exclusively at Ballydoyle Stables, having replaced the legendary Vincent O'Brien – no relation – when the great trainer retired in 1994. The 2001 season had seen a whirlwind of big races fall to the Ballydoyle maestro, including the French 1,000 Guineas courtesy of Rose Gypsy, the Irish 2,000 Guineas with Black Minnaloushe and the Irish 1,000 Guineas and Epsom Oaks double with Imagine.

Even though O'Brien had enjoyed remarkable success in his relatively short career to date (largely thanks to horses such as the three-time Champion Hurdler Istabraq and the ultra-game, six-time Group One winner Giant's Causeway) the Derby had so far proved a frustrating experience. For the past three years, O'Brien had sent forward a series of powerful-looking challengers, only for each one to flop badly on the big day. Despite reminding many of the 2000 Derby failure Aristotle in terms of appearance, Galileo shaped as the trainer's greatest chance yet of adding the Derby to his enviable collection of big-race successes. Galileo, a powerful bay horse with a striking white face, was a natural, free-flowing athlete with a beautiful racing action. His pedigree too was exceptional, being by Sadler's Wells and out of an Arc-winning mare, Urban Sea, that was a half-sister to the 2,000 Guineas winner of the year before, King's Best. As a two-year-old, Galileo won his only race by fourteen lengths at Leopardstown and carried an unbeaten record to Epsom having won both starts at three, including the Derrinstown Stud Derby Trial at

Golan leads stablemate and fellow Derby contender Dilshaan at work on the Newmarket gallops.

Leopardstown – which Sinndar had won the year before – where he showed patience and blistering speed. The performance was enough to give the horse a share of favouritism for the Derby. Even so, there were still those that wondered – given the (albeit narrow) failures of Sadler's Wells horses before him – if Galileo was the real deal, capable of seeing out the full Derby distance or just the latest big-name colt to fail in his sire's quest for that elusive first Epsom win.

Galileo delivered a stunning Derby performance to slaughter the 2001 field.

Joining Galileo as the 11/4 market leader was the Sir Michael Stoute-trained Golan. Since the Second World War, only six horses had completed the double of the 2,000 Guineas and the Derby, yet having won the Newmarket Classic in impressive style, there were high hopes that Golan could become the seventh. A bay colt by the hotly fancied 1995 Derby runner Spectrum, Golan had shown great speed to pick off his rivals in the Guineas, thus keeping alive his unbeaten record, having won his only run at two. Golan was a class horse, well worthy of the honour of heading a Derby betting market, and he was owned by Lord Weinstock, whose previous Derby runners had included Troy, Spectrum and Greek Dance. Stoute, who also saddled the rock-hard Dante Stakes winner Dilshaan, had seen his recent 2,000 Guineas winners Shadeed, Doyoun and Entrepreneur all falter at Epsom and had been robbed of a golden chance of adding to his two previous Derby wins when King's Best had been ruled out through injury the year before. However, with speed and stamina in his pedigree, as well as Pat Eddery aboard, there was a lot of optimism surrounding Golan's challenge. There was also the feeling – given what had happened to O'Brien challengers in recent Derbys – that Golan was the 'safer' bet of the joint-favourites.

As well as Tobougg, a brilliant two-year-old that had been transferred from former England footballer Mick Channon's stable to that of Godolphin (where he had then disappointed massively at three having wintered in Dubai), the main opposition to the joint favourites came from the yard of Barry Hills. The trainer, who had agonisingly had four previous Derby seconds, sent four useful challengers to Epsom on this occasion. As well as the Sandown Classic Trial winner Chancellor and the tough Storming Home, Hills also saddled Mr Combustible and Perfect Sunday. A front-runner that stayed and battled, Mr Combustible had shown extreme guts to lead all the way when winning the Chester Vase prior to Epsom, while Perfect Sunday, a son of Quest For Fame, was an improving brown colt that had won the Lingfield Derby Trial.

Indeed, in front of a modern-day record crowd of 150,000 spectators, it was the Hills-trained pair of Mr Combustible and Perfect Sunday that set about making the early gallop, which was steady. With just twelve runners in the field, each horse was able to find a position with relative ease, and the race was bereft of the scrimmaging that had hampered some of the more recent Derbys.

The running order remained virtually unchanged as they broke round Tattenham Corner, the Hills pair churning along in front from the Michael Jarvis-trained Putra Sandhurst. It had been evident for the entire race that Mick Kinane was having a wonderfully relaxed ride aboard Galileo, and the big bay horse was positioned beautifully on the heels of the leaders entering the straight, with Golan towards the outside and Dilshaan right there too. Of the perceived chief contenders, only Tobougg appeared to be out of contention as he idled towards the rear.

Jockey Mick Kinane won on Galileo.

Galileo is the centre of attention after his Derby win.

The race, so far, had been run at a sedate pace. But now the runners were in the straight, the contest changed dramatically. Perfect Sunday suddenly weakened while Dilshaan could find no more, and as game as Mr Combustible was, he was likewise one-paced, and at the two-furlong marker, he yielded his race-long lead.

It was Galileo, commanding and ominous, that swallowed him alive, and from there on in, the racing world was invited to see the destructive power that would make the Irish horse one of the finest in recent memory. Asked to take control of the race by Kinane, Galileo's response was breathtaking, and at once, he rocketed away from the pack. Although Golan showed his quality by chasing hard after him, the moment Galileo set sail for home, the race was over. As Irish voices raised their volume to stupendous levels, Galileo swept to victory in the most convincing and dominating style since Shergar had pulverised his opponents in 1981. The three-and-a-half-length winning margin over Golan – who would finish fourth behind the 2000 Derby runner-up Sakhee in the Arc later in the season as well as winning the King George as a four-year-old – was as emphatic as could be, and signalled the emergence of a great racehorse. Tobougg had never been in the race, but he was able to stay on late, taking third place from the game Mr Combustible.

The scintillating burst that Galileo had delivered to win was good enough to give him the second-fastest time in the race's history, and with stunning looks and a superb pedigree, the Irish horse was undoubtedly one of the finest Derby winners of modern times. His victory ended the long wait for a Derby winner for the great Sadler's Wells. The much-deserved honour for the magnificent stallion meant he had now broken the world record for most Group/Grade One winners, with his total standing at forty-six.

O'Brien had won his first Derby nineteen years after his predecessor at Ballydoyle, Vincent O'Brien, had saddled his last Derby winner in Golden Fleece, and many believed Galileo's victory would be the first of countless Epsom triumphs for the trainer.

Having shelled out millions in trying to win the Derby, the partnership of John Magnier and Michael Tabor had finally succeeded. The latter had previously won the 1994 Kentucky Derby with Thunder Gulch, while at Epsom, Galileo carried the dark blue colours of John's wife Sue.

After Epsom, Galileo won the Irish Derby before commencing battle with the horse that would become his biggest rival, the Godolphin-trained Fantastic Light, a far smaller horse than Galileo but one with immense courage and a year's more experience. It was Galileo that continued to raise the level of his soaring reputation by beating Fantastic Light in the King George, but the rematch in the Irish Champion Stakes was one of the most thrilling battles in the modern history of racing, perhaps a rival for the 'Race Of The Century' that Grundy and Bustino fought out in 1975. With neither horse willing to give in, it was Fantastic Light that pulled out everything he had to defeat the Derby winner, a result that, for a while, shook the racing world to its roots as Galileo's unbeaten record lay shattered, albeit ended by a super opponent. Finally, Galileo was sent to America for his last ever race, the Breeder's Cup Classic; however, he simply detested the dirt track and was soundly beaten. Although his last two races ended in defeat and despite a lingering feeling that he could have progressed even further if staying in training at four, Galileo will be noted in time as one of the great Derby winners of the modern era. Mick Kinane admitted Galileo was the best horse he had ever ridden, and there is no doubt that he was a very special colt indeed.

**2001 VODAFONE DERBY RESULT**

| FATE / HORSE | WEIGHT | JOCKEY | ODDS |
|---|---|---|---|
| **1st – Galileo** | 9-0 | M.J. Kinane | 11/4* |
| **2nd – Golan** | 9-0 | Pat Eddery | 11/4* |
| **3rd – Tobougg** | 9-0 | L. Dettori | 9/1 |
| 4th – Mr Combustible | 9-0 | R. Hills | 20/1 |
| 5th – Storming Home | 9-0 | M. Hills | 14/1 |
| 6th – Perfect Sunday | 9-0 | R. Hughes | 9/2 |
| 7th – Dilshaan | 9-0 | J.P. Murtagh | 5/1 |
| 8th – Putra Sandhurst | 9-0 | P. Robinson | 16/1 |
| 9th – Sunny Glenn | 9-0 | J. Weaver | 150/1 |
| 10th – Chancellor | 9-0 | T. Quinn | 25/1 |
| 11th – King Carew | 9-0 | Craig Williams | 200/1 |
| Last – Cashel Bay | 9-0 | J. Carroll | 300/1 |

9 June 2001
Going – Good to Firm
Winner – £580,000
Time – 2 mins 33.27 secs
Joint Favourites – Galileo & Golan
12 Ran

| Galileo | Bay colt by Sadler's Wells – Urban Sea |
|---|---|
| Golan | Bay colt by Spectrum – Highland Gift |
| Tobougg | Bay colt by Barathea – Lacovia |

Winner bred by David Tsui & Orpendale
Winner trained by A.P. O'Brien at Ballydoyle, Co. Tipperary, Ireland

# HIGH CHAPARRAL

In comparison to some of the recent editions of the Derby, the 2002 seemed to lack strength in depth. Having seen Galileo dismantle the field for the Aiden O'Brien stable the year before, the main focus of the 2002 Derby centred on the Irishman's challenge for the race with his two colts, each one with a different style but each with mountainous potential. Not surprisingly, both were to be found at the top of the betting market.

As imposing and eye-catching a horse as one would wish to see, the giant bay colt Hawk Wing had the presence and charisma of a superstar, and this aura was present around the colt wherever he went. O'Brien had not been bashful in declaring that Hawk Wing would open up the eyes of the racing world during his Classic season, so confident was the trainer in his horse, even comparing him to the great Nijinsky. Hawk Wing had enjoyed a fine two-year-old season, winning three times, including the King Of Kings Futurity Stakes at The Curragh – a race named after another former O'Brien star – as well as the Group One National Stakes; results that left the colt as winter favourite for the Derby. Blessed with electric speed to accompany his beast-like frame and raw strength, Hawk Wing was expected to hammer his opponents in the 2,000 Guineas at Newmarket, but had to settle for second place behind a blossoming talent, the awesome wonderhorse in waiting, Rock Of Gibraltar. Even after his Guineas defeat, Hawk Wing remained the apple of his trainer's eye, and it is doubtful whether there has been – or will be for sometime – a more discussed or scrutinised O'Brien horse. There was no Rock Of Gibraltar to deal with at Epsom, and Hawk Wing, despite ground that was softer than ideal because of his undetermined stamina, began the race as favourite.

High Chaparral and jockey Johnny Murtagh parade before the 2002 Derby.

Mick Kinane, looking for his second consecutive Derby win, had discarded Hawk Wing's stablemate High Chaparral, and although different in make-up and a lot less hyped than the favourite, High Chaparral was every bit as talented. A smaller, darker-looking bay colt, High Chaparral was a son of Sadler's Wells and had won the Racing Post Trophy at Doncaster as a two-year-

High Chaparral gets the better of his stablemate Hawk Wing.

old. Indeed, High Chaparral had only been beaten once in five races prior to Epsom and had taken the same Derrinstown Derby Trial at Leopardstown that had been won by Galileo and Sinndar before their Derby wins. There was no masking the fact that High Chaparral was considered the number two challenger from the O'Brien yard, yet he had class and pedigree on his side, and seemed more likely to stay the trip than Hawk Wing. Running in the colours of Michael Tabor – who incidentally had no connection this time with Hawk Wing, who ran in the Sue Magnier colours – High Chaparral was ridden by Johnny Murtagh and started second-favourite at 7/2.

The general consensus was that the Derby winner of 2002 would surely come from the two chief contenders from Ballydoyle (O'Brien also saddled a third runner in the outsider Louisville), but others worthy of consideration were the Mark Johnston-trained pair Bandari and Fight Your Corner and the Godolphin representative, Naheef. There had not been a northern-trained Derby winner since Dante in 1945, but Johnston – who had saddled Mister Baileys in 1994 – liked the chances of his duo, both supplemented at a total

cost of £180,000. Bandari had been most impressive when winning the Lingfield Derby Trial by an incredible thirteen lengths, while Fight Your Corner had taken the Chester Vase. Having won the Oaks the day before on Kazzia, hopes were high for Frankie Dettori as he tried to notch his first Derby win, with his partner the useful Naheef.

Despite rain softening the ground even further on the day, the extremely popular Hawk Wing was able to hold his position as favourite as the stalls opened, with the winner of the 2002 Derby guaranteed over £800,000 in prize money.

It was the blinkered chestnut Moon Ballad – fresh from an all-the-way win in the Dante Stakes at York and a horse that was giving twenty-second-birthday boy Jamie Spencer his first Derby ride – that led the field merrily, a position the chestnut maintained as they approached Tattenham Corner, and he was followed by Coshocton, with a short gap to High Chaparral, the outsider Frankies Dream and Naheef. Rounding Tattenham Corner, the giant Hawk

The fall of Coshocton meant a rare Derby fatality in 2002.

The giant Hawk Wing achieved big-race glory in Sandown's Eclipse Stakes after the Derby.

Wing was locked away in mid-division while Bandari was further back and really struggling to get into the action.

For all intents and purposes, this particular Derby may as well have started in the straight, as from there, it was all about two horses: High Chaparral and Hawk Wing. Sending High Chaparral on and determined to test the stamina of Hawk Wing, Murtagh drove his mount up to and then past Moon Ballad at the two-furlong marker, while in behind, Kinane responded by urging Hawk Wing after his flying stablemate.

Like lightning, the two flashed twelve lengths clear of the rest and began a war to the line. High Chaparral had edged in front through Murtagh's decisiveness, and now it was down to Hawk Wing to justify his reputation and claw him back. Closer and closer to the line the pair got, Hawk Wing frantically attempting to scythe down his rival; for a moment, he appeared ready to blast past him, but what was clearly evident now was that High Chaparral not only possessed class and stamina, but also an iron will.

For all that Hawk Wing threw at him, High Chaparral found that bit more, and at the death, the underdog of the two had prevailed by two lengths, beating the sunken Hawk Wing fair and square to give Sadler's Wells another Derby after years of near misses. Moon Ballad took third ahead of the former Grand National-winning trainer Andy Turnell's charge Jelani. Further back though, there was tragedy. Having been among the leaders until the O'Brien pair had

taken over, the chestnut Coshocton – trying to become the first Predominate Stakes winner to win the Derby since Troy in 1979 – was in the process of battling for third place when he wavered strangely off a true line just yards from the finish. Capsizing shortly after in ugly fashion, the poor horse had fractured a near foreleg and sadly had to be put down. Fight Your Corner too had been badly injured, fracturing a cannon bone in his off-hind leg.

Aiden O'Brien had become the first trainer to saddle the first two home in the Derby since Richard Carver with My Love and Royal Drake in 1948 and the trainer stated he could not separate the two prior to the race. O'Brien's second Derby win continued a magnificent run for the trainer, giving him his

Trainer Aiden O'Brien secured back-to-back victories in the Derby through Galileo and High Chaparral.

fourth Classic inside five weeks, including Rock Of Gibraltar's Guineas success where Murtagh had been on board.

This was a Derby where the top two horses were far superior on the day to the remainder, even if it was by no means the strongest Derby field ever assembled – although Moon Ballad later won a Dubai World Cup and sixth-placed Where Or When won a Group One race at Ascot. Both High Chaparral and Hawk Wing were exceptional colts in their own right. Hawk Wing, though perhaps never fully justifying his god-like status, won the Eclipse Stakes at Sandown in his next contest before finishing second twice in the Champion Stakes at Leopardstown and then the Queen Elizabeth II Stakes at Ascot. Hawk Wing trained on at four, at times flashing brilliance, such as when winning the Lockinge Stakes at Newbury. He was one of the most popular horses of recent years, yet his wins at Sandown and Newbury aside, will leave an image of a horse that almost reached greatness – but not quite. High Chaparral proved after the Derby that he was indeed the worthy winner at Epsom, and developed into a fantastic horse. Even though he was not the athlete that Galileo was, he made up for it in heart and drive, never running a bad race. He won the Irish Derby next and was then a fine third in the Arc behind Marienbard, a position he would fill again in the same race at four, this time behind the fine Dalakhani. Later in his three-year-old campaign, he won the Breeders Cup Turf at Arlington in the States and defended his crown a year later, dead-heating for first with the locally trained horse Johar as the race moved to Santa Anita. Soon after, the wonderfully game High Chaparral was retired. In some ways, High Chaparral was overshadowed by Hawk Wing throughout his career, yet there is no doubting which horse was more successful of the two. Leaving the game as one of the most consistent and worthy Derby winners of the modern era, High Chaparral took a record of ten wins from thirteen starts into retirement.

## 2002 VODAFONE DERBY RESULT

| FATE / HORSE | WEIGHT | JOCKEY | ODDS |
|---|---|---|---|
| **1st – High Chaparral** | 9-0 | J.P. Murtagh | 7/2 |
| **2nd – Hawk Wing** | 9-0 | M.J. Kinane | 9/4* |
| **3rd – Moon Ballad** | 9-0 | J.P. Spencer | 20/1 |
| 4th – Jelani | 9-0 | F. Lynch | 100/1 |
| 5th – Fight Your Corner | 9-0 | K. Darley | 8/1 |
| 6th – Where Or When | 9-0 | J. Fortune | 66/1 |
| 7th – Naheef | 9-0 | L. Dettori | 5/1 |
| 8th – Bandari | 9-0 | R. Hills | 9/2 |
| 9th – Louisville | 9-0 | K. Fallon | 25/1 |
| 10th – Tholjanah | 9-0 | W. Supple | 14/1 |
| Last – Frankies Dream | 9-0 | Pat Eddery | 100/1 |
| Fell – Coshocton | 9-0 | P. Robinson | 28/1 |

8 June 2002
Going – Good to Soft (Soft in places)
Winner – £800,400
Time – 2 mins 39.45 secs
Favourite – Hawk Wing
12 Ran

| High Chaparral | Bay colt by Sadler's Wells – Kasora |
| Hawk Wing | Bay colt by Woodman – La Lorgnette |
| Moon Ballad | Chestnut colt by Singspiel – Velvet Moon |

Winner bred by S. Coughlan
Winner trained by A.P. O'Brien at Ballydoyle, Co. Tipperary, Ireland

# KRIS KIN

Once again, the Derby wore a very open look about it in 2003, with a maximum field of twenty lining-up to do battle. Having won the previous two Derbys with High Chaparral and Galileo, Aiden O'Brien was, yet again, the focus of most attention as he attempted to make history by training the winner for a third consecutive year.

On this occasion, O'Brien saddled one-fifth of the field, with his four runners being Alberto Giacometti, Balestrini, Brian Boru and The Great Gatsby. Alberto Giacometti was named after a Swiss surrealist painter and sculptor, while the frontrunning Balestrini was considered the biggest outsider of the quartet. But it was Brian Boru and The Great Gatsby that seemed best suited to the challenge of Epsom. A strong bay colt by Sadler's Wells, Brian Boru had flirted with Derby favouritism ever since his win in the Racing Post Trophy as a juvenile. A horse with stamina on his side, Brian Boru had been third in the much-respected Derrinstown Derby Trial at Leopardstown on his only start of the season, finishing behind another Epsom hopeful in Alamshar. Also by Sadler's Wells was the gritty, soft-ground-loving stayer The Great Gatsby. The horse had run five times at two, winning once, and on his only start at three, had finished one place ahead of Brian Boru at Leopardstown. Despite his price of 20/1, it was well worth noting that three-time Derby winner Pat Eddery had personally elected to ride the horse, indicating his chance was strong.

Perhaps the safest bet in the 2003 Derby was the highly consistent and richly talented bay colt Alamshar. Owned, trained and ridden by the same team behind Sinndar's 2000 Derby success, Alamshar was an unbeaten two-year-old

and had progressed impressively in his two runs at three, taking the Derrinstown Derby Trial on his latest run. Alamshar was well-built physically for Epsom, not being over-big, and with stamina on his side and a maternal grandsire being a Derby winner in Shahrastani, the horse seemed sure to go close.

Having been 14/1 on the morning of the race, the bright chestnut Kris Kin was the subject of an enormous race-day betting plunge. An American-bred colt trained by Sir Michael Stoute, Kris Kin had run only once before Epsom, winning the Dee Stakes at Chester. However, it was enough to convince connections to supplement him for the Derby at a spine-chilling cost of £90,000. Punters too seemed to know that Kris Kin was more than just a relatively unexposed dark-horse, as his price came tumbling down to 6/1 at the off, with the Champion Jockey Kieran Fallon on board.

The horse that started favourite for the race, however, was the impressive-looking bay colt, Refuse To Bend, a horse with obvious presence about him and one that looked in tremendous fettle before the race. Another son of Sadler's Wells, Refuse To Bend had looked splendid when winning the 2,000 Guineas at Newmarket, bringing his unbeaten lifetime streak to four. Refuse To Bend, however, had never raced beyond eight furlongs and unlike many of the leading contenders, the Dermot Weld-trained horse was one with stamina doubts.

As the biggest field since 1996 tore away, it was Pat Eddery on The Great Gatsby that set about extracting the stamina from the remainder of the runners, and he was joined for a long stretch up front by Clive Brittain's runner, Dutch Gold.

On good ground, The Great Gatsby and Dutch Gold were setting a stern pace, and horses lacking in stamina seemed sure to be caught out. The perceived key players such as Refuse To Bend, Alamshar and Kris Kin were well placed for a long way and looked set to play major roles in the finish as the field rounded Tattenham Corner, but O'Brien's chief hope, Brian Boru, was running a most disappointing race, struggling towards the rear as the straight beckoned.

Entering the straight, Eddery continued to enjoy a marvellous ride aboard The Great Gatsby and, urging his horse on, he accelerated clear of Dutch Gold, opening up an advantage of a couple of lengths. The run of the favourite Refuse To Bend now started to falter. Failing to find any extra quickness in the straight, he began to fade away tamely and soon both he and Brian Boru were out of contention.

The Great Gatsby roared on in front, but behind him, challengers were mounting daring runs to try and steal his thunder. The O'Brien outsider Balestrini had chased the leaders from the start and, with two furlongs to run, he took second place from the now-retreating Dutch Gold. Alamshar was beginning to stay on towards the outside, but the one that was really flying down the inside rails was Kris Kin. The chestnut had been pushed along by Fallon for some way, and as the final furlong loomed, he was soaring.

Kris Kin gave Kieran Fallon a second Derby triumph.

Connections of The Great Gatsby must not have been able to watch. Their horse had been so game and so positive that he would have fully deserved to win the race, but as the line came rocketing into view, Alamshar and Kris Kin were charging furiously at him. Having been switched to the outside for his final thrust, Kris Kin burst from the heavens to get up in the most dramatic of late shows, robbing The Great Gatsby of victory by a length, with Alamshar a mere short head away in third. Norse Dancer – last going into the straight – had made up huge amounts of ground to come fourth with Balestrini fifth and Dutch Gold sixth.

It had been a pulsating finish, and much like the way Kris Kin had entered the Derby picture – late and in flashy style – he had similarly won the race. Fallon had ridden him beautifully, keeping the horse – a notoriously lazy

Kris Kin (blue and yellow colours) justified the gamble on him to win the Derby from
The Great Gatsby (pink) and Alamshar (green).

Sir Michael Stoute won the Derby for a third time in 2003.

homeworker – up to his task during the race before unleashing him inside the final few furlongs with a powerful and stunning winning drive. The 'dark-horse' had won the Derby, in the process sending countless numbers of punters home happy after one of the biggest Derby day plunges in the race's history.

It was Fallon's second Derby win after Oath in 1999, and for trainer Sir Michael Stoute, a third win, seventeen years after Shahrastani. The trainer had suffered a scare two days before the race when Kris Kin had gone slightly lame. However, after a period of icing his joints, the horse was passed fit to fulfil his trainer's hopes.

Pat Eddery had ridden in his final Derby and had almost stolen the race aboard his game mount The Great Gatsby. Eddery retired later in the season, but left the Epsom scene having recorded three memorable Derby wins aboard Grundy in 1975, Golden Fleece in 1982 and Quest For Fame in 1990. In addition, he had been runner-up no fewer than six times, on El Gran Senor in 1984, Law Society in 1985, Dushyantor in 1996, Silver Patriarch in 1997, Golan in 2001 and now with The Great Gatsby. After two consecutive Derby wins, the great stallion Sadler's wells had to be content with second place again – for the sixth time.

Kris Kin proved awesome on Derby day, recording a winning time just outside the record set by Lammtarra in 1995. Unfortunately, he will not go down as one of the great Derby winners. Whereas Alamshar won an Irish Derby and a King George after Epsom to emerge as the class horse from the 2003 field and Brian Boru won the season's St Leger, Kris Kin was beaten on his next three runs. He finished third in the King George, third in the Prix Niel at Longchamp and a rather poor eleventh in the Arc. Both races in France were won by the excellent, middle-distance star of the season, Dalakhani. Shortly after the Arc, the decision was taken to retire Kris Kin.

## 2003 VODAFONE DERBY RESULT

| FATE / HORSE | WEIGHT | JOCKEY | ODDS |
|---|---|---|---|
| **1st – Kris Kin** | 9-0 | K. Fallon | 6/1 |
| **2nd – The Great Gatsby** | 9-0 | Pat Eddery | 20/1 |
| **3rd – Alamshar** | 9-0 | J.P. Murtagh | 4/1 |
| 4th – Norse Dancer | 9-0 | T. Quinn | 16/1 |
| 5th – Balestrini | 9-0 | J.P. Spencer | 66/1 |
| 6th – Dutch Gold | 9-0 | P. Robinson | 20/1 |
| 7th – Let Me Try Again | 9-0 | D. Holland | 50/1 |
| 8th – Graikos | 9-0 | L. Dettori | 25/1 |
| 9th – Magistretti | 9-0 | K. Darley | 20/1 |
| 10th – Shield | 9-0 | E. Ahern | 20/1 |
| 11th – Summerland | 9-0 | J. Fortune | 100/1 |
| 12th – Alberto Giacometti | 9-0 | C. Soumillon | 12/1 |
| 13th – Refuse To Bend | 9-0 | P.J. Smullen | 11/4* |
| 14th – Franklins Gardens | 9-0 | T.E. Durcan | 25/1 |
| 15th – Dunhill Star | 9-0 | M. Hills | 50/1 |
| 16th – Brian Boru | 9-0 | M.J. Kinane | 9/2 |
| 17th – Strength 'N Honour | 9-0 | R. Hughes | 100/1 |
| 18th – Unigold | 9-0 | S. Sanders | 50/1 |
| 19th – Lundy's Lane | 9-0 | B. Doyle | 100/1 |
| Last – Prince Nureyev | 9-0 | S. Drowne | 150/1 |

7 June 2003
Going – Good
Winner – £852,600
Time – 2 mins 33.35 secs
Favourite – Refuse To Bend
20 Ran

| | |
|---|---|
| Kris Kin | Chestnut colt by Kris S – Angel In My Heart |
| The Great Gatsby | Bay colt by Sadler's Wells – Ionian Sea |
| Alamshar | Bay colt by Key Of Luck – Alaiyda |

Winner bred by Flaxman Holdings Ltd
Winner trained by Sir Michael Stoute at Newmarket

Joint favourite with Snow Ridge was the horse that had posted arguably the most impressive performance in any of the Derby trials. On his only run of the season to date, North Light had won the Dante Stakes at York, taking the race from a long way out and winning in bold style in the manner of a fast-improving horse. North Light was expected to relish the strong gallop and extended trip at Epsom as he came from a late-maturing family and the closer the race came, the more apparent his chance appeared, as many of the top contenders over the winter months – such as the talented Aiden O'Brien-trained Yeats – gradually dropped out. Another positive was the team of Sir Michael Stoute and Kieran Fallon. The duo had won the Derby the year before with Kris Kin, and the day before the 2004 renewal they had teamed up with the progressive filly Ouija Board to win the Oaks.

It certainly appeared a sub-par field for the 2004 Derby and a number of runners – Gatwick and Hazyview – had been supplemented late on to take their chance, yet there remained a variety of horses that looked likely to fight out the minor placings. American Post, Let The Lion Roar and Percussionist were three that proved popular. American Post was unbeaten in six races, three as a two-year-old and three in the current campaign. However, many believed American Post to be inferior at three than at two, and he had seemed fortunate to win the French 2,000 Guineas. American Post was a horse that benefitted from having soft ground, and with the Epsom going officially good, it seemed unlikely that the talented brown colt would become the first French-trained horse to win the Derby since Empery in 1976. Trained by John Dunlop, Let The Lion Roar was a tough-staying bay colt by the legendary Sadler's Wells. He had finished third behind North Light in the Dante, and the first-time fitting of a visor was expected to spark the horse even further over a trip that seemed likely to suit him. Perhaps the most popular winner would have been the John Gosden-trained Percussionist. The horse had been owned by Robert Sangster, but when the legendary owner had died in April, Percussionist had been passed into the ownership of the Sangster family. Sangster's name is synonymous with the Derby, and horses such as The Minstrel, Golden Fleece, El Gran Senor, Hawaiian Sound, Blue Stag, Colonel Collins and Romanov had all carried the famous green and blue silks with merit at Epsom. Percussionist would have proved a very emotional winner, and the horse was not without a chance. Like Let The Lion Roar, Percussionist was also a son of Sadler's Wells and had looked every inch a Derby horse when winning the Lingfield Derby Trial by ten lengths.

In the absence of the highly touted Yeats, it was the remaining representative from the Aiden O'Brien yard, Meath, that was to be the pacemaker in the race. Ridden by Jamie Spencer, the 16/1 Meath would lead all the way round Tattenham Corner and into the straight. North Light had looked very good in

# NORTH LIGHT

Much of the focus for the 225th running of the Derby fell on the shoulders of Frankie Dettori. Despite a magnificent career that had included an amazing, through-the-seven-race-card performance at Ascot, as well as over 100 Group or Grade One victories all over the world, the personable and much-liked Italian had still to capture the Derby after eleven attempts. Tamure had gone closest for him in 1995, while he had finished third aboard both Shantou in 1996 and on Tobougg in 2001, although neither had seriously looked like winning. Dettori had also partnered the extremely well-fancied duo of Cape Verdi and Dubai Millenium, but both had flopped in their respective Derbys of 1998 and 1999.

Dettori's partner for the 2004 running was a horse that he felt would give him his finest chance yet of capturing elusive Derby glory for the first time. Even though he had failed in the Dewhurst Stakes as a two-year-old, the well-built bay Snow Ridge had long been considered a potential Derby winner. Formerley trained by Marcus Tregoning, Snow Ridge had been most impressive when staying-on late to finish second to Haafhd in the 2,000 Guineas on his debut for Godolphin. Whether it was because the 2004 Derby field appeared on the weak side or that it was the Godolphin/Dettori combination's powerful reputation, Snow Ridge found that particular performance good enough to to earn himself a share of favouritism. However, his true make-up appeared unclear, and many debated whether it would be his dam Snow Princess' stamina or his sire Indian Ridge's speed that would prove more prominent.

North Light comes home first from Rule Of Law and the hidden Let The Lion Roar.

the preliminaries and he tracked the leader in second on the outside, while Percussionist was being pushed along by Kevin Darley to remain with the leaders, followed by American Post, Hazyview, Pukka and Gatwick.

Meath had run boldly but, entering the straight, the horse had begun to weaken badly and he soon started to fall away. Having stalked Meath throughout the race, North Light and Fallon seized the moment to play their hand.

Kicking on fiercely straightening for home, the duo powered forward. Hazyview also passed Meath early in the straight but it was American Post that appeared the most likely to challenge North Light, making smooth progress to

close on the new leader with three furlongs to run. Next came Pukka, Gatwick and the slowly improving joint-favourite Snow Ridge.

At the two-furlong gate, North Light went on again, this time decisively. American Post could not quicken, while Snow Ridge was urged vigorously by Dettori to attack the leader, but the horse could make no impression.

North Light simply did not look like he would be overturned, and it was left to Rule Of Law, Let The Lion Roar and Percussionist to chase him home. Rule Of Law – the second Godolphin candidate – had been held up at the back and had only been twelfth entering the straight, but despite hanging to the left, he came home stoutly to snatch second on the line. Let The Lion Roar had run an unfortunate race because of traffic before being pulled wide to make his run in the straight. Like Rule Of Law, he finished with thunder, showing his obvious stamina, and swiped third from Percussionist, a horse that had kept on gamely despite having to be pushed along during the contest. Snow Ridge had proved disappointing, pouring more Derby misery on Dettori, eventually finishing seventh after not lasting home sufficiently. Sadly Snow Ridge died later in the year.

North Light had won the Derby by a length-and-a-half, yet from early on in the straight – and certainly when he powered clear with two furlongs to run – he had looked tailor-made for Epsom and ran out a fine Derby winner.

On Derby day 2004, Lester Piggott was guest of honour as it was fifty years after his first Derby victory aboard Never Say Die. What the crowd at Epsom witnessed on this occasion was the confirmation of perhaps the finset Epsom jockey since the great man, Kieran Fallon. Facing a possible charge of bringing racing into disrepute for an incident earlier in the season, Fallon again proved what a masterful jockey he was with a patient then powerful performance aboard North Light. Having guided Oath home in battling style in 1999, Fallon had produced a Derby masterclass to kick Kris Kin to victory in 2003. Now he joined modern day greats in Pat Eddery and Walter Swinburn in winning a third Derby.

It was a fourth Derby win for Sir Michael Stoute and an emotional triumph for the Weinstock family, who had shared in Troy's blitz to victory in 1979. Lord Weinstock had passed away recently, and it was he who had bought in 1960 – together with Sir Michael Sobell – the Ballymacoll Stud where North Light was bred. Fittingly, North Light's Derby victory was witnessed by members of Lord Weinstock's family, including his wife, Lady Netta Weinstock, who was the daughter of Sobell.

North Light next headed for The Curragh where he was narrowly beaten by the Dermot Weld-trained Grey Swallow before running a bold race in the Arc, but ultimately finishing fifth behind the French-trained Bago, a son of the 1989 Derby hero Nashwan.

## 2004 VODAFONE DERBY RESULT

| FATE / HORSE | WEIGHT | JOCKEY | ODDS |
|---|---|---|---|
| 1st – North Light | 9-0 | K. Fallon | 7/2* |
| 2nd – Rule Of Law | 9-0 | K. McEvoy | 20/1 |
| 3rd – Let The Lion Roar | 9-0 | M.J. Kinane | 14/1 |
| 4th – Percussionist | 9-0 | K. Darley | 7/1 |
| 5th – Salford City | 9-0 | J.P. Murtagh | 8/1 |
| 6th – American Post | 9-0 | R. Hughes | 13/2 |
| 7th – Snow Ridge | 9-0 | L. Dettori | 7/2* |
| 8th – Hazyview | 9-0 | E. Ahern | 40/1 |
| 9th – Pukka | 9-0 | D. Holland | 10/1 |
| 10th – Gatwick | 9-0 | T. Quinn | 16/1 |
| 11th – Massif Centrale | 9-0 | Dane O'Neill | 100/1 |
| 12th – Coming Again | 9-0 | M. Hills | 80/1 |
| 13th – Elshadi | 9-0 | Martin Dwyer | 25/1 |
| Last – Meath | 9-0 | J.P. Spencer | 16/1 |

5 June 2004
Going – Good
Winner – 804,117 80p
Time – 2 mins 33.72 secs
Joint Favourites – North Light & Snow Ridge
14 Ran

| North Light | Bay colt by Danehill – Sought Out |
|---|---|
| Rule Of Law | Bay colt by Kingmambo – Crystal Crossing |
| Let The Lion Roar | Bay colt by Sadler's Wells – Ballerina |

Winner bred by Ballymacoll Stud
Winner trained by Sir Michael Stoute at Newmarket

# DERBY WINNERS 1780 – 2004

| YEAR | HORSE | JOCKEY | ODDS |
|------|-------|--------|------|
| 1780 | Diomed | S. Arnull | 6/4 |
| 1781 | Young Eclipse | C. Hindley | 10/1 |
| 1782 | Assassin | S. Arnull | 5/1 |
| 1783 | Saltram | C. Hindley | 5/2 |
| 1784 | Sergeant | J. Arnull | 3/1 |
| 1785 | Aimwell | C. Hindley | 7/1 |
| 1786 | Noble | J. White | 30/1 |
| 1787 | Sir Peter Seazle | S. Arnull | 2/1 |
| 1788 | Sir Thomas | W. South | 5/6 |
| 1789 | Skyscraper | S. Chifney snr | 4/7 |
| 1790 | Rhadamanthus | J. Arnull | 5/4 |
| 1791 | Eager | F. Stephenson | 5/2 |
| 1792 | John Bull | F. Buckle | 4/6 |
| 1793 | Waxy | W. Clift | 12/1 |
| 1794 | Daedalus | F. Buckle | 6/1 |
| 1795 | Spread Eagle | A. Wheatley | 3/1 |
| 1796 | Didelot | J. Arnull | N/A |
| 1797 | Fidget Colt | J. Singleton | 10/1 |
| 1798 | Sir Harry | S. Arnull | 7/4 |
| 1799 | Archduke | J. Arnull | 12/1 |
| 1800 | Champion | W. Clift | 7/4 |
| 1801 | Eleanor | Saunders | 5/4 |
| 1802 | Tyrant | F. Buckle | 7/1 |
| 1803 | Ditto | W. Clift | 7/2 |
| 1804 | Hannibal | W. Arnull | 3/1 |
| 1805 | Cardinal Beaufort | D. Fitzpatrick | 20/1 |
| 1806 | Paris | J. Shepherd | 5/1 |
| 1807 | Election | J. Arnull | 3/1 |
| 1808 | Pan | F. Collinson | 25/1 |
| 1809 | Pope | T. Goodisson | 20/1 |
| 1810 | Whalebone | W. Clift | 2/1 |
| 1811 | Phantom | F. Buckle | 5/1 |
| 1812 | Octavius | W. Arnull | 7/1 |
| 1813 | Smolensko | T. Goodisson | Evens |
| 1814 | Blucher | W. Arnull | 5/2 |
| 1815 | Whisker | T. Goodisson | 8/1 |
| 1816 | Prince Leopold | W. Wheatley | 20/1 |
| 1817 | Azor | J. Robinson | 50/1 |
| 1818 | Sam | S. Chifney jnr | 7/2 |
| 1819 | Tiresias | W. Clift | 5/2 |
| 1820 | Sailor | S. Chifney jnr | 4/1 |
| 1821 | Gustavus | S. Day | 2/1 |
| 1822 | Moses | T. Goodisson | 6/1 |
| 1823 | Emilius | F. Buckle | 11/8 |
| 1824 | Cedric | J. Robinson | 9/2 |
| 1825 | Middleton | J. Robinson | 7/4 |
| 1826 | Lapdog | G. Dockeray | 50/1 |
| 1827 | Mameluke | J. Robinson | 9/1 |
| 1828 | Cadland | J. Robinson | 4/1 |
| 1829 | Frederick | J. Forth | 40/1 |
| 1830 | Priam | S. Day | 4/1 |
| 1831 | Spaniel | W. Wheatley | 50/1 |
| 1832 | St Giles | W. Scott | 3/1 |
| 1833 | Dangerous | J. Chapple | 30/1 |
| 1834 | Plenipotentiary | P. Conolly | 9/4 |
| 1835 | Mundig | W. Scott | 6/1 |
| 1836 | Bay Middleton | J. Robinson | 7/4 |
| 1837 | Phosphorus | G. Edwards | 40/1 |
| 1838 | Amato | J. Chapple | 30/1 |
| 1839 | Bloomsbury | S. Templeman | 25/1 |
| 1840 | Little Wonder | W. Macdonald | 50/1 |
| 1841 | Coronation | P. Conolly | 5/2 |
| 1842 | Attila | W. Scott | 5/1 |
| 1843 | Cotherstone | W. Scott | 13/8 |
| 1844 | Orlando | N. Flatman | 20/1 |
| 1845 | The Merry Monarch | F. Bell | 15/1 |
| 1846 | Pyrrhus The First | S. Day | 8/1 |
| 1847 | Cossack | S. Templeman | 5/1 |
| 1848 | Surplice | S. Templeman | Evens |
| 1849 | The Flying Dutchman | C. Marlow | 2/1 |
| 1850 | Voltigeur | J. Marson | 16/1 |
| 1851 | Teddington | J. Marson | 3/1 |
| 1852 | Daniel O'Rourke | F. Butler | 25/1 |
| 1853 | West Australian | F. Butler | 6/4 |
| 1854 | Andover | A. Day | 7/2 |
| 1855 | Wild Dayrell | R. Sherwood | Evens |
| 1856 | Ellington | T. Aldcroft | 20/1 |
| 1857 | Blink Bonny | J. Charlton | 20/1 |
| 1858 | Beadsman | J. Wells | 10/1 |
| 1859 | Musjid | J. Wells | 9/4 |
| 1860 | Thormanby | H. Custance | 4/1 |
| 1861 | Kettledrum | R. Bullock | 12/1 |
| 1862 | Caractacus | J. Parsons | 40/1 |
| 1863 | Macaroni | T. Chaloner | 10/1 |
| 1864 | Blair Athol | J. Snowden | 14/1 |
| 1865 | Gladiateur | H. Grimshaw | 5/2 |
| 1866 | Lord Lyon | H. Custance | 5/6 |
| 1867 | Hermit | J. Daley | 1000/15 |
| 1868 | Blue Gown | J. Wells | 7/2 |
| 1869 | Pretender | J. Osborne | 11/8 |
| 1870 | Kingcraft | T. French | 20/1 |
| 1871 | Favonius | T. French | 9/1 |
| 1872 | Cremorne | C. Maidment | 3/1 |
| 1873 | Doncaster | F. Webb | 45/1 |
| 1874 | George Frederick | H. Custance | 9/1 |
| 1875 | Galopin | J. Morris | 2/1 |
| 1876 | Kisber | C. Maidment | 4/1 |
| 1877 | Silvio | F. Archer | 100/9 |
| 1878 | Sefton | H. Constable | 100/12 |
| 1879 | Sir Bevys | G. Fordham | 20/1 |
| 1880 | Bend Or | F. Archer | 2/1 |
| 1881 | Iroquois | F. Archer | 11/2 |
| 1882 | Shotover | T. Cannon | 11/2 |
| 1883 | St Blaise | T. Cannon | 11/2 |
| 1884 | St Gatien & Harvester (dead heat) | C. Wood S.Loates | 100/8 100/7 |
| 1885 | Melton | F. Archer | 75/40 |
| 1886 | Ormonde | F. Archer | 4/9 |
| 1887 | Merry Hampton | J. Watts | 100/9 |
| 1888 | Ayrshire | F. Barrett | 5/6 |

| Year | Horse | Jockey | Odds |
|------|-------|--------|------|
| 1889 | Donavon | T. Loates | 8/11 |
| 1890 | Sainfoin | J. Watts | 100/15 |
| 1891 | Common | G. Barrett | 10/11 |
| 1892 | Sir Hugo | F. Allsopp | 40/1 |
| 1893 | Isinglass | T. Loates | 4/9 |
| 1894 | Ladas II | J. Watts | 2/9 |
| 1895 | Sir Visto | S. Loates | 9/1 |
| 1896 | Persimmon | J. Watts | 5/1 |
| 1897 | Galtee More | C. Wood | 1/4 |
| 1898 | Jeddah | O. Madden | 100/1 |
| 1899 | Flying Fox | M. Cannon | 2/5 |
| 1900 | Diamond Jubilee | H. Jones | 6/4 |
| 1901 | Volodyovski | L. Reiff | 5/2 |
| 1902 | Ard Patrick | J.H. Martin | 100/14 |
| 1903 | Rock Sand | D. Maher | 4/6 |
| 1904 | St Amant | K. Cannon | 5/1 |
| 1905 | Cicero | D. Maher | 4/11 |
| 1906 | Spearmint | D. Maher | 6/1 |
| 1907 | Orby | J. Reiff | 100/9 |
| 1908 | Signorinetta | W. Bullock | 100/1 |
| 1909 | Minoru | H. Jones | 7/2 |
| 1910 | Lemberg | B. Dillon | 7/4 |
| 1911 | Sunstar | G. Stern | 13/8 |
| 1912 | Tagalie | J. Reiff | 100/8 |
| 1913 | Aboyeur | E. Piper | 100/1 |
| 1914 | Durbar II | M. MacGee | 20/1 |
| 1915 | Pommern | S. Donoghue | 11/10 |
| 1916 | Fifinella | J. Childs | 11/2 |
| 1917 | Gay Crusader | S. Donoghue | 7/4 |
| 1918 | Gainsborough | J. Childs | 8/13 |
| 1919 | Grand Parade | F. Templeman | 33/1 |
| 1920 | Spion Kop | F. O'Neil | 100/6 |
| 1921 | Humorist | S. Donoghue | 6/1 |
| 1922 | Captain Cuttle | S. Donoghue | 10/1 |
| 1923 | Papyrus | S. Donoghue | 100/15 |
| 1924 | Sansovino | T. Weston | 9/2 |
| 1925 | Manna | S. Donoghue | 9/1 |
| 1926 | Coronach | J. Childs | 11/2 |
| 1927 | Call Boy | E.C. Elliot | 4/1 |
| 1928 | Felstead | W. Wragg | 33/1 |
| 1929 | Trigio | J. Marshall | 33/1 |
| 1930 | Blenheim | H. Wragg | 18/1 |
| 1931 | Cameronian | F. Fox | 7/2 |
| 1932 | April The Fifth | F. Lane | 100/6 |
| 1933 | Hyperion | T. Weston | 6/1 |
| 1934 | Windsor Lad | C. Smirke | 15/2 |
| 1935 | Bahram | F. Fox | 5/4 |
| 1936 | Mahmoud | C. Smirke | 100/8 |
| 1937 | Mid-day Sun | M. Beary | 100/7 |
| 1938 | Bois Roussel | E.C. Elliot | 20/1 |
| 1939 | Blue Peter | E. Smith | 7/2 |
| 1940 | Pont l'Eveque | S. Wragg | 10/1 |
| 1941 | Owen Tudor | W. Nevett | 25/1 |
| 1942 | Watling Street | H. Wragg | 6/1 |
| 1943 | Straight Deal | T.H. Carey | 100/6 |
| 1944 | Ocean Swell | W. Nevett | 28/1 |
| 1945 | Dante | W. Nevett | 100/30 |
| 1946 | Airborne | T. Lowrey | 50/1 |
| 1947 | Pearl Diver | G. Bridgland | 40/1 |
| 1948 | My Love | W. Johnstone | 100/9 |
| 1949 | Nimbus | E.C. Elliot | 7/1 |
| 1950 | Galcador | W. Johnstone | 100/9 |
| 1951 | Arctic Prince | C. Spares | 28/1 |
| 1952 | Tulyar | C. Smirke | 11/2 |
| 1953 | Pinza | G. Richards | 5/1 |
| 1954 | Never Say Die | L. Piggott | 33/1 |
| 1955 | Phil Drake | F. Palmer | 100/8 |
| 1956 | Lavandin | W. Johnstone | 7/1 |
| 1957 | Crepello | L. Piggott | 6/4 |
| 1958 | Hard Ridden | C. Smirke | 18/1 |
| 1959 | Parthia | W.H. Carr | 10/1 |
| 1960 | St Paddy | L. Piggott | 7/1 |
| 1961 | Psidium | R. Poincelet | 66/1 |
| 1962 | Larkspur | N. Sellwood | 22/1 |
| 1963 | Relko | Y. Saint-Martin | 5/1 |
| 1964 | Santa Claus | A. Beasley | 15/8 |
| 1965 | Sea Bird II | T.P. Glennon | 7/4 |
| 1966 | Charlottown | A. Beasley | 5/1 |
| 1967 | Royal Palace | G. Moore | 7/4 |
| 1968 | Sir Ivor | L. Piggott | 4/5 |
| 1969 | Blakeney | E. Johnson | 15/2 |
| 1970 | Nijinsky | L. Piggott | 11/8 |
| 1971 | Mill Reef | G. Lewis | 100/30 |
| 1972 | Roberto | L. Piggott | 3/1 |
| 1973 | Morston | E. Hide | 25/1 |
| 1974 | Snow Knight | B. Taylor | 50/1 |
| 1975 | Grundy | P. Eddery | 5/1 |
| 1976 | Empery | L. Piggott | 10/1 |
| 1977 | The Minstrel | L. Piggott | 5/1 |
| 1978 | Shirley Heights | G. Starkey | 8/1 |
| 1979 | Troy | W. Carson | 6/1 |
| 1980 | Henbit | W. Carson | 7/1 |
| 1981 | Shergar | W.R. Swinburn | 10/11 |
| 1982 | Golden Fleece | P. Eddery | 3/1 |
| 1983 | Teenoso | L. Piggott | 9/2 |
| 1984 | Secreto | C. Roche | 14/1 |
| 1985 | Slip Anchor | S. Cauthen | 9/4 |
| 1986 | Shahrastani | W.R. Swinburn | 11/2 |
| 1987 | Reference Point | S. Cauthen | 6/4 |
| 1988 | Kahyasi | R. Cochrane | 11/1 |
| 1989 | Nashwan | W. Carson | 5/4 |
| 1990 | Quest For Fame | P. Eddery | 7/1 |
| 1991 | Generous | A. Munro | 9/1 |
| 1992 | Dr Devious | J. Reid | 8/1 |
| 1993 | Commander In Chief | M. Kinane | 15/2 |
| 1994 | Erhaab | W. Carson | 7/2 |
| 1995 | Lammtarra | W.R. Swinburn | 14/1 |
| 1996 | Shaamit | M. Hills | 12/1 |
| 1997 | Benny The Dip | W. Ryan | 11/1 |
| 1998 | High-Rise | O. Peslier | 20/1 |
| 1999 | Oath | K. Fallon | 13/2 |
| 2000 | Sinndar | J. Murtagh | 7/1 |
| 2001 | Galileo | M. Kinane | 11/4 |
| 2002 | High Chaparral | J. Murtagh | 7/2 |
| 2003 | Kris Kin | K. Fallon | 6/1 |
| 2004 | North Light | K. Fallon | 7/2 |